GOD
WITHOUT
THUNDER

AN UNORTHODOX DEFENSE
OF ORTHODOXY

BY JOHN CROWE RANSOM

ARCHON BOOKS
HAMDEN, CONNECTICUT
1965

215
R17g

51115

Oct. 1965

LIBRARY OF CONGRESS CATALOG CARD NUMBER: 65-17410
PRINTED IN THE UNITED STATES OF AMERICA

TO MY FATHER

CONTENTS

A LETTER

Dear Friend:

I have finished a book, and now I write an apology. This book makes some representations about science, and also some representations about religion—in neither of which branches do I pretend to be an advanced scholar. Are there not then two apologies needed? There may be. But the one chiefly due, as I see it, is to the religionists.

I am the son of a theologian, and the grandson of another one, but the gift did not come down to me. When I handle the venerable symbols of an ancient faith, I am well aware that my touch is too heavy, and does some outrage. I will gladly say therefore to the learned and loving scholars who are versed in the mysteries that this work of mine is mere lay work, and meant for laity.

But I have felt that this sort of apology is a little too cheaply paid—released without effort upon such a universal air and carefully aimed at nowhere in particular. Therefore I write thus especially and personally to you, the most fitting of men, in order to explain that my book will not communicate to you any fresh religious truths, and that there has never been behind it any presumption on the author's part that it might do so. I shall never write the book that might do this. The one which I have written is done in the hope of edifying the novices, whose advancement I have not myself exceeded very far; not those who have passed into the higher degrees of the religious brotherhood.

I have some confidence that you will think my view of religion to be the true and orthodox one. But my policy of frankly analyzing the religious experience is certainly not so orthodox, and it is not unlikely that you will question its expediency. It is as if I had said here of the sacred objects and the supernaturalisms of the faith: Behold these myths! Then I have defined the myths, in the cold and not very fastidious terms of an Occidental logic. That has never been the way, I understand very well, of the true priests. But it is a policy which is at least permitted to me, and which is at the moment, I judge, the most appropriate one. For, after all, look and see how roundly the world has of late been disabused of the most and the best of its myths—and as a consequence been stricken with an unheard-of poverty of mind and unhappiness of life. What a sorry reputation the true priests, the devout keepers of the myths, enjoy now in this Western world, and particularly in this most Western world of America! It has occurred to me therefore that I might undertake to explain to it, as if in simple untechnical monosyllables, the function of the myths in human civilization. This seems to me an important thing to do; and going with it is the task of explaining why one myth may be better than another.

The predicament of religionists today may be stated as follows: they have not much more to lose. But it is possible that there is something which might yet, by new tactics, be won back.

JOHN CROWE RANSOM

Vanderbilt University,
Nashville, Tennessee,
June 1, 1930.

Part One

THE DYNASTY OF HEAVEN
CHANGES

CHAPTER ONE

THE NEW GOD

IS RELIGION a cause or an effect, when we look at its relation to the whole conduct of life?

It is usual to take it as a cause, and a powerful cause too. For consider the usual meaning of religion. We mean by religion, usually, a body of doctrine concerning God and man. But the doctrine which defines God, and man's relation to God, is really a doctrine which tries to define the intention of the universe, and man's proper portion within this universe. It is therefore his fundamental philosophy, it expresses the conviction he holds about his essential destiny, and it is bound to be of determining influence upon his conduct.

In nearly every external respect, the conduct of life in the Western world has changed during modern times, for better or for worse, to a degree which is revolutionary. But while that change has been going on, it is interesting to inquire what religion has been doing.

Religion seemed during this time to change very slowly, and very little. The scientific successes of Western man were rapidly altering his attitude toward the world, and altering the program which he elected to carry out for himself in the world. But these alterations evidently were taking place in spite of his religion—his doctrines continued to make about the same demands as ever upon his attitude and upon

3

his program. Westerners therefore seemed to be submitting themselves to a curious dichotomy: half of their minds was making a profession which was one thing and half was indulging in a practice which was another. The inevitable result was that religion fell into disrepute, for on these terms it clearly did not have the force which had been claimed for it in determining conduct. But probably the simple matter of fact was that an original body of religious convictions was being progressively disbelieved, while other religious convictions were forming unconsciously which would eventually rise to consciousness and call for expression. Inevitably the time would come when men would have to profess the principles which really governed them, and leave off the painful effort of adaptation which was required when they said one thing and tried to make it mean another.

That time has about come. The old doctrines are being more or less quietly dropped, the new doctrines are being more or less openly published. The war is nearly over, and the new doctrines have all but won. We are being invited now to abandon frankly a faith in which we really hadn't for a long time believed—and to subscribe to one in which we must have been believing very powerfully in secret, if our conduct means anything at all.

I will have to be much more specific.

The religion that is about to be superseded is orthodox Christianity. But since nearly every variety of Christianity is capable of claiming that title, let us apply the term severely: orthodox means the religion of the historically elder varieties that antedated modernism. Orthodoxy—the religion which now is losing in the Western world—is therefore such a religion as that of the Eastern or Orthodox Church. Perhaps a little less, it is that of the Roman and Anglican Churches, and perhaps still less that of several major nonconformist communions. From there orthodoxy tapers off towards the vanishing point, by varying degrees which I could not define, into Unitarianism; into many local Congregational units; into Christian Science; and into philanthropic societies with a minimum of doctrine about God, like the Young Men's Christian Association, welfare establishments, fraternal organizations, and Rotary.

And what is the characteristic doctrine of orthodoxy which is losing its ground? We may as well put this quite concretely: The doctrine which is now becoming so antiquated with us is that of the stern and inscrutable God of Israel, the God of the Old Testament.

The new doctrine which is replacing it is the doctrine of an amiable and understandable God. We wanted a God who wouldn't hurt us; who would let us understand him; who would agree to scrap all the wicked thunderbolts in his armament. And this is just the God that has developed popularly out of the Christ of the New Testament: the embodiment mostly of the principle of social benevolence and of physical welfare. The new religion makes this God the ruler of the world, reduces the God of the Old Testament to a minor figure in the Godhead, or even now and then expels him altogether.

Such a religion as this is clearly the one which adapts itself to the requirements of our aggressive modern science. It is the religion proposed by the scientific party. It is characteristically Occidental and modern. But as far as a religion can be, it is fundamentally irreligious, or secular, both in its doctrine and in its works.

The scientists, so much admired for the marvels they have worked, so very imposing in their unusual singleness of mind, have been steadily acquiring an ascendancy over public opinion. Their progress has been so regular that they have not generally found it necessary to resort to open battle with those who still defended the old doctrines, and the way of life which the old doctrines would have required of them. A change in religions is of course a revolution of the first importance in society, and might well be attended with violence. And in fact we have had a little of that. There was Dayton, Tennessee, which scared us with its revelation of the deep passions that might be involved. There is now the public religious conflict in Communist Russia. But on the whole, the new religion is on the point of having established itself in America, and in most Western societies perhaps, with unusual tact and with the minimum of outrage. The war has been fought now nearly to its finish, and yet it has been a war that grew more and more polite in its latter stages, with the purpose that at its conclusion nobody need openly admit defeat.

This point may be illustrated.

The American Association for the Advancement of Science held its annual meeting at New York in December of 1928. Mr. Harry Elmer Barnes, a scientist of quite regular scientific doctrine but far from gifted in the higher strategy, read a paper demanding in belligerent language that science forthwith define and set up her new God, to take the place of the antiquated and unworthy God of Israel. But his colleagues were disturbed. They were perfectly aware that the new God had practically been set up already, and was enjoying the receipt of his revenues and homage. But he had been established on the throne in much the same manner as the supposititious child was slipped into the cradle —he took the name of the supplanted God, and was careful to keep up most of the usual court ceremonial. And the old religionists could see as well as the scientists, if they cared to look, that their God had been supplanted, but they were being invited to participate in the optical illusion that no change had been made, they were being persuaded not to make a scene.

When Mr. Barnes would have exposed this sham, he

received the abuse that he must have expected from the irreconcilables of the old religion, but he was perhaps chagrined at being deserted by his own party, the scientists. Mr. Henry Fairfield Osborn, President of the A.A.A.S., rebuked him officially. Other important scientists followed suit.

Mr. Harry Emerson Fosdick, the liberal clergyman, prominent as one of the clerical party who had gone off pretty far after the new theology, failed Mr. Barnes also in this emergency, for he said: "The foremost religious minds are becoming more scientific, and the foremost scientific minds are becoming more religious. It is the little minds in both camps that cause the trouble."

Mr. Barnes was hardly the representative scientist in his willingness to cause the trouble. He was of those men who define issues, and it was unfortunate if other men were not quite ready to discuss them as frankly as he defined them. He only offended Mr. Fosdick, he did not get him to make an alignment directly on the critical question. Nor did he succeed in compelling the scientists to record the revolutionary departures of their new theology from orthodoxy. They strongly preferred to emphasize the points of likeness, and their own general piety and reasonableness. They were already winning by these pleasant tactics—why should they change them, and force their enemies to take the field in strength against them? They might have benefited their enemies' cause, but hardly their own.

And since this rebuff Mr. Barnes has come out more powerfully and uncompromisingly than ever in his book, "The Twilight of Christianity." He undertakes to tell with perfect frankness the position that science really holds in the religious controversy: it is positivism—it is naturalism, and anti-supernaturalism—it is anti-religion, unless you are willing to take religion as a secular establishment or society for morals—and it does not require a God at all.

He does not conceal the scorn he entertains for the Reconcilers—the apostate scientists who are willing to go through the forms of a supernatural religion for the sake of an agreement with the clericals. He quotes a sufficient number of scientists of his own belief and profession to throw some doubt upon the assumption that the scientists on the whole have gone in for reconciliation. But I should think his vigorous movement comes rather too late, and I shall continue for the present to believe that science now wants the sentimental and aristocratic sanctions of religion just as much as religion wants the industrial and financial prestige of science. The odor of sanctity has pleased the nostrils of the scientists.

His honesty is admirable, even if it has embarrassed both the scientists and the clericals. His view of a scientific religion makes a useful document.

The strategy of the scientific camp, concurred in by many of the clerical camp who could read the drift of the times, required a peace without victory. In May, 1923, a document was signed and issued from Washington which will serve better than another as the official American treaty of peace. Forty-five prominent men gave their signatures to it. They were taken about equally from three groups: the scientists, pressing gently but insistently for their reform; the clergymen, supposed to be the depositaries of the religious tradition, but latterly of more and more enfeebled loyalty; and the bewildered neutrals, such as educators and men of affairs.

More active than any other in the issuance of this manifesto, if not actually writing it, was Mr. R. A. Millikan, Director of the Norman Bridge Laboratory of the California Institute of Technology. His scientific distinction appears sufficiently from the fact that he has received a Nobel prize in physics. He has probably been more energetic and more influential than any other American scientist in campaigning for a new religion to suit the scientific temperament.

There was a preliminary statement, of a semi-formal nature. Mr. Millikan announced the purpose of the manifesto in these words: "To assist in correcting two erroneous impressions that seem to be current among certain groups of persons. The first is that religion today stands for medieval theology; the second that science is materialistic and irreligious."

Let us look hastily at this preliminary announcement.

Its function was like that of Mr. Wilson's Fourteen Points, which preceded another and even more famous treaty. It stated the considerations upon which the principals were agreed, as policies that would determine them in forming the actual instrument of peace. It seemed to represent certain reciprocal concessions on the part of the combatants.

On the part of the clericals, the concession was that they would cancel the medievalism in their faith, or modernize it. This meant that they would abandon those features in it that were most historical, institutional, and in the strict sense orthodox. It was a sweeping if not a fatal concession.

The concession made by the scientists, on the other hand, was that they would cancel any materialistic doctrines that might be still extant in scientific circles, and abandon all further opposition to religion as such. Let us examine this concession.

As for materialistic doctrines, I take that term as covering, to be exact, just those doctrines which hold that the ultimate category of all existence is material, and that biological and psychic phenomena are reducible to the phenomena of physics and chemistry. These doctrines have produced the well-known mechanistic views that are widely held among biologists. They have produced among psychologists similar views, of which the latest variety is behaviorism.

I do not elect to challenge the honesty of Mr. Millikan, or of any of the signers of the document from the scientific party, if they judge that this concession is one that science is really prepared on the whole to make. But it has been evident, with or without the notice that Mr. Barnes has served, that they will have trouble delivering the contract. Perhaps most of the British and European scientists would agree to it, although it was against these mainly that anti-mechanists like Mr. J. S. Haldane and M. Bergson have campaigned. There is much more doubt with regard to the American scientists. But the issue of materialism, as it is popularly debated, is rather obscure and difficult. The trouble is that it takes a philosopher to determine whether a scientist is a materialist or not, and it doesn't mean much if the scientist, when you tell him that materialism is a wicked thing, is sure he cannot be guilty. Perhaps we may say simply that the scientists do not intend any longer to be materialistic in some aggravated style that has given notorious offense to religionists in the past.

As for the willingness of science to be religious, the point lies in what the official meaning of that term is going to be. If you let the scientists give their own meaning to it, it is obvious that they will consent to be religious. If you ask them to be religious in the historical and orthodox sense, it is fairly certain that they will decline. But that is the issue that I wish to discuss throughout this book. It is my thesis that religion in the new sense, as science would now elect to have it, is a comparatively poor kind of religion—that it is barely religious at all, that it is as irreligious as can be.

With this sort of background, the Washington Agreement of 1923 read as follows:

We, the undersigned, deeply regret that in recent controversies there has been a tendency to present sci-

ence and religion as irreconcilable and antagonistic do-
mains of thought, for in fact they meet distinct human
needs and in the rounding out of human life they supplement rather than displace or oppose each other.
The purpose of science is to develop, without prejudice or preconception of any kind, a knowledge of the
facts, the laws and processes of nature. The even more
important task of religion, on the other hand, is to develop the conscience, the ideals, and the aspirations of
mankind. Each of these two activities represents a deep
and vital function of the soul of man and both are necessary for the life, the progress and the happiness of the
human race.

It is a sublime conception of God which is furnished
by science and one wholly consonant with the highest
ideals of religion, when it represents Him as revealing
Himself through countless ages in the development of
the earth as an abode for men, and in the age-long inbreathing of life into its constituent matter, culminating in man with his spiritual nature and all his God-
like powers.

The first of the three articles is excellent, and worthy of
anybody's indorsement. It is a pity that science and religion
should fight! And it has not been the fault of science alone
that they do. Let us see.

Religious doctrines are embodied in myths, and myths
attempt to express truths which are not accessible to science.
They are necessarily super-scientific, or super-natural, but
they are not necessarily anti-scientific and un-natural. The
myths which our historic orthodoxy employs are very old
ones. It was their intention to be accurate so far as their
scientific or natural content went, and only after that to
transcend science or be supernatural. But scientific knowledge has advanced, until now these myths are definitely an-

tiquated and objectionable on their scientific side. For instance, they represented God as presiding over a Ptolemaic universe. When science substituted the Copernican for the Ptolemaic universe, the defenders of the faith were placed in an embarrassing position. They might conceivably have modified the myths and represented God as presiding over a Copernican universe. They elected to dispute science so long as they could. The myths in their hands did not prove sufficiently elastic, they were not modified gracefully in points that were not quite critical. But the obstinacy of the religionists invited retaliation. Science proceeded to dispute the myths *in toto,* because it overestimated the importance of their purely natural features. It was mistaken in supposing these to be of the religious essence. And so the issue was joined. The controversy between two such unyielding opponents was a tragic one.

It has forced upon us now the necessity of choosing between a religion which seems to repudiate science from the start, and a science which seems never to rise into a religion.

What is the solution proposed in the second article of the Washington Agreement? It is not a solution at all; it is an evasion. The purpose of science as set forth there is to develop a knowledge of nature. But it is not intimated in the least that the purpose of religion is to develop upon this natural knowledge a practicable supernaturalism. Rather, the purpose of religion is said to be to develop "the conscience, the ideals, and the aspirations of mankind." These expressions are exquisitely vague, but I believe they mean to say that the purpose of religion is simply to attend to the morals of mankind. Science for knowledge, and religion for morality. It would suit Mr. Barnes precisely, but it is not good enough for religion. No historian of religion will concede that it has made its characteristic movement when it has only made moral men out of the faithful. Morality has reference to the conduct of man towards man, but religion has reference to the conduct of man towards the universe, or towards nature, or towards God. Religion is not a secular code of conduct but a form of worship. You cannot have a religion without a God. The "even more important task of religion," as I would have liked to see it phrased in the second article, would have been: "To develop a suitable supernaturalism, a theology, or a system of myths, upon the scientific knowledge of nature as its base." But Mr. Millikan does not risk such a non-scientific concept as that.

To justify my interpretation of this article, I will quote a remark that Mr. Millikan has now made in a context dated 1930.

> My conception then of the essentials of the Christian religion, and no other need here be considered, is that those essentials consist in just two things: first, in inspiring mankind with the Christlike, *i.e.*, the altruistic *ideal*, and that means specifically, *concern for the common good* as contrasted with one's own individual impulses and interests, wherever in one's own judgment the two come into conflict; and second, inspiring mankind to *do*, rather than merely to think about, its duty, the definition of duty for each individual being what he himself conceives to be for the common good. In three words, I conceive the essential task of religion to be "to develop the consciences, the ideals, and the aspirations of mankind."

If Mr. Millikan seems sometimes to speak with two voices, this is probably the real one. For here he is quoting, as literally as he can recall, from the second article of the document of 1923; and the construction that he puts upon it is that the function of religion is merely a social, man-to-man, and secular function, and requires no God at all.

The human economy is fully provided for, in the judgment of the authors of the article, when man has been furnished with science to win knowledge and power, and altruism to use them for the common good. In the technical economic terms: science for the production of goods, and altruism for their fair distribution. But where is religion in the meantime?

There is no more essential religion here than there is in the system of Auguste Comte, who banished theology from it expressly. There is nothing in Positivism and nothing in perfect atheism that would forbid a man to subscribe to such an article. As a religious scheme, this is "Hamlet" without the Prince of Denmark.

Of course the document does not stop there. It goes on to a final article which undertakes to put the God into a religion that was on the point of forgetting about the formality.

Where does he come from? Strictly speaking, science does not "furnish" to scientists any God at all. That is the first exception to be taken to the article. Science, in the language of the previous article, was entirely occupied with furnishing "a knowledge of the facts, the laws, and the processes of nature." Science deals with the natural—but a God is a supernatural. That is the elementary consideration in the logic of religion. In vain we pretend to the contrary. It is even in vain we elect to speak of God in pseudo-scientific or professional terms, which look hard and naturalistic. We may refer to him as a God, a Person, a Mind, an Intelligence, a Purpose, an Agent, an Activity, a Force, a Principle—but he is necessarily behind, over, above, in, or under nature, and there he is inaccessible to science. Scientists are in no better position than anybody else to circumvent this logical consideration. They have no apparatus for detecting God in any factual or demonstrative sense. In the language of Kant, they must find God by the exercise of the "Reflective Judgment," whereas, when they are strictly scientific, they are engaged in the exercise of the "Determinant Judgment." I do not know whether insincerity or shabby thinking is the worse charge to bring against the scientists. But what shall we say of the very broad intimation made by many recent scientists (and repeated by many preachers under the scientific influence) that they have suddenly got hold of a God that can be demonstrated, whereas the old-time religionists never attained to this privilege?

The God who appears in the third article of the Washington Agreement is born like any other God—he suits the scientists temperamentally, but he is far from being a product of natural science, he is just as supernatural as other Gods are.

And now to see how the scientists represent their God: as one "revealing Himself through countless ages in the development of the earth as an abode for men, and in the age-long inbreathing of life into its constituent matter, culminating in man with his spiritual nature and all his God-like powers."

A great many objections might be taken to this representation by grammarians and lexicographers. And for example, to the dodge by which "revelation" is piously introduced. The word is not honestly used. The idea that means to be conveyed, I am inclined to think, is that God has revealed himself now in something better than the usual way, and indeed in some demonstrable manner that science professionally approves. This is the intimation that I have just objected to. But never mind that. Does God reveal himself to the scientists of countless ages, or has he revealed himself suddenly to modern scientists as having been working for countless ages on his projects? And what is an "age-long inbreathing of life into its constituent matter"? And when is matter constituent and when is it not? And is it not a little ludicrous to picture God as making the abode for man, and then making man out of the abode, or out of a certain fraction of its constituents? And what is it here, grammatically or logically, that culminates in man with his spiritual nature? And is there no tautology in defining God as one whose creature has God-like powers?

Mr. Millikan and his colleagues are quite professional in their scientific utterances, but evidently as theologians their amateur status will not be questioned.

But these objections are perhaps too quizzical, and there is something more serious deserving to be said. What specific doctrines emerge from this obscure credo? It lacks a great deal of being precise; but I believe there are at least two doctrines implied here which are of all importance in the new religion.

The first of these is that God as the ruler of the universe governs it in such a manner as to make it accommodate itself to the welfare of man. The earth is for man's abode; and God "developed" it; this phrase suggests that his instrument was an evolutionary or scientific process. Thus God is a scientist; the universe is his workshop; but among his productions he has produced man, and all the other productions are for man's benefit.

The second doctrine would seem to be this: Man is God-like himself. God is the great original scientist, but man is himself a little scientist. For he can understand God's scientific technique, and he can actually in considerable degree apply it in the human sphere, anticipating God, and hastening the course of his good works.

The doctrines just formulated may or may not be the doctrines implied in the Manifesto of 1923. But they are the doctrines preached more or less openly from a great many modern pulpits, and they are surely the doctrines which Mr. Michael Pupin, the physicist and inventor, elaborated a few years later in his book, "The New Reformation." Mr. Pupin is perhaps second only to Mr. Millikan as a scientific expositor of the new religion. I take this book as a good text from which to discuss its theology.

Who is Mr. Pupin's God, and what does he do? Briefly, he is a super-scientist, working the world on scientific principles, and having consistently one objective: the benefit of man. Mr. Pupin examines all the known fields of modern scientific theory, only to find that this definition always applies. The universe would be, without God, a mere chaos of whirling electronic granules. But that is only its primordial aspect. Now the way that a chaos may be put to rights is through some coördinating device that performs work, and God has several of these of his own invention: Mr. Pupin calls them God's "coördinators," understanding by the term the scientific processes of utmost generality. In certain areas and through certain periods, God harnesses primordial chaos through his coördinators, so that the aimless but vast energies of the chaos become directed, become transformed into suns and planets, into the stable chemical elements that constitute matter, into vegetation, into animal and human life. The last transformation is the grand climax of the whole series, "the last for which the first was made." The divine coördinators are such as the laws of electro-magnetism, of thermo-dynamics, or gravitation, of chemical affinity, of vegetable cellular structure, and of animal forms.

And man, the highest creature, is served by the other creatures of God. Mr. Pupin asks the question, for example, "What is the terrestrial mission of solar radiation?" He replies that its mission is to vaporize the surface of the sea and produce rains and streams for watering man's crops.

"The sight of the stars should remind us," says this scientist, "that there are in the physical universe inexhaustible stores of opportunities for rendering service similar to the service which solar radiation is rendering to our terrestrial globe. With this axiom in mind we shall always find the word 'service' written across the starry vault of heaven."

It is only fair to observe that the service which the fixed stars render, according to Mr. Pupin's conception, is not so much to the humankind which inhabits this planet. Our rainmaker is the sun. The fixed stars can be the rain-makers only for the nameless men who inhabit whatever hypothetical planets may be attached to these. But at least it is his belief that the solar system operates, in God's beneficent science, for men on earth; and that the solar systems of other suns operate to secure, if not the same, some vaguely analogous objectives. And if we observe the emphasis laid on that word "service" in Mr. Pupin's doctrine, we shall be the less at a loss to know why the new theology has at last rather suddenly and overwhelmingly prevailed. Its persuasive watchwords had already been sown thick upon our Western air. I do not know what more up-to-date recommendation could be cited in favor of a theology than to say it renders service. The God of Mr. Pupin, we are given to understand, is a God who serves. The beneficiary, of course, is man.

And now for the second of Mr. Pupin's doctrines. God, as we have seen, is a super-scientist. But fortunately he created man in his own image; for man is a scientist, and his scientific powers are, in the words of the Manifesto of 1923, "God-like." So it is man's privilege to understand God—or to understand God's coördinators, which is the same thing —and to serve himself as well as to be served by God.

Look at the steam-engine, for example. Here is a specifically human invention. But when it is analyzed, it turns out to be simply the application of one of God's own coördinators. The French physicist Carnot first had the wit to comprehend this coördinator, and therefore to tell just how the molecular chaos that is mere heat is given a uniform direction and made to perform work in the service of man. But the steam-engine is only one of many such applications; and God may be assumed to approve thoroughly of them, since he allows man to work them so successfully. Man is invited to take a certain initiative, to help himself to the coördinators, and make them go as far as they will. Of course they would be working for him in any event, for they were designed expressly in his favor. But he is not altogether obliged to wait and conform to their leisurely schedule.

Science is either theoretical or practical, according to a convenient division. But the theory and the practice bear a close and spontaneous relation to each other; they are like father and son, bound each to each in natural piety. The theory is science the revealer—revealing God in his aspects of service, in the processes by which he makes his benevolence prevail. The practice is science the worker—borrowing these processes, and using them, without waiting any longer, to realize at once a multitude of human desires. If theoretical science is the contemplation of God's goodness, practical science is an applied religion. The former is a sort of Sabbath worship. If the Sabbath continues to be observed under the new dispensation, it will have to be the day for understanding and praise, the day on which the theorists expound and extol the manifold works of God—which generally turn out to be less recondite and inscrutable than the laity might have supposed. The workaday routine, on the other hand, would be the authorized religious exercise of the practical man, putting into effect the Sabbath lessons of theory, and pursuing zealously his gainful occupations in order to get himself into close partnership with God.

It might be suggested by some cynic that the theoretical meditations of the Sabbath would be conducted in quite too avid an expectancy of the gainful occupations to follow. That is entirely because the cynic is applying to the new religion a standard of judgment that was born under the old. The old religion did not possess a God whose simple function was to serve. Religious instruction was not peculiarly in the technique by which desirable work can be done efficiently and cheaply, and religious living was regarded as something a little apart from actually getting one's work so done. But now that it is God's will that mankind be served, it becomes holy living if mankind proceeds to serve itself as hard as possible.

The God of the new religion is anthropomorphic. So, doubtless, are the gods of most other religions. But the present anthropomorphism is peculiarly tame and ingenuous. When God was pictured in the likeness of a fabulously Great Man, of marvelous technique and uncertain favor, it was fairly difficult for one to be at ease in Zion; for his fiat was unaccountable and unpredictable; and man worshiping him was necessarily humble, and for the time being neglectful of the ordinary routine of practical life as a very vain thing. But the new religion represents God as a Great Man with all the uncertainties left out: a Great Man whose ways are scientific and knowable and whose intention is amiable and constant. The net result of holding by this religion is just to be encouraged in attending to one's own human concerns, secured of God's favor and finding no propriety in burnt offering and sacrifice.

God as a Great Man is even better than that: he is the modern scientist glorified and apotheosized. And what is a modern scientist, or any scientist? He is first the man who knows the processes by which things work; and he is also— an important corollary—the man who by this knowledge possesses a handle of human control, an instrument of action. There is no scientific process that does not have as its logical end the attainment of some human good. And when God has once been conceived as a scientist, he is also conceived as one whose processes likewise aim at human good.

So the new God defines and sets in motion—"promulgates" is Mr. Henry Pratt Fairchild's word—those efficient and reliable scientific laws which move the universe. He is committed to the attainment of humane objectives. To this end he compels the stupid chaos to fall into line. The only question that still impugns our happy destiny is as to how fully man will grasp God's secrets, and hasten his own benefits. Conceivably, if man renounced science, or if he failed to prosecute science with all his might, he might delay his happiness. But evidently it is a common opinion among scientists that this misfortune is not too likely. They know now that the universe is ruled by a scientific God, and his science is very largely revealed to the mundane scientists already. The remainder doubtless awaits revelation in the near future.

For instance, the atoms, once as impenetrable as the name denoted, are soon going to be laid bare to human understanding and control, and made to bear testimony to the goodness of God. Out of the knowledge of the atoms some profitable mechanical lessons are sure to come. For a while it was expected that in the artificial dissolution of atoms a new and inexhaustible source of energy would be made available for doing our chores. That idea is passing now. But there is no doubt that it will be worth our while to know the atoms.

We have heard a good deal about the quaintness of the Ptolemaic cosmology that once so firmly enshrined our orthodox religion. Actually, it was held that all the celestial bodies occupied themselves with whirling dizzily about our little earth, in order to provide it with heat and light—it meanwhile sitting still in the center to be served in idleness. That was a rather cool assumption, we hear it said, in favor of the dignity of man and the flattering attentions of his Creator.

Modern science, we are told, has changed this ingenuous

conception somewhat. Modern science requires the earth to run its humble course like the rest of the heavenly bodies, and even in a disgracefully subordinate capacity. The whole celestial apparatus, as science re-constructed it several centuries ago, seemed to become a completely mechanical, inhuman, and inhospitable affair to look at. When they first contemplated the revolutionary alteration in their physical universe, the hearts of the faithful must have sunk within them. The scientists who could actually propose such a scheme must have seemed to them as going to suicidal extremes, with a strange indifference to obvious consequences. For under this scheme the divine favor disappeared, and God seemed to be relieved of any humanity which might have been imputed to him. The scientists must have rated as a peculiarly heroic breed of monsters, whose singular motives did not include the motive of their own human advantage.

But the alarmists were quite mistaken. Evidently it was the destiny of Copernicanism quickly to become a body of doctrine more flattering to humanity than the supplanted Ptolemaic system, and much more profitable. Did Copernicus and Galileo, Kepler and Newton, seem at first to be thrusting this planet and its population into a status of horrible impotence? But science was far from stopping there: to arrive so far and no further would have been a most unscientific procedure. All the sciences, even the most abstruse ones, even celestial mechanics itself, have their practical objectives, and we may rely upon them with confidence not to pursue any of their speculations disinterestedly, or at a human sacrifice. Sciences are essentially pragmatic; they are instruments of practice. They aim of course at reducing natural phenomena to human understanding, and to that extent they may seem disinterested and innocent. But they also aim, perhaps slyly and half-consciously at first, and then greedily and openly as soon as they can, at reducing them to human prediction and control. And now the scientists in a long and brilliant succession have built on the early Copernican foundations, in such a manner as Mr. Pupin describes in his book, until Copernicanism has become definitely and frankly useful.

The formulation which Ptolemy worked out was very flattering at first sight to the dignity of man, but it was comparatively useless. The center of the universe was the earth; the apparatus was evidently intended to promote the life and comfort of man. But the whole business was mysterious. It happens that in that period when the universe was pictured so prettily by the Ptolemaic scheme, God was being consistently represented as one whose intentions were not to be presumed upon. His large aims were not simply the benefit of man, since they entailed very seriously, and invariably, our human sufferings. Just this much humanity could be predicted of him, that he had magically arranged a universe fit for human habitation. There the matter stopped. Man enjoyed this divine dispensation; he could not improve it, he could not make a further use of it. He could not understand the secret of its process.

But this condition was altered when the Copernican theory supplanted the Ptolemaic. The great Hegel thought that theology had necessarily been revolutionized by the acceptance of Copernicanism as scientists defined it. For, to the extent that the universe through Copernicanism became intelligible to the human mind, God became rational and knowable, and ceased to be magical and irresponsible. Only the sternest philosophical qualifications kept Hegel from descending to the flattest pronouncements about the glory of the human mind—with all its "God-like powers," as it is described in the Credo of 1923. As the scientific mind came to look more and more like God's mind, God began to look more and more like a simple scientist. So the revolution which is now issuing in the triumph of the God of Science over the God of Israel had its beginning in that illustrious scientific period when scientists were winning their Copernican view of the universe. The new knowledge brought a temptation to his conceit to which proud modern man has proved unequal.

For the new universe proved not only flattering to man, since he could understand it, but profitable also, since he could use it. Do not Newton's mechanical principles, meant to account for the motions of the heavenly bodies, underlie all subsequent science of the industrial and useful kind? And have we not now become thoroughly acclimated to the Copernican universe, and found it wonderfully complete as a "development" project for our habitation?

Mr. Millikan himself addressed some remarks to the New York Chamber of Commerce in November, 1928:

> Do you practical men fully realize that the airplane was only made possible by the development of the internal combustion engine, and that this in its turn was only made possible by the development of the laws governing all heat engines, the laws of thermo-dynamics, through the use for the hundred preceding years of the steam engine, and that this was only made possible by the preceding two hundred years of work in celestial mechanics, that this was only made possible by the discovery by Galileo and by Newton of the laws of force and motion which had to be utilized in every one of the subsequent developments. That states the relationship of pure science to industry. The one is the child of the other. You may apply any blood-test you wish and you will at once establish the relationship. Pure science begat modern industry.

It would be absurd to wish that the Ptolemaic universe had not fallen before the Copernican, and that the numberless achievements of modern science had never been won.

Our modernism will justify itself without any difficulty for the New York Chamber of Commerce, as for anybody who examines it with respect to the practical goods it has produced.

But we were talking about religion. Our mechanical successes have altered deeply our attitude toward the world, and toward the God who embodies its direction. This alteration is quite like that which overtakes the spirit of a man who has found prosperity too quickly. When the modern scientists discovered that the mysterious secret of the celestial universe was nothing but a simple gravitational principle which they themselves could apply, they had taken, apparently, the measure of God. It seemed after that that everything was humanly knowable and practicable. So we have Mr. Pupin declaring that the universe, for all its scope and contingency, travails continually for the benefit of man. I should say that this is being at ease in Zion. This is a pitch of confidence to which the worshipers of a sterner and more awful God did not aspire.

In the new religion of science God is supposed to have had the goodness to invite man to profiteer upon the universe.

CHAPTER TWO

THE OLD GOD

THE WESTERN world, as it is constituted by Europe and the Americas, inherited richly from the East, and its principal heritage was—a Hebraic religion. The Roman Empire and its successor, the Roman Catholic Church, were the executors of this inheritance. The Roman Empire was in an excellent position to discharge this office, for it was a Mediterranean empire—it was as much Eastern as it was Western.[1] The religion which was thus handed down to us was superior in its depth and in its subtlety to any of the religions native to the West. The fact is, of course, that Asiatic soil has been peculiarly the home of superior religions, and for us the importation was likely to be superior to the home-made product.

But was this Semitic religion really appropriate to the genius of the Western communities? And could they adopt it in more than a superficial manner? Nietzsche and many other extreme Occidentalists have thought not. They have thought that the West made a mistake in trying to make

---

[1] We will ask ourselves at once: Was not the Greek or Orthodox Church more faithful as the depositary of the Eastern tradition than the Roman Church? Its patriarchs lived in Eastern cities: its contact with the Eastern influence was direct. But its Eastern nature was even deeper than that. This Church was simply Eastern more that it was Western. It was not *our* Church. It was Rome that had bridged the gulf between the East and the West, and its rôle was not only to carry the Eastern idea westward but also to adapt it to the Western mind.

use of Christianity, and consequently fell into a monstrous hypocrisy, because its principle of conduct did not actually come out of its formal faith.

The jarring element in our life, which makes us inhospitable to the religiousness of the East, is peculiarly modern and peculiarly Western: it is the scientific spirit. The scientific drive in the West is but little more than three centuries old, but in that time we have more and more deeply abandoned ourselves to it. It is now our theoretical scientists, our applied scientists, and our practical men of affairs, who mostly decide the conduct of our intellectual life.

The Old and New Testaments, the God of Israel and that modification or transformation at the hands of Jesus which Spengler calls "Magian," inspired and informed the early Christian Church. It held together till the close of the period called medieval.

But upon that date rose Protestantism, and rose also modern science. The two have been quite contemporaneous, and it is hardly possible to find in this fact nothing but a coincidence. For Protestantism has always figured to itself as a determination to rationalize the antiquated religious doctrines. And as for modern science, that, of course, is the sweeping rationalization of the universe under a minimum of definitive principles known as "scientific."

The conviction under which Western science labors is naturalism: the belief that the universe is largely known, and theoretically knowable, as the "nature" which science defines; and that there exists no God or other entity beyond or above this demonstrable nature. Naturalism is as antitheological, or as atheistic, as is honest Positivism. And in fact naturalism and Positivism are the same thing.

But by way of preëmpting the field against a God of another and hostile variety, modern science would adopt a God of its own whom we have just attempted to describe: he is merely the spirit presiding over the universe and making it the intelligible, tractable, and naturalistic universe it is. And we appear to be witnessing today the almost total conversion of Protestantism to this naturalism. Protestantism, whose history has been marked by the destruction of so many features of the original faith, has evidently been preparing itself to come at length to a completely naturalized religion—whatever anomaly that may be.

It is notable that Roman Catholicism, however, is not yet prepared to make this surrender. There were no Roman priests among the clericals who signed the Washington Agreement of 1923. The Roman Church has held on to its medievalism, and could hardly have promised that its religion should no longer "stand for medieval theology."

To renounce the medieval in theology was to renounce the Oriental elements in our religion.

Our historical orthodoxy was an aggregate of supernatural stories, or myths. As soon as I make this statement, I remember painfully that there is a certain state of mind which will reply: "Myths are for children, and I am adult, and I do not care to hear about your historical orthodoxy." Probably this state of mind is not of the advanced mental age it supposes. But here it is enough to say: Myth is the mark of every religion that has functioned after the usual historic types. Our myths were taken partly from the Old Testament and partly from the New. We will examine in rather short order the part which was taken from the Old Testament, and which has to do with the question, Who was the God of Israel? I would fix attention upon only a few leading features, the ones which seem most peculiarly Hebraic, and the most foreign to the temper of our Occidental modernism.

I should add that our glance will have to be, so far as I am concerned, that of a layman, and not that of an expert theologian.

The old God distinguished himself from the new God in at least three important particulars. First, he was mysterious, and not fully understood; there was no great familiarity with him which might breed contempt. Second, he was worshiped with burnt offering and sacrifice. And third, he was the author of evil as well as of good.

Perhaps all these are correlative features which imply each other.

He was mysterious, and not fully understood. The God of Israel was so great a God that he was unfathomable. He talked, willed, commanded, was angered, and performed the usual functions of personality. But not exactly those of a familiar. Physically, he was proof against human observation, or inscrutable. Not even his prophet Moses could bear to look upon his face.

> And when Jehovah saw that he turned aside to see, God called unto him out of the midst of the bush, and said, Moses. Moses. And he said, Here am I. And he said, Draw not nigh hither: put off thy shoes from thy feet, for the place whereon thou standest is holy ground. Moreover he said, I am the God of thy father, the God of Abraham, the God of Isaac, and the God of Jacob. And Moses hid his face; for he was afraid to look upon God.

So God appeared to his prophets in visions which never revealed his face. He spoke Hebrew words to them, which were a concession to the limitations of their knowledge, but from which they were not supposed to presume that they understood his whole nature and purpose. When they described him they did it in scrupulously mystical or fantastic terms, as in the visions of Ezekiel and the apocalyptic writers.

Their God was anthropomorphic but only, it was agreed,

with respect to the spirit. To prevent the idea that men could know him as a physical or even physiological entity, it was said that he uttered as the second of the commandments: "Thou shalt not make unto thee any graven image, or any likeness of anything that is in heaven above, or that is in the earth beneath, or that is in the water under the earth: thou shalt not bow down thyself to them, nor serve them." This famous prohibition served for the touchstone of fidelity in the ancient history of Israel—a people surrounded by idolaters, whose Gods were more tangible than theirs, and very tempting to that part of the mind which wants a hard factual definition in its thinking. There were many cases of Jewish apostasy. But the commandment prevailed. The God of Israel survived in his original nature, as one who could not be limited and compassed by sensible representation.

(Most Gods, by the way, are anthropomorphic, and the best Gods are anthropomorphic with this same reservation: with respect to the spirit. For example, the God of the Washington Credo of 1923, in reference to whom it is said that man has his "spiritual nature" and his "God-like powers.")

But the most reverent of the usages of the Jews was in their refusal even to pronounce his sacred name. Out of several generic terms the Jews adopted as peculiarly the name of their own God the sacred tetragram JHWH. In their ritualistic observances they never used it. When they came to it in the reading, they substituted one of the other names, and read Athonah, Lord. This practice perhaps resulted from the excessive scrupulousness with which they observed the third of the commandments: "Thou shalt not take the name of the Lord thy God in vain." They guarded against this danger by not taking it on their lips at all.

But how was their God different from that of the moderns? I do not pretend that the moderns are idolaters, and

have committed themselves to some definite pictorial representation of their God. The difference between the new God
and the old God may appear more clearly later. But already
a difference begins to appear.

The new God also denies himself form and professes to
be non-representable; nevertheless, he is much more defined
than the old God. This is a naturalistic age, and its God is
nature. But then there are two natures—depending on the
temperament of those who behold nature. By poets, religionists, Orientals, and sensitive people, nature is feared and
loved—hardly the one without the other. But by scientists
and modern Occidentals nature is only studied and possessed.
They are aware only of the nature which conforms to the
laws they are able to formulate; the nature of the naturalists. Mr. Millikan tells us:

> The idea that God, or Nature, or the Universe, what-
> ever term you prefer, is not a being of caprice and whim
> as had been the case in all the main body of thinking of
> the ancient world, but is, instead, a God who rules
> through law, or a Nature capable of being depended
> upon, or a universe of consistency, of orderliness and of
> the beauty that goes with order—that idea has *made*
> modern science, and it is unquestionably the foundation
> of modern civilization.

Mr. Millikan intends here to simplify God. He appears
to reject a certain universe because he could not depend
upon it. Suppose it turned out that the actual universe was
essentially undependable, so far as human purposes are concerned: is that an upset too grievous to be borne? Is the
universe under obligations to the scientist to be scientific, or
is the scientist rather under obligations to the universe to be
truthful and to represent it as it is? Mr. Millikan does not
claim in the least to prefer a certain variety of the universe
because it is the more actual, but because it suits him better.

This is not the fortitude of the ancients. The Jews did not concede that God, or Nature, or the Universe—"whatever term you prefer"—was a God, Nature, or Universe on whom you could depend to act according to your predictions, to be orderly, and to subordinate himself, herself, or itself to the laws which your human science had formulated. To them God was superior to formulation. To the naturalist God is the essence of the formulas.

The issue is one of fact. Is the actual universe amenable to the laws of science, or is it not? Of course the truth is that it partly is, and partly isn't. One of the consequences of too much of the modern scientific training upon us is that we finally come to the point where we mistake the Uniformity of Nature, which is only the expression of a hope, for the statement of a fact. Mr. Millikan is typical of a great many scientists in his determination to force upon us the dogma, Science works. He will scarcely consent to the qualification, Sometimes.

His peculiar God accordingly has a dominion which is, if we may try a rather flat generalization, just one-half that of the old God of the Jews. The old God was the genius of a whole universe. The new God is the genius of just that part of the universe which is, to our intelligence, intelligible. The old God was the author both of the rational and of the contingent, the new God is the author only of the rational. Therefore the old God was a whole God, and the new God is half a God, or a Demigod.

Who then is this God who, to quote some other terms used by Mr. Millikan, is the "unifying" influence, or the "integrating" factor, behind nature? God is pictured here—so far as he is pictured—as a Big Scientist behind the scenes, applying the formulas as in a laboratory, making the cosmic engine run, imposing the intelligible or universal behaviors upon the natural objects as he pushes them out into created existence.

The topic is open to endless comment. I think of but one other distinction between the old God and the new which seems to require saying at this point. The old God worked by fiat: the new God works by law. The difference is that the former conveys to us something of an act that is arbitrary and contingent, so far as our calculations go: very well described by Mr. Millikan as the caprice or whim of some person whose motivation we cannot understand. How the moderns have hated that power of fiat that was supposed to reside in the inscrutable God of our ancient orthodoxy! But of course the fiat might issue also, as it actually did, in works that would seem to us highly rational and regular. The law of the new God, on the other hand, conveys to us the possibility of only those works which we may calculate in advance. A God with a power of fiat is clearly better furnished than a God committed to a law.

The old God was worshiped with burnt offering and sacrifice. He was more than the embodiment of just those communicable principles of the universe which the scientists call scientific, and the behavior of his subjects toward him was also unscientific.

We have seen what attitude men of exclusively scientific habit exhibit towards the God of Science. He is that law, or that set of terms, which they possess more fully than anything else in the world. As possessed, understood, and used, they make no mystery of him. They continue to possess, understand, and use him. Or if they must contemplate him, it is for the purpose of possessing him more completely, understanding him more explicitly, and using him more profitably. Science is an economy which is progressive. Understanding implies use, and understanding defines itself more and more precisely in order that use may take place more and more practically.

Science therefore questions the religionists very strictly

upon their program of action: Do you propose to have a whole Sabbath day lost to human usefulness? Do you intend to require ceremonial rites that cost human labor and wealth, and consume valuable time?

It is to be feared, from this point of view, that the Jews were great wasters of scientific opportunities. They imposed upon themselves substantial concessions of time and means to the worship of their inscrutable and ineffable God. They gave him one day in seven. They also gave him tithes; and these were not quite offerings to the community chest, justified as social benevolence, but offerings to God that no man could touch and use. They expended prodigiously for God's temple. They brought him sacrifices which were poured out upon the ground or consumed on the fire of the altar.

Consider the wastefulness of human labor under some typical though slight prescription, as it must appear to the modern economist:

> And when any one offereth an oblation of a meal-offering unto Jehovah, his oblation shall be of fine flour; and he shall pour oil upon it, and put frankincense thereon; and he shall bring it to Aaron's sons the priests; and he shall take thereout his handful of the fine flour thereof, and of the oil thereof, with all the frankincense thereof. And the priests shall burn it as the memorial thereof upon the altar, an offering made by fire, of a sweet savor unto Jehovah; and that which is left of the meal-offering shall be Aaron's and his sons'; it is a thing most holy of the offerings of Jehovah made by fire.

There is in this prescription a politic provision for the sustenance of the priesthood; to that extent the offerings are devoted to human service. But for the most part they are burnt upon the air, to make a savor which shall ascend to God.

The modern economic point of view, which sees a waste in ritual and offering, is represented unfavorably in a New Testament incident.

> Mary therefore took a pound of ointment of pure nard, very precious, and anointed the feet of Jesus, and wiped his feet with her hair. But Judas Iscariot, one of his disciples, that should betray him, saith, Why was not this ointment sold for three hundred shillings, and given to the poor?

But one hesitates to hold with the author of this story that the motive of Judas was something special, and not the usual economic motive of the common naturalist.

> Now this he said, not because he cared for the poor; but because he was a thief, and having the bag took away what was put therein.

The modernist leaders in our midst, issuing religious manifestoes to repeal the old ordinances of sacrifice and ritual, are certainly not thieves. They are rather, I should imagine, only the "sophisters, economists, and calculators" before whom Burke considered that the age of chivalry had passed away. Their recipe for successful human action is simply to "produce," to "get results," to apply science, and then more science.

Today, in the degree that scientific naturalism has dispossessed religion, the service of God has become merely the service of man, and there are no offerings required of the believers which are not scrupulously accounted for as contributions to human welfare. Mr. Julian Huxley, the bearer of a name illustrious in modern science, has expressed this parsimonious view: "When men believe that they are surrounded with magical powers, they spend half their lives in ritual designed to effect the operations of these (wholly hypothetical) influences. When they worship a God whom they rationalize as man-like, they sacrifice a large proportion of their produce on his altars, and may even kill their fellow-creatures to placate his (again imaginary) passions."

With regard to this sharp passage. Whenever religionists invest the universe with powers that cannot be drawn within the net of science—and realistic observation testifies that the universe eludes the ideal simplicities of science at every point of experience—these powers are inscrutable, metaphysical, supernatural, contingent, unpredictable, superscientific, or divine. Unfortunately, to the lowest order of believers, they are simply magical, or powers amenable to magic control. The ritual is regarded by these believers as the magic key by which the ritualist secures their services. Magical pretenses have nowadays, however, been rather thoroughly exploded, and Mr. Huxley is using the term here with the most unfavorable intentions. He means to point out that it is believing in magic to think there are supernatural powers which you can bribe by ritual and offering to do your chores for you. I shall come back to that point presently. In the meantime: I am afraid it is true that some believers have exactly the attitude which he describes.

The worshipers of the God of Israel may certainly stand up and exchange taunts with the worshipers of the new God of science about motives, if such a performance seems pretty to them. We will be struck by the fact that the motives which Mr. Huxley ascribes to the antiquated believers are precisely the ones which he as a naturalist must entertain and must recommend. They are the motives of the practical man and the economist. The antiquated believers may deny these motives; Mr. Huxley cannot very well do so. His argument is simply this: We both are worshiping for the benefits that attach, but you are deluded and I will be the one rewarded.

The best motives of the religious Jews were, I think surely, religious or metaphysical motives. Their ritualistic practices, their Sabbath observances, and their burnt offerings were a sort of mnemonic discipline. By its help they reminded themselves ceaselessly of their metaphysical destiny as men. They observed ten major commandments, of which no less than four were prescriptions concerning the man-to-God relation exclusively—and six concerned the man-to-man relation. They devoted a considerable amount of their time to meditating God, and they hallowed this allotment because they knew of the dangerous encroachments of the secular interest. They did not propose to degenerate into naturalists, and they had a policy which was to prevent that. It was evidently a good policy. The steady slipping of the Protestant bodies into naturalism shows what is likely to happen when the ritual observances begin to chafe us, and are relaxed.

If a religious institution is sincere, and means to be effective, it will never be able to do without ritual, holiday, and sacrifice. These are the observances which defend the rights and honors of the God.

Of course Mr. Huxley is a wise man according to his lights, and he cannot help pronouncing some truth in his strictures. All religionists must testify in shame to a degree of justice in his charge, which is as follows: there were Jews who mistook the purpose of ritual, and thought it a device for gaining benefits from the God for whom it was performed. They were, as I have charged in return, the naturalists who had taken employment with the wrong house— with religion instead of with science. In numbers they may have been legion—they are many in every communion. It may even be, to put it flatly, that there are three men capable temperamentally of naturalism to two men capable of metaphysics. They take part in religious exercises, supposing that they are practicing a very marvelous kind of magic, which knows how to manage those intractable forces in the universe which notoriously have resisted the efforts of the common sciences.

It is only just if the scientists should feel professionally aggrieved at losing their customers to fakirs. It is certainly true that magic can never compete with science in the performance of practical projects. Limited as the powers of scientific technique may be, they are the only powers which are practically effective. But as forms of worship they are not effective at all. They destroy worship. The God of science can be used much better than he can be worshiped. When you have mastered the secrets of your God, you will not need him any further as a God, but you may keep him for a servant.

Religious leaders are probably like the leaders of the Masonic or some other mystic order. They are sensitive to the mysteries behind the world, and they desire to perpetuate in human kind the sense of mystery in order that men may not become completely brutalized, conceited, and blinded. They pack their rites with the most provocative suggestions that they can devise. But in order that no man may go without the advantage of these suggestions, and lapse into naturalism when he might have been saved, they open their communion or their fraternity to many believers, even though these must begin at a very low plane of religious understanding. There are men who mistake the purpose of the institution, and enter it in the hope that it will give them a new weapon of practical accomplishment, and yet the leaders of the institution permit them to enter. Perhaps something in the ritual may strike the curiosity of these hopeful naturalists, and lead them into the mysteries; but the instruction may scarcely be said to be forced upon them. A Church like Roman Catholicism, therefore, or a Masonic order, or even a proper educational institution, contains in its membership men of many grades of metaphysical power, and is careful not to limit its hospitality too severely, for it might exclude some who look unpromising, but who might attain if they had the opportunity.

Naturalism, even if it calls itself religion, is founded on quite a different principle. It has little patience with the mystic nonsense of the fraternal orders, if this is understood to suggest the existence of entities with which science is not acquainted. It is definitely committed against those elements of religion which are Hebraic, Oriental, or medieval, because they are reminders of the mysteries. And as for educational policy, it fiercely opposes those studies in the curriculum which are not scientific or practical, and proselytes the beginners with the claim that they will get more physical profit from positive sciences than from moonshine.

What is the good of ritual, devotion, offering, or prayer, say the naturalists, if it does not produce?

The old God was the author of evil as well as of good. This is my orthodox version of the God of Israel at the point where it is most challenging and critical. But temperamentally it does not suit us very well today. It does not flatter that universal dream of human power which our recent science has taught us to indulge, and by which we say that evil has been overcome.

The Jews were scarcely prepared to say, with the moderns, that they possessed a God whose simple function was to promote their good. They found too much realistic testimony to the contrary. The God who governed their universe was a spirit so inscrutable, so contingent, so mysterious, that his works could never be fully accounted for, and among these works of his will were evidently works that brought suffering upon human beings. To put this into words of one and two syllables: *God is the author of evil as well as good, and one can never be sure which of the two is coming next.* The language of this proposition is not according to the conventions of modern theology, which has been highly tainted with naturalism. But it is the proposition which any historical survey of the old religion will establish.

The theology of the Jews was, speaking very roughly, monotheistic. Now in polytheistic religions there may be good Gods, and bad Gods, but a monotheistic religion attempts to incorporate the many into the one, and in that one has to vest all the capacities of the universe for doing good to man, and also all its capacities for doing evil. An intelligent religion cannot very well cancel the celebrated fact of evil, however it may try on ethical principles to do so. Suppose then that a religion, trying to be monotheistic, represents its God strictly as the author of good, imposing upon him the ethical standard of a human being: then it has to qualify its monotheistic bias and set up a second God to serve as the drastic author of evil. A true monotheistic God is one of whom humanity is not a property since he authorizes the evil with the good.

The new religionists, however, would like to eat their cake and have it too. They want One Great God, yet they want him to be wholly benevolent, and ethical after the humane definition. What will they do about evil?

They will do nothing about it. They will pretend that it is not there. They are not necessarily Christian Scientists in the technical sense, for they do acknowledge some evil, of a kind which is now or prospectively curable by the secular sciences. But they are virtually Christian Scientists so far as they gloze the existence of incurable evil. They represent evil in general as a temporary, incidental, negligible, and slightly uncomfortable phenomenon, which hardly deserves an entry in the theological ledger. They have no God for it.

The Mosaic God is stern and awful, and his people suffer at his hands. There is of course an attempt to represent God as the author only of good, and to foist off on another the responsibility for evil. But to have a second God is to diminish the authority of the first; and consequently it was understood by some of the Hebrew theologians that the author of evil is only a serpent, one of God's own creatures turned ingrate and traitor. This is the Mosaic account. With magical powers the serpent corrupts the purpose of creation. But being himself a creature and a subordinate, he is destined not to have his way forever, and even upon the commission of his first evil deed God pronounces the curse upon him and dooms him to eventual destruction.

Alas, the serpent's doom was so very indeterminate of date! And in the meantime his operations were so flagrant! In the non-Mosaic and later Scriptures we speedily make the acquaintance of Satan, a much more formidable figure than the serpent. Indeed, it was he who had masqueraded as the serpent on the occasion of his adventure into Eden.

The first mention of Satan in the Scriptures is in First Chronicles, the twenty-first chapter:

> And Satan stood up against Israel, and moved David to number Israel. And David said to Joab and to the princes of the people, Go, number Israel from Beer-Sheba even to Dan; and bring me word, that I may know the sum of them. And Joab said, Jehovah make his people a hundred times as many as they are: but, my lord the king, are they not all my lord's servants? Why doth my lord require this thing? Why will he be a cause of guilt unto Israel?

The temptation which Satan offers to David here is the characteristic Satanic temptation, about which we shall see more in a subsequent chapter. The military glory of Israel is at its height, after a series of brilliant victories; so King David is going to count his military resources and Prussianize his kingdom in order to cut a great figure in the world of nations. It is a proud and wholly secular program of self-help. But it is quite opposed to the less strenuous, and indeed the pacific and easy-going statecraft of Abraham, the founder of the nation, to whom in a vision God had given the amiable promise:

> And I will make thy seed as the dust of the earth; so that if a man can number the dust of the earth, then shall thy seed also be numbered.

It is also, as events were to prove, a ruinous piece of policy.

But even more interesting than the consideration of why David's project is an evil one, is the remarkable fact that the same story has been told once already in the Scriptures by a theologian with very different terms. In Second Samuel, twenty-fourth chapter, the story is substantially the same with the exception that Satan does not appear, and his function is discharged by God himself:

> And again the anger of Jehovah was kindled against Israel, and he moved David against them, saying, Go, number Israel and Judah.

Satan is not present on this occasion to bear the responsibility for evil; the onus devolves upon God himself.

But one theology is as realistic as the other. If you have no Satan in your system, you must make God the author of evil. If you have a Satan you may clear God, but you make a serious invasion upon his omnipotence. The fact of evil is in either case allowed for.

On the whole, the Satanic theology has plenty of vogue in the Old Testament, and even more in the New. It does not matter to our argument whether the Jews originated it on their own theological initiative, or took it from a Persian source during the Captivity, as modern scholars have maintained. The Hebrew word means Adversary, and seems thoroughly at home in Hebrew thought. The notion of a

God whose works are, from the human point of view, evil, is a notion of universal religious value which scarcely requires the sanction of the Persians. The opposition between the God of good and the God of evil is a common one. The Manichean heresy, against which Saint Augustine later battled so gallantly and ineffectually, was one of its forms: this uncompromising doctrine made the two Gods equal and co-eternal, and held out no prospect of the defeat of the one by the other.

In the Book of Job Satan is a well-known power, and disputes dangerously with God for the allegiance of man. In the Gospel according to John xiii, 31, Jesus himself refers to Satan as the "prince of this world." In the Second Epistle to the Corinthians iv, 4, Saint Paul refers to him as the "god of this world."

In the Book of Revelation there is an estimate of the extent of Satan's dominion which is doubtless an underestimate, but which may be rather appalling to sentimentalists. There are visions in which this dominion is seen to be one part in three of the earth. One-third of the earth's inhabitants are doomed to destruction; two-thirds are reserved for God's benevolent offices; the balance of power is in his favor, but the casualties are horrifying. A third part of trees are burnt up, a third part of the sea is turned into blood, a third part of the ships are destroyed, a third part of the sun and moon is darkened, and a third part of earth's human inhabitants are devoted to fire and smoke and brimstone. These unhappy visions pronounce realistically upon the manifest limitations of the Author of Good. There is also in the twelfth chapter of this remarkable Book a vision of the cosmic origin of evil. "There was war in Heaven." The rebellious angels numbered a third part of all Heaven's host; they were cast out of Heaven; their prince was the dragon, "that old serpent, called the Devil, and Satan, which deceiveth the whole world." And thus Heaven itself was an empire never thoroughly consolidated under God's rule. Before the creation of man there was revolt, and hardly had man been set down in Eden before the powers of evil appeared and assailed him. Naturally they did. There had been no immunity even in Heaven.

It is true that Satan is generally regarded in the Scriptures as the cause of evil indirectly, by persuading man to sinful disobedience to God's commandment. Satan tempts, man is persuaded, and the evil that follows is God's punishment. This view is the attempt to save the goodness of God, to give an ethical cast to a universe that appeared to permit the irrational prevalence of evil. But realism was forced to declare, even so, that God's punishments were not entirely proportionate to the crimes. However justly aroused, God's anger was slow to quench: it had a way of visiting even the succeeding generations. If the fathers ate sour grapes, the children's teeth were set on edge. Indeed, all men were cursed in Adam's fall, and evil was the common inheritance of all mankind thereafter. Under this doctrine, any extreme of suffering was within the limits of expectation; at any time; and anywhere.

Objection has been heard to be advanced by fastidious moderns to this latter doctrine: It is not a pretty doctrine; this is a religion of fear! But prior to that, perhaps, is the consideration: Does it not represent a body of hard fact? If it does that, it is likely that religionists will find time to defend it against contemporary processes of prettification. Jewish theology was not rationalistic, but perhaps it was something better: it was realistic. Does God authorize the sufferings of the righteous? It is easy to say impulsively that God does not permit any such thing. But one is obliged to remember that, if God doesn't, somebody does. The Jews divided the responsibility rather equivocally between God and Satan.

Whatever may be the bias of the different writers, the Old Testament is a book provided plentifully with intense lamentations. In the world's literature the Hebrew Scriptures are doubtless as woeful as any other document, not excepting Dante's epic or Shakespeare's tragedies.

The sufferings which are lamented are in part the universal wretchedness of men, and in part the national humiliation of Israel. The Jews had reverses as a people, and in these a prime occasion for lamentation. (Our own opportunities in this respect have been nothing like so rich.) The defeat of their nation by more powerful nations never became acceptable to them, for it was not in them to become oblivious and capable of a relaxing hebetude under oppression. Whenever the chronology of a book in the Hebrew Scriptures makes it appropriate, that book laments the fall of Israel and the seeming forgetfulness of God, and speculates with a passionate, and generally realistic, philosophy upon the ways of God with his people. I shall cite only once, and in this case a Psalm illustrating those lamentations which do not reflect the national disgrace but private and universal distresses—lamentations which might seem appropriate to all men in their due season. A mortal sickness lies upon the poet who sings as follows:

I am reckoned with them that go down into the pit;
I am as a man that hath no help,
Cast off among the dead,
Like the slain that lie in the grave,
Whom thou rememberest no more,
And they are cut off from thy hand.
Thou hast laid me in the lowest pit,
In dark places, in the deeps.
Thy wrath lieth hard upon me,
And thou hast afflicted me with all thy waves.
Thou hast put acquaintance far from me;

Thou hast made me an abomination unto them:
I am shut up, and I cannot come forth.
Mine eye wasteth away by reason of affliction:
I have called daily upon thee, O Jehovah;
I have spread forth my hands unto thee.
Wilt thou show wonders to the dead?
Shall they that are deceased arise and praise thee?
Shall thy loving kindness be declared in the grave?
Or thy faithfulness in destruction?
Shall thy wonders be known in the dark?
And thy righteousness in the land of forgetfulness?
But unto thee, O Jehovah, have I cried;
And in the morning shall my prayer come before thee.
Jehovah, why castest thou off my soul?
Why hidest thou thy face from me?
I am afflicted and ready to die from my youth up:
While I suffer thy terrors I am distracted.
Thy fierce wrath is gone over me;
Thy terrors have cut me off.
They came round about me like water all the day long;
They compassed me about together.
Lover and friend hast thou put far from me,
And my acquaintance into darkness.

In these lamentations Jehovah is not denied; but it is evident to the sufferer that his favor has departed. Jehovah has not made it his intention to work those simple human benefits that are clamored for. His intention was always inscrutable; here it is cruel.

This is the God who reduces strangely if at all to the understandable and beneficent God of our modern science. One cannot help wondering how one's contemporaries, comfortably provided with this tractable God, will express themselves theologically when a mortal sickness lies upon them too.

But I do not approve the document I have cited as the last word in the expression of a completely religious experience. I admire its realism: there is no Christian Science in this outburst, but a sense of hard—very hard—fact. Yet it is not quite submissive to the fact. We do not know what the writer is going to do. It is not, in the noblest sense of a word which is more religious than secular, a Stoic utterance. It is not quite equal to a spirit which is always religious or nearly so: the tragic spirit.

I would define the tragic spirit. Tragedy exhibits always the inevitable failure of secular enterprise. In tragedy the mind makes the critical confession that human goodness, and intelligent work, a combination popularly supposed to be the sufficient cause of prosperity, do not actually produce their triumphant effect upon the material world. Or: *The moral order is a wished-for order, which does not coincide with the actual order or world order.* And having made this confession, what can the mind do about it? I would suggest the simple answer: the mind must accept the world order. It must "accept the universe," even as Margaret Fuller accepted it—only that she probably was not quite sensible of the indifference and unrighteousness and inhumanity of the universe she was accepting.

To give a logical completeness to the situation of the above Hebrew poet, there are several options that have been historically tried. One is that of Christian Science, which reiterates: "Do not fear—do not mind—all is well." This is the philosophy of the ostrich. The prescription regards its patients much as the keeper of a certain institution regards his charges: feeble-minded folk in whom it is an act of kindness to encourage their delusions. But our new religion, as advanced by our regular and secular scientists, and defined in the preceding chapter, is not far removed from this position—putting forth tirelessly its precepts of action, work,

science, efficiency, amelioration, progress, and the conquest
of nature. The militant Occidentals acknowledge no limits
to their power. They gladly accept the universe in the degree they think they can manage it. But they cannot find
much to say about an actual concrete suffering like the above.

Mr. Bertrand Russell would exercise another option. He
knows that the moral order is broken against the world
order, that the universe works evil to humankind. His answer is: "I defy the universe then." He would be a sort of
anti-Fullerite. He is the contemporary Prometheus, a twin
to the poet Henley with the doctrine of the Invincible Soul.
His confession of faith occurs in his famous "A Free Man's
Worship." Mr. Russell will not have a God that does not
practice a decent human morality in the operation of the
universe. One would never suspect from the fury of his
rhetoric that Mr. Russell is one of the hardest and driest
thinkers of our day. Under this abstract thinker there is a
man who has the gift of flying into a rage. In this condition
he writes:

> Brief and powerless is Man's life; on him and all
> his race the slow, sure doom falls pitiless and dark.
> Blind to good and evil, reckless of destruction, omnip-
> otent matters rolls on its relentless way; for Man,
> condemned today to lose his dearest, tomorrow him-
> self to pass through the gate of darkness, it remains
> only to cherish, ere yet the blow falls, the lofty
> thoughts that ennoble his little day, disdaining the
> coward terrors of the slave of Fate; to worship at the
> shrine that his own hands have built, undismayed by
> the empire of chance, to preserve a mind free from the
> wanton tyranny that rules his outward life; proudly
> defiant of the irresistible forces that tolerate, for a mo-
> ment, his knowledge and his condemnation, to sustain

alone, a weary but unyielding Atlas, the world that his own ideals have fashioned despite the trampling march of unconscious power.

I do not think Mr. Russell in this position understands either the spirit of religion, as he suggests with his peculiar title, or the spirit of tragedy about which he says a good deal in the essay. He is as realistic as an Oriental in that he declines to deceive himself about the fact, but he is pure Occidental in his disapproval of it. I started to say that this is quixotism; but quixotism deceives itself and thinks its cause is going to prevail; Mr. Russell doesn't.

The Oriental and the ancient wisdom is superior to Mr. Russell's wisdom. For it is religious: it makes that adaptation of the mind to reality which becomes so difficult and so imperative when it is seen that reality is not committed to morality, to humanity; that it is "beyond good and evil." It enlarges the God it worships, upon finding that the God That Is will not reduce to the God That Is Good.

The third option for the poet in his tribulation would consist in acquiescence.

The purest single work of theology that I find in the Jewish Scriptures—I suppose I may exercise the usual privilege of picking my texts from so vast and various a context —is the Book of Job. It is there that I would concentrate the "wisdom of the Old Testament."

The friends of Job, as philosophers, are not equal to the task of confessing that moral order and world order are not two names for the same thing. They have made God good in their peculiar human sense, and if Job is in distress they tell him it is because he has sinned, since God would never do anything that wasn't "right." But Job is intellectually an honest man and he denies the charge. It is not an instance where the punishment is proportionate to the crime and,

ethically, Job's sufferings are perfectly unaccountable. The
debate is extremely full and competent. The superior young
Buzite man enters into it after a while, and is like John the
Baptist preparing the way for the Son of God: for at last,
after proper preparation, God himself speaks magnificently
out of the whirlwind.

> Hast thou entered into the springs of the sea?
> Or hast thou walked in the recesses of the deep?
> Have the gates of death been revealed unto thee?
> Or hast thou seen the gates of the shadow of death?
> Hast thou comprehended the earth in its breadth?
> Declare, if thou knowest it all.

God recounts his powers and his works uncompromisingly,
as powers and works which are on another foundation than
the ethical and scientific order of Job's mind. He has not
bargained with Job, he has never acknowledged any responsibility for making himself intelligible or amenable to Job,
and Job, becoming smaller and smaller, at length testifies:

> I know that thou canst do all things,
> And that no purpose of thine can be restrained.
> Who is this that hideth counsel without knowledge?
> Therefore have I uttered that which I understand
>   not,
> Things too wonderful for me, which I knew not.
> Hear, I beseech thee, and I will speak:
> I will demand of thee, and declare thou unto me.
> I had heard of thee by the hearing of the ear;
> But now mine eye seeth thee:
> Wherefore I abhor myself,
> And repent in dust and ashes.

This is the climax of Job's religious experience. For I
exercise my privilege again, and pass over as an unworthy

anti-climax the epilogue in which God, who has thus hum-
bled the pride of Job, relieves his sufferings and gives him
twice as much of worldly prosperity as he has had before.
This is somebody's "happy ending" which spoils a tragedy.

CHAPTER THREE

NATURE AND THE SUPERNATURAL

But why do we have to have any God at all? Some scientists do not recognize the necessity. Laplace is said to have replied to Napoleon, when the latter was asking about a God behind the stars: "I have no need for that hypothesis."

The scientists profess, as a rule, that they are wholly taken up with nature, and have no concern with the supernatural. As the scientific preoccupation has grown in the Occident, there have developed, as we have seen, two scientific attitudes towards religion. One is the attitude of Mr. Millikan and others, who might be said to compose a "soft" variety of scientists, and who are willing to have a God of a sort—that is, provided he be divested of medieval or ancient or Oriental properties (including his thunder) and become a good creature, not *very* supernatural, whom they can manage. The other attitude is that of the belligerent or "hard" scientists, who don't want any religious institution at all, and would persuade society to go without Gods entirely.

Under the steady fire of natural scientists of both varieties, the supernatural features which are of the essence of religion have steadily diminished in public repute.

The anti-supernaturalism of scientists has had its effect of course upon the Bible. This book consists of an older part which was written by Jews in Hebrew, and a later part which was written by Jews in Greek. It is still, nominally, the documentary basis of our religion.

But only nominally. Our regular Western religionists have practically repudiated the Old Testament. A modern American preacher may feel a little need of knowing his Greek, but he no longer has any particular need of his Hebrew. As a distinguished clergyman said to me, "The Old Testament is not considered now to be of any doctrinal importance." On the whole, the Old Testament would seem to serve Christians today only in certain rather dubious functions: perhaps in the tolerably unimportant function of an interesting "literature"; or in the function, a less innocent one, of a set of misguided doctrines which can be employed as a foil to set off the superior doctrines of the New Testament.

And as for the New Testament, the Christians of our days have grown quite choice in electing from it the parts to suit their taste. They accept, to a certain extent, the account of the deeds and words of Jesus. But this account is taken preferably as an account on the pure secular plane, where there are no supernatural or theological complications, as a body of examples for our emulation, a set of admirable expressions of our common humanity.

If the Bible is somewhat unpalatable to the modern Occidental mind, this is probably for several reasons, of which at least two are obvious. I cannot tell which of the two is the more naïve.

In the first place, the God of Israel—who was, I should think, the God of Moses and the God of Jesus alike—cannot be identified with a principle of human service. He is awful, unpredictable, unappeasable, and his works issue frequently in human suffering. So he is repudiated on strictly humane or ethical grounds as a God not to be worshiped, or even approved. I have already expressed my suspicions of the validity of this attitude. It ignores the question whether this is or is not the God that really is, so far as either one of them is; a question whose answer would seem to be fairly independent of whether he suits us or not.

But in this chapter I would consider the second and more usual objection to the Jewish Scriptures. The historical critics have examined them, and disputed their authority as history. The scientific critics have joined in, and disputed their authority as a scientific record. In the place of the history which ought to be there, and of the science, they find tall stories of a primitive, marvelous, or mythical sort. The second objection to the Bible is that it deals in myths.

Myths are construed very simply by the hard Occidental mind: they are lies. It is supposed that everything that is written in serious prose ought to be historical or scientific; that is, devoted either to authenticated facts or to sober generalizations about these facts. Myths, like fairy tales, like poems, are neither. They are therefore absurd. We are given to understand that their effectiveness can be only with some simple and primitive population, that they are not nearly good enough for the men of our twentieth century generation, brought up in the climatic blessedness of our scientific Occident.

But there is another possibility which rather rarely, it would seem, occurs to the contemporary Occidental mind. It concerns the meaning which the Jewish Scriptures actually intended to convey. And how do I know what meaning they intended to convey? All I can do is to choose between the rival authorities who have interpreted them. The interpreters have fallen into two general classes, of which one class has a Hebraic, Oriental, symbolistic cast of mind, while the other class is Occidental, scientific, modern, and anthropological. I feel compelled to take the former group as the better authority: their credentials impress me.

But I must make this disclaimer: I have not a proper background for valuing these authorities, especially the former one—I am far from learned in Oriental studies. My acquaintance is quite insufficient with the Talmud, which was the work of the learned rabbinical commentators upon the Scriptures; with the Cabbala, which represents the learning of still more learned and esoteric religionists; with the Hebrew language, which was so evidently the construction of priests, and crowded with esoteric meanings; with the labors of the neo-Platonists of the early Christian era, who eagerly interpreted all religious myths whatsoever, including the Scriptural—and it is only from an Occidental remoteness and with an Occidental backwardness that I can define what seems to be distinctive in the Oriental mind generally, skilled as it obviously is in the creation and understanding of myths.

The interpreters who belong to the Oriental school are deeply persuaded that the Jewish myths were not composed by simple men who thought they were composing history and science, but by initiated men who had very different purposes in view. And it seems to me necessary to admit that these interpreters are much closer to the composers of the myths, whether by race or by habit of mind, than our modern Occidental scholars can possibly be. I suggest, in other words, that they are right. It is altogether too likely that they have easily understood the intention of the Scriptures where we, who have condescended to adopt them for our own, do not.

I believe that religious myths, including those of the Bible, are unhistorical and unscientific, precisely as our gallant historians and higher critics have recently discovered; but that their unhistorical and unscientific character is not their vice but their excellence, and that it certainly was their intent.

This suggestion takes us at once into a theory of myth.

What is the intention of a myth? And how does it relate to history and to science? These are fundamental questions that the defenders of a religious tradition must raise and answer.

Let us define history, as strictly as we can. When may a story expect to receive the approval of the historian, and take rank as "historical"? And what is that kind of judgment which is called a historical judgment?

The primary rôle of the historian is to establish the "facts." It has evidently not changed in the least from the rôle which was assumed by Herodotus, the Father of History. To his account of peoples, politics, and wars he gave the title *historia*, because the method by which he secured it was described in the verb *historeo*, to ask questions. Herodotus went, asking questions, about the world of the Greeks and their barbarian neighbors. If he could find an eye-witness to the event, he used his testimony. If the event was too remote in time or place, he got the nearest testimony he could; and if there was a conflict in testimonies, he was careful to say so. Often in his narrative, where the account he received had come a long way, he declines to sanction it, and is content to tell us, "These say it is so."

His effort was always to get as near to an eye-witness account as he could. And this permits us to define what fact meant to Herodotus, and what it has meant to historians ever since. A fact for him was evidently the impression of an event which he could establish as having been registered upon the senses of an honest and sound observer. But this is the same meaning that fact bears for all the sciences and all the philosophies, no matter how recondite they may appear to be. *Fact is the sensible event.*

Today the historian is still engaged primarily in the business of validating his facts, by carrying them back to the point where they first appeared, as events for the genuine eye-witness or sense-witness. The historic judgment is the simplest of all the judgment forms, and consists in affirming the simple evidence of the senses: "This is as I saw it." The historical method consists in asking questions, or taking testimony from those who have participated in the sensible event. This is the method of the American census-taker of April, 1930. It is also the method of the genealogist; of the man who conducts a modern industrial, social, or educational "survey"; of the newspaper reporter; and of His Honor the Court, trying to establish the facts of some mooted "case."

Such is history proper; so it is defined philologically and historically. But what the historian does with his facts, once they are established, is another matter. For he does more. Herodotus is greatly exceeded in these days by historians who are as much interested in the interpretation of their facts as in their validation. These historians deal in "principles," "laws," and "causes," much as the physical scientists do. In fact, they emulate these sciences in method and purpose—though of course their subject-matter is so intractable that they have to be content with a different order of precision in their generalizations. Their field is human conduct in its social, ethnological, military, economic, political manifestations—it is humanistic rather than physical. Their general remarks are correspondingly the more precarious. But with this business of generalization history enters upon a second or scientific phase, and ceases to be the pure function which I have just described. In the primary sense history is still concerned with the sensible fact; but in a secondary sense it is scientific, or interpretative.

The pure historian brings to bear upon the Bible his usual genius for facts as sensible data. With his technical training in comparative evidence, he boldly questions whether the Scriptures testify to actual sensible data. His findings are often adverse. The data furnished are sometimes pre-historic, or beyond the reach of historical evidence, as in the account of the doings of Adam and Eve: it is not possible to discover a reputable hearsay tradition which leads back to any eye-witness account. Again, there may be discrepancies between two Scriptural accounts of the same event, or between the Scriptural account and the account by some independent secular witness: the difference has to be arbitrated. The conclusion may leave a Scriptural passage without any historical standing—sometimes to the amazement and mortification of those who "believed" their Bible, but considered it was nothing if it was not historical.

But perhaps even more frequently does the historian disapprove the Bible as interpreting the sensible facts, or giving their rational causes. The historian considers that some parts of the narrative testify to the sensible data, while other parts represent the Scriptural author's explanations. The sensible data may not be open to question. As historical scientist, however, the historian questions the explanations. Granting the fact that Joshua besieged and took Jericho: yet the historian is accustomed to explain the conquest in the regular terms of military science, he is unfamiliar with the principle that the celestial economy suspends its operations in favor of a military project. The Israelites prospered, on occasion at least, and won territories and tribute from their enemies. So much is fact. But is it historical to conclude that the favor of God surged out to them, and interfered physically on earth in their behalf?

For history as science deals with a system of natural causes. It has no room for supernatural causes.

Science is never independent of history, since it has to start out with its attested facts or data from which to generalize. Nor does history usually stop with its facts or its pure chronicle of events, for to some extent it always proceeds to generalize or to "compose." History is a record of particulars, but they are necessarily defined as instances of rules or generalizations. Science is the whole systematic body of rules or generalizations, but of course they were derived from actual instances, and they are worthless if they are not applicable to fresh instances.

The generalizations of science and those of history are not different in kind, they cannot be distinguished with regard to their essential technique. I will try to define the meaning of generalization, considered as the fundamental act of science. This section will necessarily be somewhat technical.

Some generalizations are descriptive, and some are causal. The descriptive generalization is simply the one which takes a multitude of similar objects and defines the set of constant features by virtue of which they are similar. This generalization produces the concept, the skeleton, the class, the type, the rule, or the universal. Under the influence of this concept, we simply observe the particular objects as indifferent instances: they all illustrate the concept equally.

And this way of thinking is science. A scientific concept is a fine thing, but science has to pay for it. When our thinking is scientific or conceptual, we fail to observe the particular objects as particulars, or as objects which are different, and contain a great many features not at all covered by the given concept. We attend only to what is constant or like among them, or to what has repetition-value. Of course we are enabled by this method to cover ground, and to attend to a great number of objects quickly. For we may dispose of them immediately as instances. This is to attend to them in the most ruthless and the most practical manner, and to proceed with the greatest economy.

No doubt the class-concept has plenty of dignity, so far as dignity attaches to sheer magnitude and extent. The concept man, for example, represents an essence so enduring and so fertile that there are at this moment a billion and a half of dutiful specimens on earth which answer to its every requirement, while an indefinite number of billions of other specimens are presumed to have obeyed it in the past. There are indeed no theoretical limits upon the extent of its rule.

So great, yet so small. Great in its fertility, in the indefinite reach of its reproductive power as it stamps so many instances with its constant likeness: small, and exceeded by the nearest and meanest of its actual instances, in the finite simplicity of its quality. For we are obliged to remark that the generalization never exhausts or begins to exhaust the quality of the particulars which it generalizes, but abstracts from all that quality only the little part which is constant, and which repeats itself. Qualitatively it is as limited as quantitatively it is formidable. In the language of the school logics, you can define man but not Socrates. Your definition of man is peculiarly finite, handy, and intelligible, but it is not Socrates.

We do not flatter the world in calling it rational or intelligible, if we remember the qualitative poverty of all our descriptive formulas. If the particular objects were perfectly submissive to their classifications, if the members of every class were uniform in every respect and never exceeded their class-constants, then the world would be perfectly understandable. But this is not the testimony of a disinterested observation.

So much for the class-constant or descriptive generalization. Very similar considerations hold for the scientific cause. Its only peculiarity is in the fact that it represents a type or constant of time sequences, and is therefore a little more compound than the constant of a group of static objects. It is the constant of events, the other is the constant of objects. A flower has a class which is timeless, and an explo-

sion has a cause which is in time: but the class and the cause
are both, and equally, generalizations or abstracts.

We must bear in mind what we have learned from the
critics of science, such as David Hume first, and latterly
such writers as Karl Pearson and M. Bergson. We must
construe the cause-seeking processes of science for exactly
what they are. A cause, if it is reputable for science, is *simply a portion of a whole actual stream of events*. The cause
of gunfire is the assemblage of the gun, the projectile, and
the powder, and the concussion supplied to the powder. Any
event in time may be taken as standing at the end of a sequence of events, or may be regarded as an effect with a
temporal or causal background. History establishes the background. Science picks out from this background—which in
any particular case is an inexhaustible one—a set of items
which are common to the backgrounds of all similar events:
this becomes the cause of the event. Karl Pearson puts it
very neatly: *the shorthand of routine experience*. Emphasis
on the *short*: the causal concept is an abbreviation, a con-
densation, an abstract. The cause, like the class, comprises
but the finite part of an infinite particularity.

So a scientific law is ordinarily a generalization about the
cause of an event, and we may always observe with respect
to it:

(1) That it never goes out of the natural history of the
event to find its terms;

(2) And that it never takes more than a part or abstract
from the whole of that natural history.

But a myth is different from this. It is a representation
of the event which jumps clear out of the natural background. Its terms are pure fictions: supernatural terms, or
terms which history knows nothing about. This is why science
and religion conflict—this is why a Bible composed by Eastern religionists is unsatisfactory to Western scientists.

For it is evident that science is not much agitated when it hears that generations of men lived, bore children, and died; that Israel conducted migrations and wars, and went into captivities; that a temple was constructed and a ceremonial instituted;—these are common types of historical fact, and if history is ready to accept them, science does not care.

But many of the Biblical stories are quite different from such narratives. For example, we hear that God created the universe by a certain act and produced simultaneously all the animal species which we now know; that he commanded a whale to swallow Jonah, who lived unharmed in his belly for three days; that Elijah was caught up into Heaven by a chariot; that a virgin immaculately conceived and bore a son. The scientist does not deny that at the bottom of these stories there may have been genuine sensible phenomena, or historical facts, which needed to be accounted for as caused. These were, respectively: a material universe, with an animal kingdom of vast variety; a sea journey that one Jonah unsuccessfully attempted from Jaffa to Tarshish; an Elijah who ought to have been wonderfully distinguished from his unworthy generation, and rewarded signally; and a young man so noble that no ordinary genealogy would easily account for him. But the scientist knows no such causal explanations for these events as alleged in the Scriptural account. He asks for natural causes strictly.

For example, the cause of the natural universe of today, so far as science can say, is simply the natural universe of yesterday; or that of the day before yesterday; or of the days before that,—a recession that continues *ad infinitum* except that it can never go back behind some natural universe whose existence is demonstrable, for whose existence there is historical evidence. Behind Jonah's unsuccessful sea-voyage, science says, there must have been some sequence of natural events, such as a storm at sea, the casting of Jonah

overboard even, and the swallowing of Jonah by a whale—
but not a supernatural God's command to the whale nor his
supernatural protection of Jonah from the whale's digestive
processes. Elijah became deservedly a great figure to the
Jews after his death, but for very good natural reasons—
not because he was miraculously translated. And Jesus had
a remarkable mental and spiritual development, perhaps,
but it was a human or natural development.

Nevertheless, the life of Jesus was remarkable, and so
were all the other events I have named—and how can the
"shorthand of routine experience" ever explain satisfactorily
what is remarkable? It will never cease to be difficult for
science, with its naturalistic principles, to account for any
remarkable event. Such a particular tends too obviously to
exceed its type, too spectacularly to strain against the confinement of its law. *It tends always to exhibit more particularity than type.* It tends, that is, to be *unique,* and to escape from science altogether. Science of course does not give
up too easily. It pretends that nothing is wrong, that this
individual is not really an individual but only another indifferent instance. But the extreme cases are so poorly han-
dled by science that we may be sure science lacks the technique to handle them. Not that we had to wait on the spectacular case before we came to this conclusion, however:
for anything, either object or event, is ineffable, and exceeds
definition, if we care to attend to it sufficiently—if we love
it, for example. But it is all the easier to see that science,
sticking to natural history and abstracting from its fullness,
does very badly for the individual who is remarkable.

Yet to those who would boldly account for this individual
in supernatural terms, science opposes a skepticism which is
invincible. Science reiterates tirelessly: All the background
to this individual that you can observe is a natural or historical background. Where is your supernatural item?

This is safe ground for the skeptic to stand on: the name

of this ground in the vernacular is Missouri. The moment we observe with our physical eyes a supposedly supernatural item, that moment it becomes a natural item. Those items that stay supernatural are the unwitnessed ones. Science refutes them all with the utmost ease, by asking them please to be circumstantial! All facts have to substantiate themselves. If God spoke to the whale, what language did he employ, or by what physical means did his thought get access to the whale's sensor-motor mechanism? By what power was Elijah's chariot propelled, as it moved through the air; if by wind, where was its sail? Describe the ovum in process of fertilization in the woman's womb without a material spermatozoön attaching to it. Picture these events in process, if you please!

Lacking such evidence as would make these events historically probable, science rejects them.

The scientists are quite within their professional rights, and even within their professional responsibilities, in rejecting the miraculous portions of the Bible when the matter is referred to them for scientific judgment. These portions do not constitute a scientific record. The scientists have to take their choice between regarding them simply as false or incompetent, and regarding them as a record whose intention is foreign to their own understanding as scientists. It is not strange if they have generally elected the former of these alternatives. They have assumed that the myths tried to be scientific and failed, or that they pretended to be scientific and lied.

These, then, are the myths, put forward by Hebrew writers, rejected by modern Western critics. I imagine that the Hebrew writers, and even modern Orientals who might be brought into the controversy, would be quite surprised to see with what earnestness these old myths were being refuted. It would occur to them that the labors of the ancients had come to be thoroughly misunderstood, and that there must have passed completely out of the intellectual life of our race and period the capacity for a kind of experience once invested with sufficient dignity.

A myth is frankly a fable: it calmly alleges a miracle or impossible occurrence: it is a *tour de force* which intends to take its representation of the object out of the fatal confinement of science and routine. The myth-maker offers us the Far-darting Apollo, saying, Catch him, define him, if you can. The scientist offers us sunlight; or light-energy; still better, or at least more to Mr. Pupin's mind, the process of solar radiation,—trying always to define and narrow the thing a little better. The myth of an object is its proper name, private, unique, untranslatable, overflowing, of a demonic energy that cannot be reduced to the poverty of the class-concept. The myth of an event is a story, which invests the natural with a supernatural background, and with a more-than-historical history.

Let us recall: the scientific account of an event (1) never goes out of its natural history, and (2) uses only an abstract or part of that history. But its myth, on the other hand, (1) leaves its natural history altogether and yet (2) attempts to imply the whole of that history. This seems odd. But we study it a little. Then we see that these two features of myth are one and the same. *Myth resorts to the supernatural in order to represent the fullness of the natural.* The myth-maker is a desperate man, for he has a memory. He remembers the remarkable individual in the richness of his private existence. He sees very little relation between that individual and the dry generalization into which science would fit him. He would do the individual the honor of a representation which will leave him somehow with that fullness of being which by right he possesses. Unwilling to testify to the individual through only some of his terms, after the method of science which lets the most of his being escape, the myth-maker abandons the idea of any natural or historical formulation, and tries one that is meant to look non-natural and unhistorical. This is for provocation. The myth-maker would sting us into awareness by this device, and compel us to perform the critical act of recollection, to restore the individual image, or else to go back and seek a fresh experience.

Evidently this procedure is one in which the so-called "primitive" thinkers are well versed, but it is nevertheless a rather subtle one, and far from the animal order of mentality. In fact, it would seem to be a trifle advanced by comparison with the acts of the naturalistic temperament, which fails to understand it. The myth-maker is an older man mentally than the scientists, for myths arise as an act of revulsion against scientific generalizations.

The examples are innumerable. "I will do anything for you," says the lover to his lady in the story. "I will get you whatever treasure you desire." But suppose the lady wants a treasure guarded by a dragon at the bottom of the sea. The lover is represented as making his way there, killing the dragon, and returning with the treasure to lay at the lady's feet. This story employs a common literary device for the representation of the superlative: the lover performs the biggest labor that his author could invent for him and, to make sure it is big enough, a labor that no mortal man before him ever achieved.

The poets are constantly creating little local myths, in their rebellion against the destructive terms of a routine presentation. "The waves outdid themselves in glee." They did not actually. It is simply a way of saying to the reader, "Look very hard—did you ever see waves laughing—try them for yourself."

Humor is more privileged than poetry and religion; perhaps because it knows how to retaliate upon its enemies. The

grotesque effects in which it indulges go commonly uncen-
sured, though they are miraculous. "What he wants is the
world with a fence around it." This statement will not for
a moment bear analysis: it is not intended to. And perhaps
what the humorist would most relish is to have it challenged
in its detail by the literalist, whose mind does not work on
the same plane as the humorist's. It will be the literalist
and not the humorist who will have to bear the ridicule of
the company.

There is the story of Socrates. I assume that Socrates was
impatient with the idea that he was a simple being who
could be defined, predicted, and therefore discounted. He
represented himself as divinely directed by a personal
daimon, or demon: the meaning of demon being evidently,
"A spirit you'll never understand, not within the compass
of any generalization you can make."

Now for a far more important example, which is of the
essence of the religious myth. The myth-maker sets him up
a God. Why a God? I am sure that there are, at one time
or another, two motives for a God as the explanation of
the universe. First, to represent its indefiniteness in extent
of time or of space. For here is the visible portion of the
universe in space, but we are constantly going a little farther
out, and evidently the universe flows on beyond the bounds
of observation. And here is the universe as it has had its
successive states within the limits of historic time, but each
new day has added another state, and we desire a universe
that had states before history began and will go on having
states tomorrow and thereafter. Let us have an entity to
represent this out-and-beyond and this before-and-after
universe, let it be God, and let his name mean when we
pronounce it: A universe of a magnitude exceeding its own
natural history. Few can resist, even among the regular
scientists, the need of that entity.

But there is another motive for having a God that is

quite imperious, especially perhaps among Orientals and people with a powerful esthetic sense. The universe might be defined in the terms of its own natural history, and yet no item within it was ever fully explored by natural history; while still less, of course, did its fullness get into that abstract of natural history which is the scientific generalization. The universe in every local detail is evidently of inexhaustible fullness or particularity. The universe is not therefore a simple cosmos, or the sum of its constants and cores-of-repetition. Let the universe then be the body and manifestation of an inscrutable God, whose name shall mean: Of a fullness of being that exceeds formulation.

These are two Gods, an extensive and an intensive. Sometimes they merge, in the thought of the expert myth-maker, into one very great God.

The fault of myth-makers is therefore simply that they try to do justice to their objects, as they have actually experienced them. They cannot do this in systematic terms, in the usual generalizations. So they use the supernatural, to indicate that these objects are to be experienced and not defined: "Do not try to verify: not demonstrable, not historical: go and try them."

To put this very briefly: *The myth is not descriptive, it is prescriptive.*

Science is professionally opposed to myths. And yet there is much persuasion for us, if we are squeamish about them, in the fact that the scientist himself is often a fertile myth-maker. By a movement of mind which is spontaneous and uncontrollable, he leaves his scientific generalizations high and dry and fabricates myths.

His discontent with generalization is the ordinary one which I have already pointed to. It simply binds up a few of the actual features of the historical objects in order to compose a pattern, without beginning to represent their fullness; and it represents only the historical or observed instances of the pattern, with no indication of its indefinite reach, out and beyond, before and after, the field of history. The myths of the scientists would like to remedy these two limitations. They are like the two Gods of the religionists: they represent either the infinite particularity of the objects, as opposed to the type or definition; or the infinite magnitude of the type, with its universal and eternal capacity for producing its instances. That is, they make up entities which are *fabulous in intension* or entities which are *fabulous in extension*. Generally, I should say that the flair of the scientists is for myths of the latter variety. Anyhow, they are fabulous, they are not statements of fact, they are not capable of demonstration.

A chemical formula, let us say NaCl, is a definition with a convenient and specific yet a limited and finite meaning: a law about the cause or composition of something. This something has unit molecules in the creation of which a unit atom of Na joined with a unit atom of Cl. But that is intolerably bare. How did the atoms unite? What united them? Resting on what ground were they when they united? In what busy little world did the atoms pursue their private businesses when they came into contact? What attendant circumstances made the moment of union a rich circumstantial moment, as moments to our actual observation sometimes are? The scientist cannot get this detail into his formula NaCl: so he indicates it with a gesture. He points to it when he utters the mystic word: Substance! The doctrine of substance is a mythical one which says: Under every NaCl is a ground which supports it and provides it with plenty of accessory detail; but do not look for it; I am only supposing it. (*Substance* is that which stands under, and *supposition* is the act of putting it under; my supposition is the origin of yonder substance.)

This will read perhaps as rather metaphysical and difficult. Many scientists are capable of talking mysteriously about Substance without seeing that they have to suppose it. The act of supposition is a perfectly human one, but often only a half-conscious one.

When a scientist is conscious of his supposition, he prefers to call it a hypothesis. A scientist may be generally trusted to prefer a Latin term to an Anglo-Saxon, and a Greek term to a Latin: he relishes the one that is bigger and rarer, and the one that conceals its meaning the better from the laity. Science often resorts to hypothesis, which means on the whole that science makes a myth. It revolts against the impossible poverty of a generalization as the account of an object, and invents a background, or an underground, in order to complicate it. The law of the medieval William of Occam, known as Occam's Law of Parsimony or Occam's Razor, prescribes that "entities must not be multiplied beyond absolute necessity." It sounds very strict. But what sort of necessity did Occam have in mind? From the pure scientific point of view the Parsimony of Occam is excessive liberality. Why suppose any entity at all? The necessity for it is hardly scientific, but human, esthetic, or religious.

Cause itself, as the scientist actually rather than theoretically conceives it, has whatever private meaning the fertile imagination may choose to give it, but certainly a great deal of fictitious meaning. As Hume perceived, it is something quite fabulous and a departure from the field of sober history. It invites us to think up a substantial background in the midst of which, by the aid of which, the given sequences of fact may have taken place. Try to see for yourself, this notion of causation directs us, how A acted on B, and B on C, and C on D; supply the fullness of their inter-organization, their crowded commerce with each other; feel it, revel in it; but don't stand off and be content to tabulate the bare results. This is esthetic causation, not practical and not scientific. But scientists come to it like the rest of us.

And as for the second sort of myth, the one that gratuitously enlarges the boundaries of the kingdom in which the generalization rules its instances, that is still commoner, and in fact so common that scientists have even less awareness here of what they are doing. A generalization, so far as it is a statement of fact, comprehends its observed instances and nothing more; and the moment it is expected to comprehend some further instances, not in the field of observation, that moment it has enlarged the kingdom and made a myth. It has assumed a power, a reach, a set of dimensions, that is not demonstrated. Then it has gone beyond the "shorthand of routine experience," and improvised a Ruler, a Governor, a Law-maker, who has not exhibited nearly all of his dominion, but proposes to exhibit some more. This dominion may be in kind a very mechanical and monotonous one, and consist in producing simply one indifferent instance after another. Nevertheless it is made quantitatively a greater dominion than facts will justify. Therefore it is myth.

The myths which science composes on this order are those expressed in such terms as the Universe; Gravitation; Energy; Law; Mechanism. I write them in capitals to make sure they are intended as myths. There is also: God,—for the soft variety of scientists.

In a later and perhaps more formidable section, entitled "Ghosts: Including the Holy," I will try to examine these common lapses into myth more strictly.

Of course we must include the scientific historians with these apostate scientists. We read for example: "Then began a struggle which is far from ended yet, a struggle between political tradition and political progress, between the principle of religious conformity and the principle of religious freedom." The combatants in this struggle are not behaving like the docile abstract generalizations they were supposed to be. They are far too animated, and the passage is like an echo of the Homeric warfare of the Gods. But there is hardly a page of readable history which does not take recourse to such mythical representations. History revels in animated principles, spirits, tempers, movements, cultures, and Zeitgeists. They are all quite fabulous. The truth is that the mind, no matter how intimidated by discipline, cannot admit that the generalizations of events comprise the events, but seems determined, in spite of all its naturalistic canons, to point to the real events through sly forms of mythical expression.

Before the sciences can approve themselves in rejecting the myths of honest religions, they will have to look to their own houses. And it will be interesting to see what remains of a passage of general scientific exposition or a chapter of scientific history when the mythical features have all been taken out by the censor. It may turn out to be a procession of bodies so incredibly finite—dehydrated, eviscerated, enervated, and chemically broken down into their "elements"—that no public currency can well be expected for such literature.

It is even worse than that. There is simply no meaning in a science which has no supernatural meaning. There are supernatural assumptions which science has to make right from the beginning, and as long as it undertakes to be science.

The effort of the sciences therefore to follow the advice of Comte, and to be pure or Positivistic, is not successful and cannot be. It is the effort to limit the mind to the Determinant Judgment, and never make the Reflective or Legislative Judgment. It is a heroic effort—but a quixotic. The scientist as a man is at war with the scientist as a naturalist.

CHAPTER FOUR

PRINCIPLES OR GODS?

THE POSITIVISTS are Comte's disciples. They are the scientists most strict in maintaining the attitude which is supposed to be professional for science: they hold no traffic with religion, they have no Gods.

But what is more, they will not even profess to having any metaphysics if they can help it. Comte considered that first the theological concepts had to go, and then the metaphysical ones, only a little less crude than the theological, till science was left alone in its purity. The Positivists therefore declare that they know nothing but nature, do not pretend to know anything else, do not believe there is anything else to know: that, in short, they are not superstitious.

Sometimes they put it in this way: Physics (or natural science) is possible, and in fact very actual and true; but metaphysics is impossible and will not bear analysis. I would like to look very hard at these assertions for a minute.

Positivists realize that many of their brother scientists, of course, unguardedly make metaphysical assumptions. One of them remarks, by way of deploring this error: "The physical scientists today are giving up the notion of cause, for in spite of themselves this notion tended always to be more than a mere generalization, and to suggest some fabulous undercurrent of connections which assisted the unborn facts to issue according to order; and in the place of cause we are now contenting ourselves simply with the notion of Pure Probability."

The answer to this is that their Probability is not at all pure. Believing in Probability is not "getting back to the facts." Probability says that statistical history is going to repeat itself. It assumes that behind the historical facts is something which produced them, but which is not through with producing, and which has adopted our generalization of the historical facts as its guide—so that it is going to produce some more facts, and make them fit in with the already prepared statistics. This Pure Probability is not a scientific principle but a faith.

For generalizations, which are the characteristic act of science, are demonstrably valid only when they are *ex post facto*. Speaking strictly, or after the manner of Positivists, there is no science of the pre-historic past, and none of the future. Nature is for history the aggregate of observed facts. Nature is for science the aggregate of facts arranged in groups, or displayed as instances of types, or classified under headings. But what lies beyond the ordered and classified facts? What lies out in further space beyond the immediate limits of visibility, what lies before and after the period of time which dates the observations? And what lies at the heart of any individual object, which makes it so much more complex than all the formulations the historian can ever give to it? What lies there must be assumed, it cannot be demonstrated. And when we push the logic of the assumption to its limits in the assumer's mind, we find him dallying with a metaphysic, and almost trembling on the verge of a religion and a creed.

It may be fortunate or it may be unfortunate, but the Positivists are only human; they are living creatures and embodied wills; they must look before and after: they must act. Facts are facts, they are past participles, they are gone forever. Positivists cannot stop with generalizing that which is past. They too must meditate their destinies and formulate their careers in this world. They must take a leap into the dark like other men, for the light of the Positive knowledge is directed only backwards. They must make the metaphysical assumption.

Having made it, they leave it there—undefined, and mostly out of consciousness. They do not know that they have expanded their physics into metaphysics.

Perhaps the Positivists do not know that they are obliged to be metaphysical whether they like it or not. But they do know that they are not religious, in the ordinary sense of that word—they are sure about that. A religion consists in the frankest and most explicit enjoyment of the common metaphysical assumptions. You may have a sort of metaphysics without having a religion, but not *vice versa*: you cannot have a religion without having a metaphysics which you understand to be other than your physics.

The intelligent religionist knows something which is evident to every adult person who has not "hardened his heart" against it, or hardened his head—to every one, in other words, who is not a Positivist. And this is, that nature is made and kept natural only by the virtue of a supernatural being that compels it; or, that one cannot account for the facts except by appealing to something not fact. To the metaphysical entities of this sort the religionist gives supernatural names: God, his hosts and ministering angels, Satan, demons, and the like. The names mean to be undemonstrable. And this is one reason why they are superior to the quasi-scientific names through which scientists grow metaphysical without knowing it. Gods are better than Principles, because you know that with Gods you are dealing with entities not phenomenal, while it is possible for you to invoke and use Principles, thinking that you have merely picked them up somewhere in the natural world.

And so we may define at least one of the differences between metaphysics and religion: Metaphysics names the supernatural entities in terms that look physical or natural and tend to conceal their character; but religion names them in terms that declare their supernaturalism. Metaphysics sticks close by physics, where a confusion between them is the most likely, while religion is openly mythical.

Comte considered that the progress of human enlightenment was by the successive steps: from Gods to metaphysical Principles, then from metaphysical Principles to pure science. And he documents this thesis by showing how the improvement of the specific sciences had apparently come about as first the Gods, and then the Principles, had been overthrown. But there is some truth and some fallacy in the argument.

The fallacy in the argument is in assuming that the perfection of a scientific knowledge has anything to do in the way of diminishing the necessity of the metaphysical Principles. There is clearly just as much metaphysics involved in an exact science like physics as in an inexact science like politics. Any single one of Kant's books will show the actual place of the metaphysical assumptions in promoting any science whatever. Science never gets rid of its assumptions, and the utmost success it will have in this direction will be the doubtful success which consists in covering them up. Nobody with any philosophical standing nowadays would care to defend the Positive thesis that science can ever dispense with metaphysical implications.

But there is some truth in the contention that certain Gods, as men have defined them, have hindered the progress of secular knowledge. Gods are the mythical counterparts or expansions of the metaphysical Principles, incapable of expression in natural terms. When we set up Gods to keep, we elect to consider the Principles regularly under certain forms *as if* they were natural forms. Then we sanctify the forms, or impose a taboo upon them which is to guard them from familiarity. But it may happen that the taboo operates to keep natural science from exercising its legitimate functions. The classical example is the God of the ancient or Ptolemaic cosmology. God was the creator and ruler of a Ptolemaic world. He was protected in this capacity, so that it was blasphemous if anybody questioned him, or any of the facts about him as represented in the myth. So the scientists who for good reason preferred a Copernican world were in the position, a rather painful and heroic one too, of being heretics. And this is how a God may hinder science from attending to its proper business. But the fact that men abandon a Ptolemaic God does not mean that they need no God at all, or have found a substitute which is not a God at all but just as good. A Copernican universe requires a God just as much as a Ptolemaic one.

Mr. Huxley laid down his famous Three Hypotheses respecting the origin of nature, with the remark that every man must make one of them his own. But these were simply three metaphysical assumptions; and as soon as some man might begin to elaborate the one of his choice, it would be on the point of becoming his myth and his God.

The progress which moderns need now to make—especially those very pure and representative ones who are Positive scientists—is just opposite to that recommended by Comte: they should bring to full consciousness the metaphysical Principles to which they habitually run in the course of their sciences; and then they should set up the very best Gods they can to embody the Principles. And I suppose this is really the true and regular sequence of progress anywhere, at least so far as logic might have anything to do with it.

The generalizations of science come quite logically, and

often enough actually, before the generalizer knows what metaphysical purpose underlies his work. The geometry of Euclid held up for more than two thousand years before anybody noticed that it was all based on a postulate which was metaphysical, hypothetical, and incapable of demonstration. So there is no question about the justice of the first of these steps. A scientist is not up to his times if he now cannot tell what presuppositions he makes in his work; that is, he is only an ordinary, professional, old-style scientist, like the majority perhaps. Scientists now, if they are "enlightened," are like Mr. Eddington—they try to tell the metaphysical Principles that they use.

But the need of the second step, to myths and Gods as the forms of the metaphysical Principles, will not be so easily agreed upon.

Kant, who has the place of highest honor in European history as an apologist of metaphysics, has no such place as an apologist of religion. He had a Protestant and Puritanical fear of myths, along with a passion for metaphysical Principles. He illustrated in his own person a weakness which is almost professional in philosophers: they are just as afraid of committing themselves to a concrete religion as scientists are afraid of committing themselves to metaphysics. Kant had much to say about God, but he was God-in-general, not God-in-particular. Kant, and the philosophers generally, translate the Gods downwards from persons into Principles. They *elevate* science into metaphysics; but they *reduce* religion into metaphysics. "Nature is conceived," says Kant, "as if the unity of its manifold empirical laws were due to an intelligence." There he elevates science. "We cannot, however, assert that there actually is an intelligence of this kind, for judgment does not give a law to nature but only to itself." That is, you can never demonstrate the intelligence you have assumed behind nature; and there Kant reduces religion; for this is hardly the tone in which a serious religionist refers to his God.

But metaphysics and religion deal with the same thing—they are two different techniques which aim at the same result. A Principle may grow a little dangerous in becoming a God, as Comte's evidences would go to show. But it is improved in most respects: it becomes vastly more effective as an expression. Presently we shall continue this subject, and see why and how we make Gods out of Principles.

The realm through which metaphysics and religion would conduct us is the realm of *als ob*, As If. Our experience of nature points to it incessantly: we cannot keep from entering it and traversing it. But how different are our two guides!

"This is Mirage Land," says metaphysics. "There is nothing here which you can demonstrate; the senses cannot actually perceive anything; and all the sense-images which you have are phantasms. The realm exists, but not one single thing you find in it exists. Therefore make no notes, draw no maps, and leave your camera behind you when you enter."

But religion is a much more comfortable attendant. It encourages us with our pictures, our maps, and our notebooks, fictions though they offer. It expects us actually to make a selection of the best of them and hold on to these: they will serve us poorly but they will serve. This is a counsel of desperation, but it is the most practical counsel we shall receive.

So the second step is from metaphysics to religion, or Principles to Gods. This is the progress which the world needs now to take, above all the other progresses which are being urged upon it by its prophets, some of whom are vociferous and most of whom are necessarily false prophets.

This is just the progress which many a thoughtful man wishes now that he knew how, or had the courage, to take. With all our sciences we know very well that something is lacking.

But the need of our Western society for a religion is only, for the most part, *felt:* not understood: only a rather unlocalized *pain;* for religion does not have much support from the articulate philosophers. The function of philosophy with respect to religion has been, just as Comte saw, a destructive one. Philosophy has tended to disestablish religion, by reducing Gods to Principles. This means that the service of philosophy has been critical, not creative, and that it scarcely lies in the power of the philosopher ordinarily, or as a member of the profession, to be a leader of society, but rather just to castigate its errors—his vocation is not that of prophet but of dialectician.

How then shall Gods come out of Principles, and the descent which has been engineered by the philosophers be reversed? For I assume that the Gods have now for us been rather egregiously disestablished, and have lost their identity at the point where they first received it: in the metaphysical Principles.

I know how the priests, the professional keepers of religion, would establish their Gods: by pointing us to a Divine Revelation. "God spake unto Moses . . . And Jesus said . . . The inspired word of Saint Paul tells us . . ." Such expressions show the style of approach which the priests use. And they have used it long, they have used it for the length of a very old tradition. The fact is, significantly enough, that this tradition goes back to the time when the Occident had not yet emerged as a peculiar human temperament, or as a historic polity, from the Orient: it is in the Oriental manner. But Oriental priests had a great advantage. Their hearers were used to myth, and did not stumble on the supernatural. The Occidental hearers are different—instructed by their sciences always to stick to their natural facts, inclined not to know that they must live by Principles, which can never in any of their specific forms be attested as facts. As Westerners we hate lies, do not understand myths, and have the greatest difficulty in seeing that myths do not propose to compete with natural history.

Therefore I should say that Revelation and Authority do not serve the priests as an effective approach to the Western mind today. These terms are misunderstood—except by initiated religionists who do not need any fresh approach from the priests. They seem to set up the God in competition with the sciences over issues of fact, and they arouse a very deep suspicion. It is vain to tell the Western world how God's nature has been told by Divine Revelation, for the Western world sees shrewdly that this is tautology; it begs the question; it defines the myth in mythical terms. It is my idea that the myth should be defined for the modern unbeliever in terms of its psychic necessity—by a sort of natural history of supernaturalism. This is a quite unorthodox way to justify orthodoxy, but I imagine it is the only effective means of persuasion that remains now.

I presuppose the Principles.

For our purpose, the metaphysical Principles with which we have filled in the world, and which many of us now acknowledge, are on the general order of the following:

Substances, which underlie certain phenomenal fields in order to support them and keep them from falling apart;

Causes, which permit the disparate items of a natural sequence to touch and affect each other;

Hypothetical Forms, which are assumed for objects of such magnitude as to be too great or too small for the senses to grasp—like the microcosm which Bohr assumed for the infra-sensible atom, and has now recalled;

Souls, minds, or *selves,* to which the conscious states are referred for the sake of constancy and permanence;

Ideas or *Universals,* as Forms endowed with the power and the will to create or reproduce their likenesses;

Individuals, as the cores of privateness or uniqueness in objects that we sense as exceeding their own recorded history;

An Intelligence, behind the whole of the phenomenal universe to give it unity and stability.

The list is neither systematic nor complete.

To these Principles we are driven, by a necessity which seems to be twofold. First, it is according to the requirements of our logical constitution; and second, it is a necessity which is practical, or which conditions our reasonable conduct. We legislate such Principles into being when the time comes for us to perform our legislation. There is no use in repining: this is the task which devolves upon us.

So we legislate; and now shall we have the courage of our legislation? Shall we mean or not mean those Principles which we have called into existence? Shall we legislate once in a long while, and intend our legislation to last, or shall we stop and make a fresh legislation every time the original situation recurs? It is the way we answer this question that makes us religious, or that leaves us only metaphysical.

A Principle insisted on, stuck to, meant, developed in detail, defined, professed, becomes a God. A Principle half-heartedly enunciated, apologetic, indefinite, not intended to persist, fades out of consciousness, and has to be re-legislated into its embryonic existence as soon as we need it again.

The issue of Principles *versus* Gods is an issue for our spiritual economy, and the two sides are sufficiently near equal to make it a contest. In favor of mere Principles this much can be said: Principles are so vague and shadowy that you do not commit yourself in them to any particular detail, and so you do not run the risk of any future embarrassment. Professor Niels Bohr's version of the atom as a pretty microcosm was in a fair way of being stabilized as a quite hard little Demon, and was canceled just in time: this improvisation meant to consist with the phenomenal events, but actually it began to conflict with them: it would have forced the scientists to deny the facts. The circumstantial God who had Ptolemaic properties suited for a while but finally lost his innocence and competed with the admirable Copernican generalizations of science for our allegiance. There are a good many other cases of Principles whose detail has proved unhappy. (It is of course my own feeling that this peril is not so mortal as the scientists seem to suppose; but it is a peril.) The God is the Principle made circumstantial, and it is to be hoped that his circumstance is always harmless, but that may not be so.

And on the other hand, what are the advantages of Gods over Principles? I think of at least two that are major. In the first place, the Gods are concrete, they have sensible quality, they furnish us with esthetic experience. This is no small benefit. The scientific processes are terribly confining. They crucify our organic sensibility while they drive furiously towards their abstracts, and their exclusive aspects. Science as a mental habit is an obsession which is quite unhealthful. While engaged upon it, we may stop it momentarily to resort to the Principles, but that relief is too fleeting: the Principles are just a *gesture* towards fullness, towards the indulgence of sensibility. As soon as we have made the gesture we are back at our abstractions. Gods, on the contrary, are nothing if they are not full-grown objects, concrete, and inviolable. We set them up at critical points in the heart of our secular world and worship; that is, we enjoy their independent fullness of being, and we make a point of returning to them periodically, according to a self-imposed ritual which is to secure us in their enjoyment.

Then we lay aside the fearful responsibility of sustaining our pure abstract systems, and in leisure contemplate existences which we propose not to dominate and reduce.

In the second place, and perhaps even more obviously, Gods are better than Principles in the respect that legislation is always superior in the practical sense when it is specific. Laws, if the legislative technique behind them is competent, are plain, they have wide publication, they succeed in being perfectly understood. Principles are as vague and slippery as they can be. Gods are, comparatively speaking at least, explicit. The Gods who have been legislated into official existence by the will of the whole society are defined in myths which tell what they are like; how they have performed in the physical universe and in human history; what sort of conduct they require from their subjects, the members of the community. The sanctity, majesty, divinity, taboo, with which they are invested, are to represent in the most binding way possible the power and determination of the social will that lies behind them. Their commandments are the oldest and most fundamental prescriptions which society has imposed upon itself. Under the picturesque terms of the myth this ancient body of legislation comes down to us translated into Divine Revelation, and this old and continuing will of society becomes Divine Authority. These are the mythical sanctions of the myth.

The myths are therefore the frank development of the metaphysical Principles. But not all myths become religious myths, not all attain to the honor of becoming dogmas. Perhaps all are candidates for that honor, when they first appear for inspection before the mind which has created them. At that moment they are likely to seem solemn and expressive enough. But generally the mood passes and they do not return many times more for review. These myths do not quite wear, they will not stand up under usage; they prove to have been just the most convenient forms we had to give to the Principles upon a certain occasion.

The psychology of myth-persistence is the psychology of religion. It must be a branch of study far more delicate and complicated than is usually admitted. At the beginning of such a branch of study we should have to admit that we would probably never quite succeed in defining the grounds of our deepest tastes and distastes.

An ordinary myth is enjoyed for the time being, since it expresses something that needed to be expressed and could not otherwise be expressed. But the myth that stands at the base of a religious institution is more than enjoyed. It is repeated over and over, both spontaneously and as an act of deliberate ritual. And it is not merely repeated, it is professed, it is practiced, it is believed, it is held firmly before us as a guide to conduct, and it is passionately defended from competition. Men will fight for their religions. If the most fundamental thing to fight about is one's economic existence, or one's life, it seems reasonable to think that one's religion is, very likely, the next best thing. Evidently we are not playing when we participate in our religious myth, we *mean* it intensely, and perhaps fiercely.

A persistent or religious myth must have survived several requirements, which will be evident enough for the psychologist. I shall name some of them, without trying to do it too systematically, or to anticipate his labors.

(1) *The myth must be important.*
The late Professor J. A. Stewart in his excellent book, "The Myths of Plato," has some terms for this effect which are a little too fine for my present purpose: he speaks of myths which are Aitiological, and Eschatological. That is, they refer the universe as a going concern back to its first cause to see what it intends to do; then they picture the destiny of man as a consequence of this intention. So the Scrip-

tural poet first apostrophizes the glory of God, and then asks, "What is man, that thou art mindful of him?"

Religious myths, in other words, must deal with no lesser objects than with Gods. And these Gods must be complete Rulers and Causes, cosmic in dimensions, comprehensive in their operations. It is not possible to find a philosophy of life in the contemplation of Gods who represent less than the whole of the universe.

What then of polytheism? If the Gods of the myths are not great and cosmic, but little and local, then there must be correspondingly many of them, in order that the system of myths be comprehensive enough to be of service. If one God only is represented, he in his turn must be comprehensive.

Fairyland, or the world of dreams, may furnish us with a literary entertainment but hardly with a religious experience. Fairies are pretty objects, and occasional dragons give a variety, but our minds will not be exercised very seriously with such myths. And poetry is crowded with little myths. The brooks are made to babble, the daffodils to dance, and the mountains to brood. Under these representations we experience the objects very genuinely, as objects exceeding in their fullness any lesser representations—for example, exceeding their usual representations as things with certain practical uses, or their scientific representations as typical flora, or fauna, or geological specimens. But the objects are insignificant and the myths are unimportant.

Furthermore, the God needs to be fully equipped with his thunderbolts: a philosophical religion will not forget its realism and fail to make testimony to its Jupiter Tonans. Without this provision no religion will have much of a life. This fact is proved today: the softer and more benevolent the representation of the God of Christendom, the more he is neglected, the less need of him the believers find they have. The importance of the God takes in not only his physical magnitude, as the most obvious requirement, but also his inscrutable variety and the uncertainty of his favor. It is not important thinking if we are impeded by fear or by sentimentality to the point of refusing to invest our God with his proper sternness, or even frightfulness. A certain severity therefore attaches to religions which are full and expressive. The myths of savages excel in their realism, and reflect a primitive courage which we have not always maintained. The ritual with which they invest such leading facts as birth, sex, kingship, disease, natural catastrophe, and death, is likely to compare too favorably with the euphemistic rigmarole in which the race indulges its hopes in its effete stages. Savages are in direct and sustained contact with a nature over which they know they have a very limited power. Their God is a Thunderer. In their myths they often express a tragic sense which represents the highest philosophical enlightenment, whether it is the property of a youthful race or not.

In general, the God who survives must embody our fullest idea of the universe.

(2) *The myth must be vivid and energetic.*
Religion cannot dispense with Gods, and the Gods must be quasi-natural, or frankly circumstantial. The dogma in which we believe must have plenty of sensible quality, or quasi-historical concreteness. "I believe in God the Father Almighty, and His only begotten Son our Lord, who was crucified, dead, and buried . . ." That is genuine dogma, a myth with a content. "And God said unto Abraham . . ." That is, too.

Many of the persons who want a religion, and seem unable to explain why they have not one, are really too afraid of the vigor of a concrete myth. They dare not risk the charge that they are guilty of anthropomorphism, or of idolatry, and so they deny to the God all his substantial existence. The anthropologists, exposing the foolishness of primitive super-naturalism, have made them very sensitive on this point—they do not want anthropologists pointing to their errors! So they attempt to have a God without having any God in particular. But they will not get them a religion until they get them a ritual, and a ritual requires a particular God, and some particular history about him.

To these fastidious persons religion will not come in any full sense, but only a vague yearning like that which was experienced by Wordsworth, looking at nature without the benefit of a creed, and trying to satisfy himself with a metaphysical taste that had no concrete image to feed upon. Wordsworth did not commit himself to myth even as readily as the ordinary lyric poet—his poems read astonishingly tame, whereas the ordinary poet creates one myth after another to serve his momentary desires. He wrote a great deal about the God behind nature, but almost never tried to invest him with any properties.

And a myth which has flourished once will perish when its devotees become too squeamish, and begin peeling off its wrappings of concrete detail, saying that they are interested only in the "heart" of its mystery—but finding in the end that the heart which they arrive at is only an abstract essence that has no blood in it. The modern preacher now addresses his public prayer to an abstraction, and is careful not to require of the worshipers more than the minimum of that indignity that consists in entertaining a lively image of the God. In this way the priest abdicates his function—though I do not doubt but that it often seems to the priest that he must choose between losing his myth and losing his constituency.

Primitives never make this error. Their Gods are tangible.

(3) *But the myth must, on the whole, be in keeping with our taste.*

This is the converse of the foregoing requirement. Number 2 and Number 3 are the whirlpool and the crag between which the religionist must steer his exceptionally difficult course. It is probably in vain that we try to compel ourselves to go against the grain and profess our faith in a myth that arouses some powerful antipathy because of its peculiar associations. For example, how may a Copernican repeat sincerely the myth which pictures his God in the act of creating and conducting a Ptolemaic universe? Or *vice versa?* The myth tells of a God supporting the accepted natural phenomena: it cannot be very well adapted to the believer in whose view it seems to falsify the natural phenomena.

We respond sympathetically to a myth only if it suits us racially and culturally. We are now living in cities, for the most part. Not only do we not live in an agricultural society, but the agricultural life has come to be held in a certain scorn. We could not therefore, probably, if we were perfect creatures of our age, accept with relish as the appropriate symbol of omnipotence a mere Rain-God, or a God of vegetation. We have no longer any particular relations with the beasts, and we could not care for totemism, or a myth which defined God as an animal. We have developed a rigorous censorship with respect to expressing the bodily affections, particularly those of sex—how then could we feel happy with myths which publicly employed phallic images for God —or even mere physiological ones, as the Hebrew myths are supposed by the Cabbalists to do?

I must say this too: there are Gentiles who cannot readily adapt themselves to a myth which is Jewish in its coloring; and Occidentals who cannot adapt themselves to imagery which is too rich and foreign in an "Oriental" way.

We cannot hope to find our religious expression in a religion which causes us to blush. And this is most embarrassing. I do not know of situations much more painful than that of wishing to take part in a religious institution and feeling not quite able to go through with it, because of some massive but indistinct repulsion or disgust, which comes we do not know why.

Conditions of this sort have much to do with the rise of religions, and certainly they have just as much to do with their decay.

(4) Finally, as the climax of all its development: *A myth must be institutionalized, or become a social possession.*

This has been the understanding implied in all the foregoing requirements. There is hardly any such thing as a strictly private religion, or a dogma with but one adherent. A religion is the possession of a society. If I name a religion, you will spontaneously and immediately think the name of the people who believed it and practiced it.

And part of the meaning of a religion for the individual is in his sense of this fact. A strictly private belief does not command one's own complete conviction, while one waits to secure the adherence of others to it too. Our devotion to the myth is not finished except in the knowledge of the social sanction behind it.

But with respect to its capacity for winning the public consent, a myth is almost an unknown quantity. Nobody can predict it. The conversion of a whole society to a myth is an event as unaccountable as it is important, and we are wise only after the event.

This is unfortunate, in some ways. It leaves impotent and distressed all those modern Platos who have a gift for myth-making, and would willingly serve their age by giving it the myth which it conspicuously needs. The most creative act that a society can perform is to sanction a myth and set up a religion—most of the other decisions that it has to take

are minor to this one, and follow from it logically. Yet nobody in the influential circles of that society attempts seriously to predict a new religion, or to found one. The latter rôle devolves now and then, if at all, upon some totally
obscure and unlikely person. The genius of the race makes
its most critical manifestation in the most unexpected manner.

CHAPTER FIVE

RELIGION AND MAGIC

So the myths rise spontaneously out of the Principles, and when they have been selected for institutional purposes, systematized, and perpetuated, they produce Gods. I hope I have not indicated that the natural history of a set of Gods is anywhere or at any time an easy one to follow. What I have given is rather a logic than a history.

At last then, the Gods. But even when they are once established, they are never quite secure. There are too many people who do not know where they came from—natural scientists who resent them as competitors, and weak-minded believers who do not understand what they are doing, and play into the hands of the scientists. *The peril to which a religion is constantly exposed is that of being regarded as a magic*—greedily practiced by its own adherents as a valuable magic, scorned and abused by its enemies as a ridiculous magic. When the scientists attack religion, they attack it where it is weakest: where it seems to be a magic. I suppose there has never been a religion without a goodly number of devotees who tried to use it in that sense. The idea of magic is inseparably associated with religious practices in the West, at least; and for all I know the Eastern communities suffer from it too.

A special branch of science has evidently been developed, not quite spontaneously, but for the precise purpose of exposing magic. This branch is anthropology. It is the perfect product of the nineteenth century. It has undertaken, ostensibly, to study the culture of primitive peoples. Within the less than a hundred years of its existence it has already produced a voluminous exhibit of primitive rites, and it has indicated that all the primitive religions seemed full of magic. But then anthropology has not quite been content to stop there, and there was no reason why it should. Anthropology has made the study of primitivism the basis of a searching study of comparative religion. In this field its most telling strokes have consisted in showing that even the rites of advanced religions, like those of our own society, have their counterparts and presumably their historical origins in the magical rites of the primitives. Thus Christianity is a complex containing an element which is a survival of a vegetation-myth, and another which is a survival of a solar myth, and another perhaps which is a survival of a phallic myth—and presumably, anthropology says, these features perpetuate not only the primitive forms but also the primitive purpose, which was to work magic.

Serving in this rôle, anthropology has clearly been the handmaiden to a belligerent scientific party attacking its enemy the party of the religionists. Anthropology is bent on the refutation of religion, and the point of its attack is magic.

There is no trouble about the meaning of magic. Magic arises for the ritualist who believes in his God in the very same sense in which he believes in his king, his friend, his wife, or his horse: as a demonstrable or historical being. He is so stupid that he thinks all the detail of his myth is a part of the natural order, and has been furnished by the Determinant or finding judgment rather than by the Reflective or creative judgment. He is a pure naturalist, and a peculiarly gullible one. So it is logical that he should try to enter into profitable relations with a God of whose factuality he has convinced himself. He conceives that the ritual is a cere-monial which this God guaranteed to be effective for the be-lievers who will approach him in due order; or at least that the ritual is a form of approach which has been demon-strated to be effective. He employs the ritual in order to secure his practical ends. That is magic.

Primitive magic, as it is practiced by the rain-maker and the medicine-man for example, is perfectly vain as a mat-ter of course and has no effect on the sequence of nature. But in this sense prayer is vain too, and vain is every form of rite in the Christian communions, early or late. The idea of ritual as an effective influence upon the natural order of events is entertained today as it has always been, and it still indicates a very feeble talent for epistemology, for the analysis of the terms of his knowledge, on the part of the man who entertains it. He is scarcely informed of the sense and intention with which the myth-maker created the God. He is even a good deal more ingenuous than as a naturalist he is obliged to be.

So I, and all religionists and defenders of religion, are forced to admit it: magic is not only a primitive kind of be-havior but a perennial one. The believers in magic we have always with us. The anthropologists are quite correct in charging that the savage who beats his idol in order to com-pel it, or who puts food upon the ground in order to per-suade it, is acting with precisely the same intelligence as the modern man who thinks he secures a physical blessing by prayer, baptism, offering, or ceremony, under the forms sup-posed to be sanctioned by his God.

There are probably sorcerers, magicians, and fakirs in the pay of every institutionalized religion, as its priests, and peo-ple who are taken in by them, as its defrauded believers. I should certainly not undertake to find an exceptional re-ligion where this fact would not obtain. Nevertheless, I do not think it a fair conclusion that these classes together "constitute the Church."

And now it is time to discuss Fundamentalism. My own view is that all first-class religionists are Fundamentalists, and that it is the Fundamentalists, properly speaking, who constitute the Church. These Fundamentalists, as I see it, do not believe in magic. And yet I would feel obliged to define them in the usual terms. The Fundamentalists are those who regard their God as an actuality, and treat their supernatural fictions as natural objects. How then is it possible to clear them of the usual reproaches heaped upon them by anthropologists?

I will try to imagine the religious history of a good Fundamentalist as a perfectly intelligent course of action. There seems to be nothing preposterous in that combination.

The Fundamentalist is a man who, in the first place, had the metaphysical acuteness to rise from the scientific laws to the Principles. To get that far he employed philosophy, in its most ordinary kind of service.

But he was not only a philosopher, for he had religious desires; and so he allowed his Principles to take their spontaneous mythical forms. There was some courage and decision involved in this step too. He had to release his imagination, and honor the forms under which it represented the Principles.

And still he had not done all. The enjoyment of myths in general does not quite make a Fundamentalist. The act that yet remained for him was *to pick out of all the myths a particular one to profess and to keep.* This act he performed; and at that stage he became our full-fledged Fundamentalist.

For a single Principle is capable of generating a dozen images in quick succession, which will constitute a dozen myths, and the number of possible images is limited only by the fertility of our imaginations. But dogma is not made out of a dozen equivalents at once, dogma is built upon the one myth preferred of all. The Fundamentalist commits himself to it, and desires it to prevail in the minds of his generation. You do not found a living religion by preaching with the completest impartiality all the myths of men indifferently: in that way you found comparative religion, which is a literary exercise, or a theosophy, or a pleasant game. You must concentrate on one myth and say to it, "I believe." And this demands an old-fashioned kind of "character," which agrees to say to all the others, "I don't believe." The other religions will have to be left to shift for themselves. The God of Israel was said to have commanded: "Thou shalt have no other Gods before me."

Versatility in myths is, for religious purposes, a defect of the poetic temperament. It is only a little less fatal than the fear of any myths at all, which is the professional defect of the philosophical temperament.

Between having Principles and having Gods, therefore, there is an intermediate state which is more than metaphysical, and less than religious. I imagine that this state can be identified historically with Gnosticism. The Gnostics saw a great deal more of the light than did the Agnostics. Their trouble was, in fact, that they saw rather too much of it. They knew so many beautiful myths! And every one of them a perfectly legitimate development of a Principle. So they ran from one to the other without ceasing. But necessarily they were impotent, for no religion came out of the synthesis of all religions at once, and they had to go without the benefits that one good religion might have offered them.

Gnostics were very common in the period just following Christ—they were intellectually very able men, but without practical decision. But the present age also is producing

Gnostics at a great rate. Men of metaphysical capacity and of sensibility are not unaccustomed to admire the Gods to whom the peoples of the earth have sworn, and to see behind them always the justice of the Principles out of which they have developed. But that is not enough; they know too well that is not enough. Gods are not Gods except when they are treated as Gods, and myths do not work in human civilization except when they are dogmas, tolerably hard, and exceedingly jealous of their rivals.

In the Greek language we find an instructive word derived from *mythos:* it was *mytheomai,* a verb in the middle voice which means, "to mutter to oneself." The word *mythos* has a favorable connotation, but there is something a little ridiculous about this verb. It defines the essential practice of the theosophist, or the Gnostic. To perform the action a man had only to be a versatile composer of myths. He went about immensely preoccupied with the mysterious supernatural beings behind the natural world, and incessantly giving them their bodies and forms. But the poor man knew so well that these were incompetent, and not fit to publish to the world, that he only talked about them under his breath.

You have to simplify your stock of myths if you want to found a dogma and preach it to the world. If your imagination exercises too riotously it will have to conduct a private enterprise strictly. This is a kind of literary enterprise, such as rhapsodical poets are given to: it does not produce a responsible social deliverance.

Dogma is the simplification of myth. The church needs only a few great raving mystics in its exhibit at a time: for its ordinary public purposes it needs saints and theologians of a more conservative order.

The Fundamentalist does not babble to himself. His mythology is practicable and communicable because it is unitary, consistent, and dogmatic.

So the Fundamentalist took the most critical step in his career. There may well have been the utmost deliberation and reluctance behind it. It was not a decision to take hastily. But eventually he subscribed to his elected myth by saying, "I believe." He required it at the very center of his practical life, as a myth to go by. And ever since then, he has honored his subscription by his willingness to repeat, whether spontaneously or on the prescribed or ritualistic occasions, "I believe." That tells his subsequent history, that defines his present status, and it is that which makes him a Fundamentalist. A Fundamentalist is after all a believer. He has convinced himself, and he has the courage of his convictions.

I hardly believe that he would be either nobler or more intelligent if he elected to cross his fingers whenever he repeated his creed. It would be asking too much to require him to take the pains to say to himself each time: "Remember, this is myth, not fact; this is *als ob*, my hypothesis; don't be taken in." If he did that he would seem only pusillanimous. The patriot who is caught in the act of saluting a striped rag does not feel obliged to stop and offer the qualification that he honors it only as the symbol of something else, especially when he could not define that something else to save his mortal life. He would be a pedant if he felt obliged to be so delicate. The only excuse for him would be that he was being constantly abused by a public which contained a very large percentage of pedants. The Fundamentalist, to borrow Kant's phrase again, has *legislated* his God into being, not found him somewhere, and if he means business he will stand by his own legislation. He makes himself a little bit absurd if he continues to suspect it, to demand its credentials, and to force himself to go each time through the agonies of his original decision.

The uses of religion are esthetic and practical. Of the first of these uses the Fundamentalist is eminently in a position to avail himself. His opposite, the Modernist, is the man who is afraid of the vigorous detail of the concrete myth, and will not let himself go in order to receive its esthetic benefit. He is too busy "defining his position"— and pre-occupied, fearful that somebody will misunderstand him, and fidgeting all through the religious ceremony. The present movement away from Fundamentalism is simply the form which the destructive tendency of Protestantism takes for this age. It is a "philosophical" movement in the old sense that it prefers the Principles to the Gods. It is the movement of people who have not the imagination and the courage to enjoy the excellent Gods they have inherited. And as there is nothing new in Modernism, so there is nothing new in Fundamentalism either. The Fundamentalists are simply those of our period who still find it easy and natural to profess beliefs, and then to hold to them.

The other use is practical or economic. The religion which the Fundamentalist has adopted contains the decision he has taken with respect to his career. He has elected it because it seemed to offer him the best definition of his humanity, the best recipe for his happiness. This practical teaching of religion is implied in the ritual, for he senses there the fullness of God, the invincible majesty against which he must not strive. But it is contained frankly in the commandments which the God imposes upon his conduct: for an effective God does not fail to lay down these commandments. A good religion intends to be proof against any folly of interpretation.

But this description of the Fundamentalist says nothing about magic. He "believed" in his myth originally in a sense that was quite deliberate and understanding, but now it is hardly much different from the ordinary believing of a naturalist in a natural phenomenon. He takes his God for actual, talks to him, obeys him, makes offering to him. If the naturalist questions him about this, he will not discuss it: for he has made his decision, and elected his belief, and he does not care what its grounds were and what he meant by it. *In effect the Fundamentalist does not any longer distinguish myth and fact.* But why should he, if the myth is worth believing in? He did distinguish when there was need of distinguishing: but he made the distinction then in order that he would not have to make it every day. In the life of belief there must be a certain economy. It is well to believe a good many things without having to conduct a continuous epistemological discussion about them; to believe without being self-conscious about it.

But as for magic, that depends on what the Fundamentalist expects to get out of his Gods, be they as actual for him as he will make them.

The magic charged most frequently against the modern Fundamentalist lies in the purpose with which he prays. When he prays, does he think he is practicing a magic, does he believe that he is making contact with a natural force which will work to his advantage? I shall be disputed, but I should answer in the negative. The Fundamentalist whom I am approving does not think so. He has been too well grounded. He guarded against this possibility when he made the God stern and inscrutable; he will not be guilty if his God is old-fashioned or Oriental in his nature. "Not my will but thine," is what the Fundamentalist says in his prayer. His private petition is frankly uttered, but under the ritualistic or directed form of his prayer he quickly perceives its absurdity. It is not that he perceives the absurdity of expecting nature to modify its course in his favor; that is not quite the form of his thought: the absurdity which he perceives is that of expecting his God, who is majestic and incalculable, to bend to his pleasure. The one absurdity has been effectively translated into the other, and none of the force of the original been lost in the process. His prayer therefore un-prays itself before it is done, and renounces his claim to a favored treatment. In fact, its purpose is opposite to that usually ascribed to it: it reconciles him to his impending defeat.

Reverting to a bit of recent religious history: there was the affair of Dayton, Tennessee.

Fundamentalism occupied itself there with defending a myth that casually included in its embrace a Ptolemaic astronomy, and some natural history which naturalists seemed to have demonstrated to be in error. Of course these features were not essential to the intention of the original myth. But the defenders of the myth did not admit to a distinction, and held all its features to be equally sacrosanct. They were confronted with a cruel pair of alternatives: whether to admit exceptions to a body of doctrines which they had loyally adopted, and possibly bring them all into disrepute; or to continue holding to them in their entirety at the cost of public ridicule, and even on pain of establishing in their own minds a painful contradiction between the natural and the supernatural. The dilemma was the consequence of the antiquity of the myth, which was no longer in harmony with the state of natural knowledge.

I have not been able to see that either of the belligerents at Dayton escaped with perfect honor. The religionists were teased into giving battle on a field which they were bound to lose. They were infatuated in their devotion, they were so brave that they were foolish.

But the scientists, on the other hand, were so naturalistic, and so obtuse, that they lost caste while they were winning the field. They succeeded in their tactics, but they lost in their strategy, for they alienated the public sentiment of the region.

This is the case for the best of the Fundamentalists. It is unfortunate that there are other Fundamentalists, much more simple in their intelligence; and that the good ones are often confused with the bad ones. These bad or simple Fundamentalists are the mercenaries of the religious army —they fight expecting to take their pay in hard quick coin.

They provoke the sneers of the naturalists, and quite properly. They have never understood the God whom they profess. They think he is a natural cause who can be touched, and persuaded to govern natural events for them. They think that in religion they have a way of access to his favor. It is quite as miserable a piece of thinking as any natural scientist cares to call it.

And they deceive themselves. But luckily, they do themselves no great harm by their religious observances. The religion which they serve is never, one would imagine, of their own invention: it has been created and elaborated by wiser men: the commandments it entails make a better thing out of the lives of the ignorant than their own devices would be likely to do. The office which a religion fulfills for a society is to inform its members of what expectations they can reasonably cherish in this life; and the mercenaries who serve religion do not get precisely the reward which they claim, but do get a code, an occupation, and a career. These are just as great blessings to a mercenary as to an intelligent patriot. The believers in religion as a magic get all they are entitled to, and probably more than they would get from any ordinary master.

To return to the anthropologists. The study of anthropology seems to have been pursued exclusively by naturalists, never by poets or by religionists. In my reading of anthropological literature—which includes its most notable single document, "The Golden Bough"—I have encountered few intimations that myths have ever been created with the intention that I have undertaken to define. Evidently the possibility does not occur to the ordinary anthropologist that

here are any entities in our minds except historical facts and
cientific generalizations on the one hand, and errors and
ies on the other. They are Positivists, and unacquainted with
netaphysical or reflective thinking, and with the representa-
ions of this thinking in terms which are mythical. One of
he few exceptions that I know is Professor Paul Radin,
vhose "Primitive Man as Philosopher" had, I believe, just
he public reception which was to be expected from a book
vith such a title: it was hailed as an irregular performance
vhen judged according to the standards of the profession.

The anthropologists may be slandering the religionists
vhen they invariably liken them to the primitive believers
n magic. But when they assume that all the primitive myth-
nakers believed in magic I feel sure they are slandering the
orimitives. It is hard to believe in their primitives. But I
hall not undertake to document this remark.

I am aware of course that anthropologists nowadays have
aken exception to the variety of primitivism which was as-
umed by Herbert Spencer, a pioneer anthropologist—his
variety now looks too, too primitive. But anthropologists still
eem to cling to their belief in a primitivism which was primi-
ive enough to take religion as a branch of natural science.

I shall be satisfied with showing the unfortunate state of
oublic opinion to which three quarters of a century of an-
hropology have now brought the public mind. It is of the
greatest importance to observe what the opinion actually is
oday about the religious project. The enemies of religion
already know what that opinion is, for it is their opinion; the
religionists ought to meditate it too.

I have before me some recent popular books which are
direct consequences of anthropology. They set forth the an-
hropological view of religion. But the remarkable thing is
that they do it so casually, and with so little commotion: they
assume that this view is a commonplace one in these days.

Here is Mr. Lewis Browne's book of 1926, "This Believing World," and here is a passage from Book One, "How It All Began."

In the beginning there was fear; and fear was in the heart of man; and fear controlled man. At every turn it whelmed over him, leaving him no moment of ease. With the wild soughing of the wind it swept through him; with the crashing of the thunder and the growling of lurking beasts. All the days of man were gray with fear, because all his universe seemed charged with danger. Earth and sea and sky were set against him: with relentless enmity, with inexplicable hate, they were bent on his destruction. At least, so primitive man concluded . . . It was an inevitable conclusion under the circumstances, for all things seemed to be forever going against man. Boulders toppled and broke his bones; diseases ate his flesh; death seemed ever ready to lay him low. And he, poor gibbering half-ape nursing his wound in some draughty cave, could only tremble with fear. He could not give himself stoical courage with the thought that much of the evil that occurred might be accidental. He could not so much as conceive of the accidental. No, so far as his poor dull pate could read the riddle, all things that occurred were full of meaning, were *intentional*. The boulder that fell and crushed his shoulder had *wanted* to fall and crush it. Of course! . . . The spear of heaven-fire that had turned his squaw to cinders had consciously *tried* to do that very thing. Obviously! . . .

What a primitive man this is! No beast was ever so incompetent. The only "obvious" thing I see here is Mr. Browne's desire to write in a background for his anthropological thesis about the origin of religion. And now comes the religion as Mr. Browne sees it.

. . . he was afraid. From experience he knew that fighting was useless, that the enemy-objects, the falling boulders that maimed him, and the flooding streams that wrecked his hut, were in some uncanny way proof against his spears and arrows. That was why he was finally forced to resort to more subtle methods of attack. Since blows could not subdue the hostile rocks or streams, our ancestor tried to subdue them with magic. He thought words might avail: strange syllables uttered in groans, or meaningless shouts accompanied by beating tom-toms. Or he tried wild dances. Or luck charms. If these spells failed, then he invented others; if those in turn failed, then he invented still others. Of one thing he seemed most stubbornly convinced: that *some* spell would work. Somehow the hostile things around him *could* be appeased or controlled, he believed; somehow death *could* be averted. Why he should have been so certain, no one can tell.

The last sentence in this passage is illuminating. No one an tell why a primitive man should have been so certain, nd in fact any one will have serious doubts as to whether ne was. But this is no primitive man of history: this is Mr. Browne's myth about a primitive man.

Mr. Mencken's book, just out, is "Treatise on the Gods." Its view also is the common anthropological one.

Mr. Mencken declines to be intimidated by the organized Baptists, the organized Methodists, or the organized Catholics: but I should imagine that he is deeply intimidated by he organized scientists, including the anthropologists. This aaving been said, his position on such matters as these is eminently predictable, and his book turns out to be exactly what might have been foreseen.

He writes:

. . . it is quite simple at bottom. There is nothing really secret or complex about it, no matter what its professors may allege to the contrary. Whether it happens to show itself in the artless mumbo-jumbo of a Winnebago Indian or in the elaborately refined and metaphysical rites of a Christian archbishop, its single function is to give man access to the powers which seem to control his destiny, and its single purpose is to induce those powers to be friendly to him. That function and that purpose are common to all religions, ancient or modern, savage or civilized, and they are the only common characters that all of them show. Nothing else is essential. Religion may repudiate every sort of moral aim or idea, and still be authentically religion. It may confine itself to the welfare of the votary in this world, rejecting immortality and even the concept of the soul, and yet hold its character and its name. It may reduce its practices to hollow formulae, without immediate logical content. It may imagine its gods as beings of unknown and unknowable nature and faculties, or it may imagine them as creatures but slightly different from men. It may identify them with animals, natural forces, or inanimate objects, on the earth or in the vague skies. It may credit them with virtues which, in man, would be inconceivable, or lay to them vices and weaknesses which, in man, would be unendurable. It may think of them as numerous or as solitary, as mortal or as immortal. It may elect them and depose them, choose between them, rotate them in office, arrange them in hierarchies, punish them, kill them. But so long as it believes them to be able at their will to condition the fate of man, whether on this earth or elsewhere, and so long as it professes to be capable of influencing that will to his benefit, that long it is religion, and as truly deserving of the name as the most highly wrought theological system ever heard of.

A curious admission accompanies Mr. Mencken's attack on the Bible as the locus of absurd supernatural beliefs: that the Jews, its authors, were at the same time the authors of the "greatest poetry" the world has seen. Of course Mr. Mencken does not attack the Jewish poets—those who wrote "the magnificent poems called the Psalms" and others that are specified—either as deluders of men or as deluded men. He does not hold the poets to the letter of their images because he knows the effort would bring ridicule not upon them but upon him. And it is very common to exempt literature from responsibility to the canons of naturalism while holding religion strictly up to the mark. But the difference between a religious myth and a poetic myth is not at all in the naturalism or the supernaturalism of the belief, but rather in the importance and the persistence of the belief. The religionist is not committed to magic any more than the poet.

There are a good many other books to the same effect, but I will cite just one more: Mr. Barnes' "Twilight of Christianity." This book contains a harder order of thinking than either of the two I have just mentioned. It is the work of an enemy of Christianity who wishes to consider honestly all the interpretations that can be put upon religion.

Christianity is full of magical practice, according to Mr. Barnes.

There is no doubt that prayer represents an attenuated contemporary manifestation of the ancient conceptions and expressions of magic. The dominant trait of magic as a phase of primitive religion was its supposed coercitive character, namely, its capacity to control the gods and secure desired results. Modern prayer implies a similar belief in the capacity of man to control and direct God's will and to modify the operation of divine wisdom. Otherwise, prayers to bless our public officials, to give us health and prosperity, to send rain or to avert cataclysms, would present no rationality whatever. It is held that in prayer the good Christian may not only sway God and modify his own destiny, but may also definitely affect the actions of others, even though the latter may not be conscious of his prayers.

But there are nevertheless Christian prayers which do not fall under this description:

Of course, not all prayer partakes of this quasi-coercitive character, but it cannot be denied that the great majority of prayers uttered by orthodox Christian preachers have as their basic theme a request to grant something which, it is implied, God would not be likely to insure or concede without this prayerful entreaty. Many prayers may be regarded as more correctly a part of worship than a hang-over from early magic. Such prayers express our appreciation of the majesty and goodness of God, and the like. Whether prayers are primarily coercitive or worshipful, the one common and basic factor remains, namely, the belief that man may get into direct contact with God and induce God to lend him very directly for the time being the divine ear.

Mr. Barnes rejects either type of prayer, however, as based on the illusion of the objective existence of God. He is a regular naturalist after all, and considers that a God or a myth is supposed to be a fact, and competes with the facts of natural science. He for his part does not wish to have any commerce with a God. He would have a religion, but it would have to be a religion without a God. It would be only an institution:

> Who, for example, could have any quarrel with religion when defined as Professor Edward Scribner Ames defines it, namely, as the search for, and realization of, the highest conceivable social values. If one identifies religion with all social decency and justice one creates a conception of religion which is highly attractive, but it is not equally accurate as a historical picture of the nature and practices of religion nor is it a reliable description of organized religion today.

This passage, in effect, construes religion just as the anthropologists have always done, but would take it and remove from it all the elements which the anthropologists have found objectionable: the supernatural God, the rites of communion with him, and the distasteful features of a myth which is now antiquated, and always was Oriental. But this is to make such radical alterations in religion that it is doubtful if the name religion would still be appropriate for what would be left. Mr. Barnes himself suggests to us that it is doubtful.

CHAPTER SIX

SATAN AS SCIENCE

I SEE no particular difficulty in finding plenty of philosophical meaning in the leading Old Testament myths. So ingenuously do I believe in my own theological system! even if I see that it is decidedly of a lay and amateurish variety. (The fact is that it is a theological homebrew.) I shall have the boldness to propose an interpretation of one of these myths.

I would even insist that my interpretation is a perfectly obvious one. I seem to be stating what was certainly the intention of the original myth-maker.

Of course it is not the only interpretation possible. I am aware that there might be other meanings than the one I advance, and I would never want to stop an exegete from his exegesis, however fanciful it seemed to me. It is both asset and liability to the myth that it is concrete: its maker may resign himself to the prospect that it is going to be the point of departure of a great many systems of thought, some of them probably far from his own conscious intention. Things release thoughts, and as things are inexhaustible so thoughts are unpredictable. The myth inevitably outgrows the myth-maker. I find it too much to believe, for myself, that the authors of the Hebrew Scriptures—J, E, P, and however they may be named and dated—could have anticipated, or would have welcomed, *all* the glosses of the learned Talmudists, and then those of the still more learned Cabbalists. Yet it seems not only charitable but even reasonable to assume that these interpreters can hardly have been entirely on the wrong track, that they were not likely to miss altogether the essential Orientalism of the originals. After all, these interpreters were Jews too; and they knew their Hebrew, and what different orders of meaning one and the same text could be made to contain. I would defer as a general thing to their judgments. It would be they rather than I, and rather than any Occidental, modern, "historically trained," and "higher" critic, who would be inside the tradition; it would be this latter-day scholar and I who would be outside.

In my interpretation of a myth I do not follow either the Talmudists or the Cabbalists. I mention them because at least they seem to me to obey the rule which I should think is the very first rule to observe in interpreting a myth: *not to construe the myth-maker for a fool.* This is a rule with which the anthropologists are scarcely acquainted. They impute foolishness readily to the myth-maker, except for the occasions when they impute knavery. They assume that he was trying to write natural history. And when their assumption has come to prevail generally, the interesting question rises whether the "enlightened" religionists of a late age can make any use of myths whose origin was in a mind so credulous and befuddled.

Some of them, like the Washington Manifestants of 1923, think not. They find the myths hopeless. Their point of view was expressed forcibly a number of years ago by Thomas Huxley, the natural scientist. He had a mind of great clarity and consistency, with a single limitation: it was a modern Occidental mind. His religious position was Agnosticism. In discussing Philo Judaeus as the bridge between the theology of the Jews and the theology of the Christians he wrote:

In order to get over the ethical difficulties presented by the naïve supernaturalism of many parts of the Scriptures, in the divine authority of which he firmly believed, Philo borrowed from the Stoics (who had been in like straits in respect of Greek mythology) that great Excalibur which they had forged with infinite pains and skill—the method of allegorical interpretation. This mighty "two-handed engine at the door" of the theologian is warranted to make a speedy end of any and every moral or intellectual difficulty, by showing that, taken allegorically, or, as it is otherwise said, "poetically," or, "in a spiritual sense," the plainest words mean whatever a pious interpreter desires they should mean. In Biblical phrase, Zeno (who probably had a strain of Semitic blood in him) was the "father of all such as reconcile."

In attacking the method of allegorical interpretation, Mr. Huxley is insisting on his own historico-scientific point of view. The Scriptural authors were deceived, or they lied. Their apologist, Philo, unable to defend their history or their science, borrowed from Zeno the pleasant but farfetched notion that, though foolish on the face of them, they might be still of some use to wiser and later men who could read into them something that would do.

But Mr. Huxley did too much honor to Philo, and to Zeno. The Jews hardly waited for Philo to tell them what their Scriptures meant—it was rather the Christian Gentiles, the early Fathers, who used him for that purpose.

Nor did the Greeks wait on Zeno to explain to them their myths. He was doubtless of service in his own generation. But Plato was interpreting Homer and composing the Cratylus nearly a hundred years before him. And there was the public scandal over the charge that Euripides had revealed in his plays the mysteries, whereas Aeschylus and Sophocles

had left them decently veiled—from which we would conclude that Greek drama was concerned with the same things
as the mystery cults were.

Many modern scholars of Greek forget that the Greeks
were as much Oriental as they were Occidental, and that
though they inaugurated Western science they also were accomplished mythologists and mystics in the Eastern sense.
Writers on Greek drama familiarize themselves with Aristotle's Poetics, a perfectly open and exoteric document. But
they might well consult "The Prometheus of Aeschylus," a
paper by Samuel Taylor Coleridge, who though a late and
Western critic was deeply involved in the traditional priestly
learning. It is a commonplace to Coleridge that Greek literature employed the legends of the mystery cults in order to
convey theological truth to those who were prepared to
receive it. The Greek drama looks like mere drama, but it
is also philosophy and religion. As for that, said Coleridge,
literature and sacred literature used to be one and the same
thing. Coleridge discovers in the "Prometheus" the fundamental doctrines of the Greek race. He takes it as a text,
with perfect or Philonic seriousness.

A good many Churchmen have the same view as Mr.
Huxley about the naïveté of the Old Testament, but do not
quite like, for the sake of appearances, to throw the book
away. But the use they would make of it is not flattering to
its authors. They say to themselves, "We shall not force the
issue, of course. We'll just interpret these ancient narratives, and we'll take care to bend them to our purposes."
For, by some lucky accident, it seems often possible for the
moderns to translate the delusions of the myth-maker into
allegory which will furnish passable religious doctrine even
today. How providential! It is perhaps on that basis that the
Old Testament still keeps a sort of semi-official status and
has any currency at all with Gentiles.

So it is an arbitrary assumption, as I see it made by the

anthropologists and the higher critics, that the myths of to-day were the natural science of yesterday. This represents one extreme of attitude toward the myth-makers. The other extreme of attitude is that of the Talmudists, Cabbalists, Rosicrucians, Masons of high degree, and the esoteric religionists, who believe that the myth-maker had in mind a metaphysical doctrine so elaborate that whole libraries have not yet exhausted his meaning.

My own feeling is that the truth about the myth-maker lies somewhere between these two attitudes: that the myth-maker whose myth was so good as to survive him must have been the wisest philosopher, priest, and statesman of his day; that it carried a profound but not too intricate meaning in a popular and accessible form; that it was the product of a mentality which would do the moderns credit at this very moment.

The myth which I wish to treat is the story of the Garden of Eden and the Fall.

In this myth the Hebrew religionists represented a first instance, therefore a fabulous instance, of the conflict between science and religion, as they sought for the favor of the human mind. In the victory of science they found the first sin, the cause, prototype, and essence of all specific and actual human sins. In the curse which followed upon man's temptation and fall, they showed the necessary and unhappy sequel. Like a true myth, this one is of universal validity; it has the easiest application to our present civilization.

The account is in part as follows:

Now the serpent was more subtle than any beast of the field which God had made. And he said unto the woman, Yea, hath God said, Ye shall not eat of any tree in the garden? And the woman said unto the serpent, Of the fruit of the trees of the garden we may eat; but of the fruit of the tree which is in the midst of the garden, God hath said, Ye shall not eat of it, neither shall ye touch it, lest ye die. And the serpent said unto the woman, Ye shall not surely die: for God doth know that in the day ye eat thereof, then your eyes shall be opened, and ye shall be as God, knowing good and evil. And when the woman saw that the tree was good for food, and that it was a delight to the eyes, and that the tree was to be desired to make one wise, she took of the fruit thereof, and did eat; and she gave also to her husband with her, and he did eat.

Then comes a remarkable feature of the story. When Adam and Eve had eaten, they must have done something else too: for suddenly they "knew that they were naked," and they sewed fig-leaves together to make themselves garments. But God immediately discovered their sin, and he pronounced upon the guilty pair his differential curse, with one penalty for the woman and another for the man.

Unto the woman he said, I will greatly multiply thy pain and thy conception; in pain thou shalt bring forth children; and thy desire shall be to thy husband, and he shall rule over thee. And unto Adam he said, Because thou hast hearkened unto the voice of thy wife, and hast eaten of the tree, of which I commanded thee, saying, Thou shalt not eat of it: Cursed is the ground for thy sake; in toil shalt thou eat of it all the days of thy life; thorns also and thistles shall it bring forth to thee; and thou shalt eat the herb of the field; in the sweat of thy face shalt thou eat bread, till thou return unto the ground; for out of it wast thou taken; for dust thou art, and unto dust shalt thou return.

Then God removed them from the Garden, in order that his curse might be fulfilled; but first he paid an ironic compliment to their new scientific attainments.

> And Jehovah God said, Behold the man is become, as one of us, to know good and evil; and now, lest he put forth his hand, and take also of the tree of life, and eat, and live forever—therefore Jehovah God sent him forth from the garden of Eden, to till the ground from whence he was taken.

A myth which is good enough to make a religion is important and practical in its meaning. It is not an idle fancy. The myth-maker is a legislator whose legislation has been adopted. The community in accepting his myth professes to a certain view of the human relation to the universe, and to an economic theory which is appropriate to that relation. *The religion of a people is that background of metaphysical doctrine which dictates its political economy.* And all its constituent myths, its ritual, its documents in their detail, have their effective part in this purpose; they serve for instruction and reproof, they bear on the economic program.

This view of religion might perhaps be called, scornfully or otherwise, an "economic interpretation of religion."

But I would feel obliged to add the reservation: Religion is not responsible for all political economies, but peculiarly for a certain kind of political economy, which we are to see in this chapter. There are in the main just two economies: the one is the religious, and the other is the secular. The former is the conservative, the latter is the progressive. In history it is always the conservative policy which the religionists favor. Philology represents religion as looking backward rather than forward: *re,* back, plus *ligo,* bind. Religion enlarges the God and limits the man, telling the believer incessantly to remember his limits, and be content with his existing condition. The secular program, on the other hand, forgets about these limitations and spins its projects for human improvement at the expense of nature, which it scorns, and of God, who is its spirit.

Secular economy is always discontented. It is based on such hope as is inspired when science has found a process or a tool that promises to win for mankind a fresh advantage from nature. But secularism is not defined merely by the proposal to adopt some specific process or tool: it is defined by a total attitude, which abandons the idea of limitations. Secularism is a wartime economy, and the war is the one which man has declared against nature. It says nothing about God, who vanishes from the picture as soon as men think they see through nature; or perhaps it mentions God, but to the effect that man now becomes the God, and will determine the world according to his will.

Here was the first human community, then, living in simplicity, taking their food from the abundance of a kindly nature, and knowing but one condition to limit their freedom: Do not eat of the fruit of the tree of knowledge. This tree was plainly science; or rather, it was the whole secularistic attitude, which scorned the simple, animal-like adaptation of man to his environment, and proposed that man with his scientific talent should remove himself visibly from the animal kind and take possession of nature as fully as he was entitled to do.

The myth also meant something more specific than that. For it seems odd, and every one remarks upon it, that the punishment of Adam for eating of the tree of knowledge is that he shall find trouble in tilling the ground—we had not been told that this was his intention. Therefore in this myth we have the story of the perilous step man had taken towards his later civilization when he introduced agriculture and ate of flesh. And elsewhere in Scripture, if not here, we find the familiar idea that here lay the origin of the strife between the animal species, when man began to enforce the fact of his superiority by militance and aggression.

Let us consider also the point involved in that part of the

curse which says, "Dust thou art, and unto dust shalt thou return." The punishment is supposed to fit the crime—what then was the crime? It consisted evidently in man's attempt to rise too high above his origin; to become an angel, so to speak, or a God, and to live on a cloud or in the ether. In this project he is doomed not to succeed. He shall go back into the dust from which he was created, but which he spurned.

In general, the myth deals with the tragedy of man's ascent to power. It is accompanied by his estrangement from the earth, and from the dumb kind to which he was cousin. Civilization had to take place—in the sense that what is had to be—but it was an outrage, and had to be punished. It has not come cheap. It is painful and expensive; and it had better stop where it is.

This will do for the beginning of an interpretation.

In this sense, the myth is consistent with many other Scriptures. The doctrine appears frequently in the Old Testament.

For example, in the later myth which distinguishes the economy of Abraham from the economy of Lot. This is another story telling how men may keep or lose their happiness.

Abraham might have been a mightier agent in human history, except that his mission was eventually rejected. Abraham founded Israel on the principles of an easy-going statecraft. When he and his brilliant nephew Lot were trekking from the East, they arrived inevitably at the parting of their ways. Abraham offered to Lot his choice of lands, and Lot made the decision that his character required. He looked at the high lands on one side, and at the plain with its lordly cities on the other. He took to the plain, and pitched his tent toward Sodom. He became a great city man, and soon the cry of the wickedness of those cities was come up unto God.

Abraham took to the hills, and his house prospered and multiplied in the regular pastoral manner. The Lord blessed
him, and made the promise that his seed should be innumerable as the dust of the earth. In this story we have an
early instance of the conflict between two economic orders:
that of an urban, industrial, and business life, and that of
a simple communal life lived in the country. But again, it
is more than an instance, a case, an illustration or allegory:
this one is the critical instance that counts, the etiological
one, the one that determined human history, the one that
was rated as official by the religious act of a nation.

Not very different in meaning is the conflict between the
policies of Abraham and David. In God's promise to Abraham that his seed should be innumerable was really contained
the commandment that this seed should not be numbered,
or reckoned for economic and military purposes, in the sense
quite familiar to our advanced modern societies.[1] The feeling
against a census or a "survey" is still quite usual in the
Orient, where it is regarded as a direct betrayal of the religious economy, and looks like the herald of vast and revolutionary changes—as it doubtless means to be. W. I.
Thomas, in his "Sex and Society," quotes the letter of an

[1] As I write this, the decennial census required by the Constitution of the
United States is being completed, and the correct figures are being released
daily. I do not carry my regard for the Hebrew theologians to the point of
proposing to amend this feature of the Constitution. But I observe the cries
of joy and the wails that go up on the air as one city exhibits a greatly increased population, while another must confess in shame to a "backwardness"
that had been imputed to it with no effect by its rivals, these last six or eight
years. This is harmless: except that the Chamber of Commerce of every city
large enough to have a Chamber, before the year is out, will be making over-
tures in all directions to the industrialists, begging them to bring their industries in on any terms, so that the city may show a better rating in 1940. And
this without any consideration, usually, of whether there is a human advantage
to the citizens in industrializing themselves. The most admirable small town
within my acquaintance has recently landed a huge industry which it cannot
begin to assimilate to its own way of life, and to whose way it is bound before
long to capitulate. Already the dignity of its physical appearance is quite
spoiled.

Oriental official to a Westerner who asked for some economic data.

MY ILLUSTRIOUS FRIEND AND JOY OF MY LIVER:

The thing which you ask of me is both difficult and useless. Although I have passed all my days in this place, I have neither counted the houses nor inquired into the number of the inhabitants; and as to what one person loads on his mules and the other stows away in the bottom of his ship, that is no business of mine. But above all, as to the previous history of this city, God only knows the amount of dirt and confusion that the infidels may have eaten before the coming of the sword of Islam. It were unprofitable for us to inquire into it.
. . . Listen, O my son! There is no wisdom equal to the belief in God! He created the world, and shall we liken ourselves unto him in seeking to penetrate into the mysteries of his creation? Shall we say, Behold, this star spinneth around that star, and this other star with a tail goeth and cometh in so many years? Let it go. He from whose hand it came will guide and direct it. . . . Thou art learned in the things I care not for, and as for that which thou hast seen, I spit upon it. Will much knowledge create thee a double belly, or wilt thou seek paradise with thine eyes?

The meek in spirit,

IMAUM ALI ZADI.

Abraham passed, and in due time came David, under whom Israel reached the height of its power. And David was tempted to go against the commandment and number Israel. This is the occasion in the Scriptures of that famous crux where one account says he was tempted of Satan, and the other says he was tempted of God. At all events he was tempted. His idea was to survey the military and economic strength of Israel, and the numbering of Israel was the census of its adult able-bodied male population for future reference. He intended to organize a little, perhaps to industrialize, certainly to imperialize—in short, to Prussianize, as we would have understood that term about fifteen years ago. His intention was very properly opposed by his counselors, but he carried it through. Shortly afterward begins the story of the downfall and degradation of his people. The moral is not hard to draw.

It is evident that Israel since then has followed Lot's and David's example rather than Abraham's. That race seems committed almost beyond all others to cities and industrialism, and to the scorn of nature and the pastoral and agrarian life. It does not seem to have been altogether a happy choice.

Others of the "historical" Scriptures tell the same tale. For example, the story of Cain and Abel. I will improvise a little at this point, by way of establishing a likely background for this story.

The writers of Genesis were patriotic defenders of the theocracy Israel. This people, according to tradition, had migrated under Abraham from the East, where they had led a simple pastoral life; and they had settled in a populous region of the Mediterranean littoral, where there was every temptation to them to fall into the economic habits of their neighbors, which they disapproved. Unfortunately, not all of them disapproved. The religionists must have been often taunted by the Liberals with this argument: "If we went by your program, there would never be any progress. If mankind had never instituted economic changes in defiance of what you call the commandments of God, Israel could not now have become the nation she is." In answer to this argument the religionists pointed to the myths which showed the steps in man's economic development in the following light: unfortunate, each one of them, at the time being, and attended with a curse; but for all that irrevocably taken, and finally sanctioned by God's will as accomplished facts, though wrong. In other words, the religionists defended the *status quo:* they did not quite propose to undo history and revert to primitivism; they only questioned any fresh and sweeping developments. *They objected to any fanatical doctrine of progress.* If this was not the temper of the religionists of Israel, it is the temper of religionists usually.

Hence the myths of Genesis. To begin with, there had been Adam and Eve, living an economic life which was the most immediate adaptation they could make to an easy and provident nature. They plucked their living from the trees. But they had become ambitious, and decided to improve their position with respect to nature, and in fact to prey on nature. They had become killers and eaters of flesh, and planters, and so a new civilization had been founded—painfully and foolishly enough, yet with finality.

The story of Cain and Abel had to do peculiarly with the establishment of an agricultural civilization to replace the pastoral. It therefore covered a little less ground than the Garden myth, in which at one bound Adam springs—or falls—from an economic status where he picked his food off the bush, to one where he kills his meat and raises a crop.

Abel was the devout son who stuck to his flocks, and made the offering of a lamb unto the Lord as according to the commandment. But Cain had become a planter, and for his offering he brought the fruits of his produce. God rejected this offering and favored that of Abel, and in despite Cain slew Abel: meaning that the agricultural order prevailed over the pastoral. For a long time God was wroth. He would not let the ground be productive under Cain's hand, and Cain was a vagabond on the earth, or reverted to a pastoralist of the meanest order. But of course the critical step had been taken.

The myth contained in Genesis iv, 1-23, must be studied closely as an alternative to the more familiar one contained

in Genesis iv, 24–Genesis v. The two myths deal again
with the critical steps taken by the race in successively shifting its economic foundations. In the first of these stories Cain
becomes, significantly, the founder of the first city. Then
are named Cain's descendants, down to the time when
Lamech, of the sixth generation, begat Jabal and Jubal by
one wife, and Tubal-Cain by another. At that point we read
how Lamech cried out, "I have slain a man to my hurt, and
a young man to my wounding." There the story stops short,
and the alternative story begins. But what young man had
Lamech slain? I would guess that he had favored Tubal-
Cain, who was "an instructor of every artificer in brass and
iron," and the founder therefore of metallurgy and the age
of industrialism; and at the expense of Jabal, who was only
"the father of such as dwell in tents and of such as have
cattle." This murder would be the analogue, at a later stage,
of the original murder of Abel by Cain.

But in the alternative story there is no posterity attributed
to Cain, and yet Abel is dead, and therefore Adam's line
must descend through a third son named Seth. The eighth
generation (instead of the sixth) produced Lamech, whom
we have met; the intervening generations, by the way, repeat some of the names found in the posterity of Cain
above. Then Lamech begets Noë, and we enter upon the
story of the Flood, the Ark, and the Covenant. Here the
myth-maker means to tell us again how serious, and almost
fatal, was the revolution wrought when the old order translated itself into the contemporary form of Jewish civilization. All the men of earth except Noë's family were destroyed! But who were these men? They were men whom
God had never liked: acquisitive, imperialistic, "mighty"
men, the descendants of the fallen angels who "saw the
daughters of men that they were fair." This was a race of
property-owners and capitalists. After the floods subsided,
however, God recognized that the insubordinate spirit of

his creatures was bent on agriculture and the private owner-
ship of real property: "And the Lord said in his heart, I will
not again curse the ground any more for man's sake; for
the imagination of man's heart is evil from his youth." So
the agrarian civilization became a fact. For God sanctioned
it, ordaining by his Covenant that the seasons would serve
men faithfully in the future, and the Flood would not repeat itself.

Much more might be written about the doctrine conveyed in the Garden myth, as one which is embodied again
and again in a whole tissue of Old Testament myths—while
it remains itself the grandest of all the embodiments. But I
must make a more general point which does not have to do
directly with myths.

The Scriptures do not consist only in "histories" or myths
or doctrine. They are the work of a race of writers who
loved nature, and a very large fraction of them consists in
pastoral poetry, or a literature about nature. Religionists are
almost inevitably agrarians rather than industrialists—they
find a God readily when they make contact with the elemental soil, and with more difficulty as their habitations and
occupations increase in artificiality and in distance from the
soil.

There is nothing mysterious in the curse which attaches to
the artificial habitation, and to the occupation with business
rather than with agriculture. There is just one thing wrong
with an artificial environment: it is much simpler than any
natural one, and it produces in the man whom it environs a
false illusion respecting the simplicity of nature. I will modernize a little. In the office room in which I write, the six
inclosing surfaces, the doors, the lamps, the furniture, the
shelves, and the books are for the most part of a severe
rectilinear pattern, or at least of such geometrical and regular patterns as lend themselves to the easiest production by

man's tools and processes. And they have textures which are smooth and homogeneous—another mark of the mechanical product. If I leave this room, I must walk through a building whose appointments are of the same simplicity. If I leave the building, I am in a city where I am almost as little in contact with nature: the streets are paved, the buildings are rectilinear, and the flora arrange themselves dutifully according to the prescriptions of the Street Commissioner and the Park Commissioner.

The modern American city or industrial district is certainly the most impressive transformation of natural environment that has yet appeared on this planet. It is no wonder if it tickles its inhabitants so pleasantly with the sense of their ruthless domination of nature, and the ease with which they can manage its God.

But any city, even a small city of the old Jewish world, approaches this degree of transformation. Its effect is to insulate its inhabitants against observation of a fact which it is well for the realist to take always into account: the infinite variety of nature. The agricultural population is constantly aware of this fact, and accordingly its temper differs from the temper of industrialists and city-folk: it is humble, religious, and conservative. Its God is inscrutable. The nature it knows is not the nature that the city-folk think they have mastered. Neither in the manner of their habitations nor in the forms of their occupation do the city-folk make contact with elemental nature. And if even the city-folk are visited sometimes by an unaccountable nostalgia for the soil, and would like to return at week-ends to visit the old nature from which they have emancipated themselves, they do it far too patronizingly, they do not really recover the old attitude towards nature: they only take what may be called a picnic view of nature.

Pastoral poetry, which reached a beautiful perfection with the ancient Jews, is perhaps nearly always the protest of a people that is being industrialized and thinks it is making a mistake. In so far as the movement has already been accomplished, its mood is that of a passionate nostalgia. It remembers, and dwells lovingly on an order of experience that has passed. And in so far as it comes out of a disquieted spirit, and has in the background some reflections on the fundamental economy of life, it is part of the general religious complex.

From this point of view I come back to the myth of the Garden. It is not pastoral poetry in detail, but it presents a thesis which has been fondly advanced by the pastoral poets of many races in their later and unhappier stages of economic development: the doctrine that there was once a Golden Age, an Age of Innocence, a Happy Time, from which mankind passed by its own fatal election. In the Age of Innocence a primitive mankind is always pictured as living gracefully on the bounty of nature. In this Age mankind did what the young lover is advised to do in the poem of William Butler Yeats: "She bid me take love easy, as the leaves grow on the tree." To turn away—to turn forward, as the progressives always have it—from this idyllic simplicity of life is to seek to improve the human position at the expense of nature as an enemy, to eat of the fruit of the tree of knowledge, to break from the definitive man-to-God relation, and to commit sin. This is the origin of unhappiness —again as in the poem of Yeats: "But I was young and foolish, and now am full of tears."

I have not used the term romantic, which is a term with esthetic associations, but it fits into this connection. The romantic attitude to nature, or to any natural object, is the one in which we regard the endless mysterious fullness of this object, and respect the dignity of its objective existence after all—in spite of the ambition to mastery that has become more and more habitual with us. Our sensibilities are too much wounded by the war of conquest which we would wage incessantly. We cannot bear the doom of Cain: never to have those moments when we are in loving *rapport* with environment. Romance in this sense probably touches us all, even the hardest. It touches us most poignantly when we have sinned: that is, abused nature, and alienated ourselves from earth. It takes the form of a nostalgia then, so that we grieve, remembering the good moments we have destroyed.

But the book of Genesis is made out of stern stuff. It is romantic not in detail but in outline—with no repinings, no outpouring of joy, no fullness of circumstance. The legend of Eden is brief and grand.

The detailed literary treatment of this outline was furnished us best in our language by John Milton. He was one who would understand it.

His credentials in this undertaking were doubtless the highest that any man of his generation could have supplied. As a young man he had renounced the busy secular life, to the extent of retiring to his father's country place at Horton, much to the disgust of those friends who aspired for him to an important worldly career. The innocent joys of this simple life he celebrated in his "Allegro." But only its economics was simple: spiritually he introduced into it meditations and studies which made him the most learned poet in English history. They are celebrated in the "Penseroso." They embraced science and humanities: the latter including the Hebrew and Aramaic, and the Greek. In these languages he pursued the myths and their interpreters. He knew his Bible, his Apocrypha, his Talmud, his Cabbala, his Plato, his Neo-Platonists, and his Fathers and saints; not to mention his Oriental religions and his Greek drama. But then, as if to keep his learning from being quite too eclectic and literary, he was caught up into the ecclesiastical controversy and into the civil war, and there he learned at first hand something of the ways of this world.

Under wretched circumstances he came finally to write his two great epics, the "Paradise Lost" and the "Paradise Regained"—heroic paraphrases, the one of the great myth of the Old Testament, the other of the great myth of the New.

Quite like any other pastoralist, Milton descants very prettily upon the original happiness of the Garden condition. The reader likes this part or he does not like it: it depends on his own personal history. The simple pleasures of Adam and Eve have not been too acceptable to many sophisticated readers. But at any rate this much must be acknowledged, that he complicated the simplicity of Eden so that it could not be mistaken for emptiness. He did not leave Adam and Eve stranded without a natural career. Nor had Genesis: for it tells how "the Lord God took the man and put him into the garden of Eden to dress it and to keep it." Milton greatly developed this provision, and gave to the man, and the woman too, a fairly realistic occupation. He goes even so far as to risk the critical suggestion that their labor came to seem to them a little burdensome, and Eve suggested they specialize their tasks; and that it was only when they had separated in the process of this specialization that the blandishments of Satan stood a chance to succeed. This is Milton's passing comment on specialization as a labor-saving device.

Adam is not without his intellectual life. The friendly angel Raphael is quite sympathetic with Adam's speculative interests. He is willing to see Adam prefer the Copernican cosmology to the Ptolemaic. He is glad to tell him all he wants to know, within the limits of his understanding.

But the primary lesson of the "Paradise Lost" is that there are limits to the human understanding. It was the same doctrine which Immanuel Kant was to use as the basis of the Critical Philosophy. There was one step which Raphael advised Adam not to take. The eating of the fruit of

the tree of knowledge was its symbol. The act prohibited
under this form consisted in the adoption of a secular attitude; in having unlimited faith in the powers of human
science; in regarding nature not romantically but posses-
sively, and as an enemy. Satan was going to tempt those two
innocents to rely on their secular brains and secular arms
(which were theoretical and applied science respectively) to
promote their happiness. That would be sin, and it would be
fatal to happiness. To scorn nature was to forget God, and
it would bring on as in a pageant a succession of evils, in
which would appear cities, wars and strife, industrialism, and
those very profligacies which disgusted Milton in the life of
the Restoration.

As a student of the literature of the early Christian period,
Milton was much occupied with his researches into comparative religion.

The interpretation I have placed upon the myth sees it
concerned with a problem which is perennial and universal,
and therefore must have had correspondent myths among
other races than the Hebrews. Milton is conscious of a par-
allel between the Garden-myth of the Jews and the Prometheus-myth of the Greeks.

He saw that he could have conveyed his thesis to the Restoration admirably through the Prometheus-myth. He preferred the Old Testament myth as the one to which he and
his audience were, by inheritance, the closer—and knowing
that it would convey his thesis too. He makes several refer-
ences to the Prometheus-myth. He also plays slyly with the
name of the serpent who tempted: his name was Lucifer, but
Milton pretends to be determined to keep the secret, and to
let it out by accident. Milton followed Jewish and Patristic
authorities in identifying the serpent with the archangel who
had revolted from God's rule and had been cast out of
Heaven. Lucifer is Light-bearer; in more prosy language,

the Scientific Enlightenment. In this capacity he is a spirit analogous to Prometheus, who is Forethought.

Prometheus was the Demigod or Man-God whom the Greeks represented as endeavoring to alienate mankind from Zeus the malevolent despot. When in defiance of Zeus he stole fire from Heaven and brought it in a hollow reed to barbarous mankind, he is to be understood as offering the blessings of science. Through science it was promised that men might be independent of Zeus, and therefore Prometheus stood for a pure secular economy. But Prometheus comes down to us in a rather different rôle from that of Lucifer: his reputation is better. The Greeks, as incipient Occidentalists, tended more than the Jews could possibly have done to approve of his office, and to resent the tyrannical prohibitions of Zeus. They made a great hero out of Prometheus accordingly, and admired him as he lay crucified against the rock to pay the forfeit of his deed in suffering. But the important thing is that they made him pay it. They observed that secularism is folly, it cannot carry out its promises. In the myth of Prometheus they expressed the unending conflict between science and religion.

This myth made perfect material for their tragic drama. So it goes into the trilogy of Aeschylus, of which only the middle play, the "Prometheus Bound," survives. But the thesis laid down in this play is the stock one of the whole Greek drama, though Prometheus in person may not appear in it. This thesis says that it is by *hybris*, the vaulting ambition of man, that the heroes bring themselves to grief. That is the staple of Greek dramatists and theologians alike.

Prometheus is no more alone as the personification of *hybris* in the Greek mythology than is the story of the Garden the only one of its kind in the Scriptures. There were many other Half-gods, often kinsmen of Prometheus, who contested the throne of Heaven with Zeus. Thus the Titans. Half divine themselves, they disapproved of the stern

God and tried to unseat him. They always failed. And the punishments they received were exquisitely appropriate. Ixion was bound to a revolving wheel, and here I think the myth-maker was saying that men who have once committed themselves to industrialism will never escape from industrialism—wheels being perfect symbols of progress yet most uncomfortable for the human physiology that is bound to them. Sisyphus—whose name looks like a satirical reduplication of the word that means wisdom—was doomed to roll the stone up the hill and see it roll down again: a Greek comment on the fallacy of work-for-work's-sake, or unlimited production pursued as a goal without any relation to the real needs of the human constitution. Tantalus was sentenced to thirst in the midst of his pool, without being able to reach the water, which receded whenever he bent to partake of it: a commentary on all sorts of artificial objectives which are attainable well enough, but which prove not to contain the real nourishment we required. Dr. Schiller has taken this last myth to illustrate the future of the American industrial society; his little book, "Tantalus: the Future of Science," is specifically on the question whether our scientific or secular program is going to produce our happiness. There are others. The Greek idea was that Demigods had better not set up for Gods, and that man himself might well claim to be half divine, but was eternally cut off from participating in entire Godhead, and was poorly advised in undertaking its responsibilities. The lesson of Greek myth and of Greek drama is what we would call in these days "reactionary." The Greeks were not yet indoctrinated with the Good God of the moderns, nor with industrialism, which is his cult.

So the Hebrew Lucifer is equated in Milton to the Greek Prometheus, and receives the benefit of many Greek and even Occidental associations.

The European Renaissance was a revival of the Greek spirit, which impressed the Church-bound European spirit as tending daringly toward secularism. It seemed to magnify the dignity of man while it minified proportionately the dignity of God. John Milton was a late child of this Renaissance. He loved the Greek spirit. But he knew it well enough to know that at its best it had gone only so far and no further; for he was steeped in his Greek tragedians. He assimilated the Greek learning to the pattern of his own religiousness.

Then there had come to Europe the beginnings of an Enlightenment which was quite spontaneous, under the auspices of a secular science. Its hopes were high. Milton was well informed about that too. He had met Galileo; he was familiar with Copernicanism; he knew the completely secular doctrines of Hobbes about society and politics. But the new science was only the old Prometheus, the old Satan—a Half-God whom it would never do to take for a God.

Milton evidently deplored that his Lucifer could not freely bring the light, but must incur the curse. Everybody has seen how nearly Milton makes a hero out of Lucifer in the early parts of the work. The speeches which he makes in praise of knowledge are so persuasive that they come close to seeming unanswerable for some readers, and so to spoiling the story. Thus Lucifer is represented as quite surprised to hear that God has forbidden the taste of knowledge to his newest creatures, of whom he is supposed to be so fond.

> Knowledge forbidd'n?
> Suspicious, reasonless. Why should their Lord
> Envie them that? Can it be sin to know,
> Can it be death?

At this point the Garden life, which Milton has described with great relish, becomes suddenly tasteless, for it is the life of barbarous ignorance.

There was a doctrine of human perfectibility which had been advanced, as Milton knew, in some stately Greek sources. It was close kin to the religious doctrine often drawn nowadays from the theory of Evolution. Lucifer argues it:

So ye shall die perhaps, by putting off
Human, to put on Gods, death to be wisht,
Though threat'n'd, which no worse than this can bring.
And what are Gods that man may not become
As they, participating God-like food?

But eventually Milton, after nearly making out of Lucifer a heroic champion of mankind, returns to the orthodox tradition and repudiates his dangerous if specious services. He gave to the Hebraic myth the Greek and the contemporary associations to which it was entitled, and then he agreed that its issue must be as Genesis had represented it.

A hundred years ago the poet Shelley, young and militant, sang without qualification the praises of Lucifer and of Prometheus indifferently. He unbound the crucified Prometheus from his rock, and in the restoration of the unfettered powers of science he described the dawn of millennial happiness on earth. It is certain that a Greek playwright would not have ventured so far, though he might have gone further than any Scriptural Jew.

Shelley regarded Lucifer's benevolent spirit with similar esteem. In the first part of the "Revolt of Islam" we are made to witness an epic combat between an eagle and a serpent. Our sympathies, trained in a certain system of associations, are of course with the eagle. But presently we are astonished to find that Shelley's sympathies are with the serpent. When the serpent is wounded, a beautiful woman weeps upon him and shelters him in her bosom. For the eagle is the bird of Jove, the symbol of Jehovah, while the serpent is our old acquaintance Satan, or rather he is Lucifer, the spirit of secular science. It is unfortunate, says Shelley, that Lucifer, who intends nothing but good to mankind, has received at its hands an evil name, and been branded with every shameful stigma; while the eagle, who stands for tyranny and taboo, has monopolized all the names of good, and fixed his slavery through superstition upon the race.

Shelley was a very gallant crusader on behalf of the God of Science versus the God of Israel, and evidently about a hundred years ahead of his time. If he, and not Milton, had written the "Paradise Lost," he would frankly have made Lucifer the complete hero, and mourned his humiliation; that is, he would have told of Lucifer about the same story that Aeschylus had told of Prometheus; but without stopping to ask what Aeschylus might have added in the lost third part of the trilogy. And if he had written the "Paradise Regained," he would have given it a different meaning altogether; it would have been analogous to his "Prometheus Unbound"; it would have dealt with the release of Lucifer from the confines of Hell, and the triumphant renewal of those enterprises on behalf of human happiness which cowardly man in the Garden had only half supported.

Milton was old when he came to the composition of his "Paradise Lost"; his eyes were out; the second wife, whom he had loved, was as dead as the first; his cause was lost irrecoverably; he was the relict of a way of life that seemed to have departed from the face of the earth. Consequently he had great advantages over Shelley as a reliable thinker. He had realism. He found that his realistic observations of life were capable of perfect expression within the strict limits of Scriptural orthodoxy. So he concurred with the orthodox account in his rejection of Lucifer.

And even when he treats of "Paradise Regained," he does not think of making Lucifer the agent of the restoration, nor does he expect the material sort of prosperity on earth that

Shelley did. He does not look for any spectacular overturn at all of the dire and ordinary course of nature.

There is a piece of interpretation for us now which is rather more difficult. What is the connection between science and sensuality? between eating of the fruit of knowledge and indulging in sexual excesses, which seem to have been the most immediate consequence of the eating?

Milton's paraphrase upon this feature is very full, but he does not improvise altogether, for the feature was actually within the original. In Genesis the lovers realize their nakedness and make themselves aprons of fig-leaves. This is the first birth of shame. In the "Paradise Lost" the fruit of the tree inflames Adam with carnal desire for Eve, who is nothing loath. They had loved as in decent wedlock already, and been defended by Milton, who gave them a pastoral romance strictly according to literary tradition. But now for the first time it is said of them, "In lust they burn." In both accounts they find their occasion unseasonably, or in the daytime. And in Milton, the psychic history of lust is carried out to the bitter end, where the lovers awaken and revile each other.

Literary scholars, or those with whom I am acquainted, generally take the view that the lesson of the "Paradise Lost," so far as the work has a specific one and is not just a rather extended exercise in orthodox religious doctrine, is to rebuke the sin of sensuality. Or they take the view that it is the study of a fantastic test of man's obedience, under which he failed, showed his truly disobedient nature, and was punished. They have very little to say about the sin of knowledge—though there is nothing fantastic about that. They do not construe Lucifer as a Prometheus, as the voice of the contemporary Enlightenment, as the protagonist of a humanity secularizing itself in defiance of God's commandment, as the Man-God or Demigod claiming to be the God. I am afraid that is a construction of my own. They ignore the whole question of knowledge, and of the symbolism of the tree—though Milton dwells at great length on it, and it had to do with a leading issue of the age.

And I must agree that it is awkward to say that Milton's one text presented us with two morals: one the moral about sensuality, which is certainly there; the other the moral about the scientific or secular economy, which I would read into it.

Fortunately, I think the two morals are one and the same; that the myth-maker perceived this, and Milton after him.

It is my idea that sensuality, followed by disillusionment and remorse, typifies very well the spurious benefit of applying our science too hard, just as the eating of the tree typifies the winning of its theory of knowledge. But this is a conclusion to lead up to by degrees.

Religion is an order of experience under which we indulge the compound attitude of fear, respect, enjoyment, and love for the external nature in the midst of which we are forced to live. We were born of earth—why should we spurn it? But in science we cultivate quite a different attitude. Science is an order of experience in which we mutilate and prey upon nature; we seek our practical objectives at any cost, and always at the cost of not appreciating the setting from which we have to take them. Science is quite willing to lose the whole for the sake of the part.

An apple is an object of esthetic value to be appreciated, as well as a practicable object which can be used. Its useful qualities are its savor and its capacity for filling the empty belly. But in practice we fix exclusively upon these qualities, abstracting them from the whole in thought, and then extracting them from the apple in fact. And so we eat the apple, and discover we have lost it: use is a destructive process. In the same way, and with the same consequence, we fix upon the horse-power that is stored in the waterfall, the heat that is stored in the forest, the protection for the skin that is stored in the fox's fur. These are all destructive fixations which both religious and esthetic counselors alike would have us indulge as sparingly and critically as we may. The pleasures of use are self-regarding, intense, and destructive of the object, while the pleasures of enjoyment are unselfish, expansive, and respectful or conservative of the object.

On its purely theoretical side, or as a form of pure knowledge, it is just the same. Science is effective and yet brutal here too: it aims always at abstracting some arbitrary essence from the whole. What it knows, it knows hard, but it cannot afford to know much. Its knowledge is ruthless and exclusive, while esthetic knowledge, aiming at the fullness of the object, is inclusive. Science wants its universal, or its finite core of constancy; but enjoyment is of the concrete, the full particular, and it is obliged to neglect the universal, or suspend it for the time being at least.

But here we are concerned with practical science more especially. The perils of action are nowhere in human experience plainer than in the life of sex. Here we have two courses in clear opposition to each other, with all possible compromises in between. One course is love in the romantic sense, as sanctioned by religion and honored in poetry. The other course is lust, which may be defined as the pure abstract act of sex. *Love is the esthetic and lust is the science of sex.*

The true lover respects the beloved person. Modern psychology speaks of the sublimation of a single passion like love till it involves the whole mind. The experience becomes complex, important, expressive of the organic personality, and making contact with the whole fullness of the world. Plato, Plotinus, and Dante have shown how it initiates the lover into the knowledge of God. The lover treasures not merely the body of his beloved, but her looks and gestures, her thoughts, her friends and associates, her possessions, the ground she walks upon, and even the whole world in which she lives. This is an expansive experience which reveals to him the infinitude of the world's quality. But sometimes he applies to this great field of knowledge and enjoyment the destructive process with which he is well acquainted even as a scientist of amateur standing. He fixes upon the specific gratification of his desire, which is like a scientific process pure and simple. He defines his exact objective, and the technique of operation. This is to use and possess his beloved, and she, as a world of enjoyment, must necessarily disappear.

The problem of sex, like the problem in any other field of behavior, is how to realize an end which is biologically and practically necessary, without completely sacrificing its setting for religious and esthetic experience. The problem is how to perform the act of love without losing the art of love.

Milton is perfectly realistic in representing the remorse that follows upon lust. The romantic impulse, defeated in fact, takes its revenge in memories. It reminds us powerfully of our lost happiness, and curses the brutal scientific spirit that drove us out of Paradise. Much of our romantic literature is a literature of nostalgia and defeat. Lord Byron gave us romances of this description; he knew from bitter experience what he was doing.

So Adam and Eve hastened greedily to their brutal satisfaction, or lusted after each other, and their action stands for the whole range of ruthless practicality which is one type of behavior.

CHAPTER SEVEN

CHRIST AS SCIENCE

THE historical person of Jesus is certainly very hard to find beneath the wrappings of the myth. There is not one circumstantial document about him which is pure natural history, and free from mythical additions.

But why undertake the unwrapping? Have we any real interest in finding the man Jesus? He would not do us any particular good. The service of the Christ-figure in our European and American development has not been that of a man but that of a God; has not consisted in furnishing us with a history but in furnishing us with a religion. Only somebody who is peculiarly interested in the technique of mythopoeia (or myth-making) needs to make the study of how Jesus of Nazareth became a myth, and a fountain of Christian doctrine. Did it begin in his lifetime, and to what extent? Did it begin after his death? He was not the first nor yet the last of historical actual men who developed into myths. The age in which he lived was fertile in myth-making. Certainly most of the myth that came to cluster about him was the work of the century that followed his death. So much mythic detail accumulated, indeed, that one of the important functions of the ecclesiastical authorities was to make a modest selection from it all which would be about enough to go on, and to throw away the rest.

And if the myth was some while in being put together and

a still longer while in being pruned of its superabundance with many willing hands engaged upon it, it is easy to imagine that it was not going to remain constant forever afterwards—that the myth which was regularized at the time of Nicaea, let us say, was not going to be the same myth which would serve the Christian communities of Europe and America thenceforward without a single modification. Even official myths are too fluid to permit that. Too much of the initiative of the ritualist goes into it during every generation. A continuous critical spirit has played not only upon its detail, but even upon its central intention.

The present generation is in a fair way to cancel the value which the myth must have had in the ages of orthodoxy, and to substitute a value all its own.

Let me define this at once.

As I understand the myth of the Garden of Eden, it meant to express something substantially like this: Satan is the Demigod, the Prometheus, the Spirit of Secular Science, who would like to set up falsely as the God, the Ruler of the Universe—beware of him.

And as I understand the myth of Christ, it meant: Christ also is the Demigod, the Man-God, who represents the highest human development—but observe how he refuses to try to be the God; believe on him in the light of his self-confessed limitations.

Satan was the Pretender, the Archangel who aspired. Christ was the Son who had no intentions upon his Father's throne. So the rôle of Christ was of a nobility almost unparalleled in the lore of myths: *to be the Demigod who refused to set up as the God.*

But by an exquisitie irony the disciples of Christ have disobeyed his admonitions, forgotten his limits, and made him assume the throne after all—where he sits now quite incompetent to rule over the dominions of another. In this false position he cannot do them much good. They are simply doomed to disappointment.

Christ was a subordinate figure in the early Christian Godhead. He is now become, or at least he is rapidly becoming, the whole Godhead.

Of course John Milton got his theology in this matter straight. Nothing else was to be expected of him, even if he was in some respects violently Protestant, and if he wrote as late as the period of the English Restoration. In 1671 he gave his version of the Christian myth in his "Paradise Regained."

This epic does not make use of the whole of the Gospel story. Christ is represented personally as the perfect man, of great intellectual power, religious sense, and loyalty to the God of Israel. His career on earth, according to the Gospels, was a full and exciting one, all of its incident being doubtless good for the purpose of doctrine. But Milton makes a very bold selection from it. Unexpectedly he chooses one fairly slight episode as sufficient for his purpose. This is the episode where Christ is in precisely the situation in which Adam had been: he is tempted by Satan. As Adam had been tempted, so is Christ, but where Adam had fallen, Christ stands. In this difference lay his significance, and in this contrast lies the close relation between "Paradise Lost" and "Paradise Regained."

Milton had the choice of comparing Christ with Adam or comparing him with Satan. It did not matter which he did. Adam, Christ, and Satan were alike the sons of God; they had alike the divine reason, the gift of knowledge, the Logos, by which they could understand God's world so far as it was intelligible—though hardly any further. It was only a literary problem, or a problem of myth-making as a fine art, whether a Satan should appear in either story. He only embodies the secular ambition which is deep in the hu-

man constitution already. Eve talking with Satan is only
arguing with herself, Christ talking with him is only arguing
with himself. If Milton in the "Paradise Lost" has represented Adam as yielding to the blandishments of Satan, he
gets his parallelism in the "Paradise Regained" by representing Christ as resisting the same blandishments. So it is
the same thing whether we take Christ as a second Adam
or as a second Lucifer.

The New Testament also offers us alternative forms of
the same doctrine, and they are something like the following:

In the person of Satan, Adam worshiped Reason, and
fell; but Christ refused to worship him, and honored the
God of Israel instead; and we should emulate not Adam but
Christ. Or—

The men of old worshiped Satan, and fell; but now we
have a Christ to worship, who is Incarnate Reason, with a
difference; namely, that he disclaims complete Godhead and
points us to the real God.

It is the first of these two forms of doctrine that is presented in the "Paradise Regained," the second which is generally preferred by the theologians. The Church likes to say,
Believe on Christ; and I am far from dissenting from the
saying except that history shows it is a dangerous one. I
would always add a qualification which the Church sometimes forgets to make: Believe on him as he directed, that is,
as an Incarnate Reason *who was inferior to the God that
had sent him.* It might have been safer if the Church had
preferred to find his parallelism with Adam. This parallelism
the Church has seen well enough, as when it has said, Do not
fall with Adam but stand with Christ. But that is not what
it has liked to say best.

So in the "Paradise Regained" we find Christ tempted by
Satan. His temptation seems even more grievous than that

which Adam had suffered. Christ was tempted in the desert, where he hungered; Adam in the Garden of Eden, where he lived in an idyllic happiness to which nothing lacked. In Adam's time there were no economic, nor social, nor political problems; in Christ's time every sort of problem. There was national servitude, a yoke that had not grown easier with several changes of masters, and a nation crying fiercely for a Messiah who would lead it into power. Milton dwells with some plausibility on the military and political career which lay open to Christ if he desired it, if he wanted to be that Messiah. Some of its steps were: alliance with Parthia, the dreaded enemy of Rome; shrewd maneuvering which would win the fractions of the unwieldy Empire one at a time; eventually the conquest of Rome and the dominion of the world. Christ, in the poem, considers this prospect at great length—and rejects it. Milton therefore represents him in the strange aspect of an Alexander who declined to conquer. Political power is not the meaning of Christianity: Messiahship was not the career which Christ elected.

Christ also considers another career which looks very innocent, one which appealed powerfully to Milton himself, who was a scholar and man of letters enjoying the fruits of the Renaissance and of the new scientific Enlightenment. This was the career of learning, of theoretical science, of literature, of philosophy: in short, of knowledge in its purest or unapplied sense. But regretfully he abandons that too. On that road lay only another kind of irreligiousness, of forgetfulness. He saw the pride of knowledge best reflected from the illustrious period of the Greeks, but even there it had not been good enough. The Greek philosophers after all had not attained unto a religion. (Plato had been a Gnostic, reveling in many myths without the courage to profess to any; Aristotle had been a pure metaphysician, with no Gods and only Principles.) Whatever human reason could accomplish on its pure theoretical side, Christ considered its benefits and decided that it did not offer to him a sufficient life.

This was the Christ who did not intend, by taking thought, by shrewdly planning, to make much of an attempt to overcome or to understand the world whose nature is half evil in its incidence upon man. Evil would continue to rage on earth. Christ did not claim to stop it. He did not make even the natural motions of self-defense in warding it off his own person. Within three years he was to be haled to his crucifixion. This was a very extreme degree of submission to the will of God—an extremity which is incredible to modern Western minds, as something which is monstrous, antique, and simply Oriental.

In the person of Christ, Milton finds that man under the most trying circumstances possible could still refuse to secularize himself. He could still reject the Demigod for the God.

There is therefore an ironical disappointment in store for those unacquainted readers who approach the "Paradise Regained" with certain hopes inspired by its title: under the persuasion that the function of Christ was to bring visible and objective blessing to a helpless humanity—and that the function of a major poet was to hymn such an event with a very fine magniloquence and hyperbole. Such readers will look in vain to find the Paradise they fancy in process of being regained by Christ's heroic exploits. It will seem to them a rather hollow victory that Christ wins over Satan. (Satan does not stand for what they think; the victory is not too decisive in its true sense; it is even less decisive if it is taken as a victory over the irrationality and evil of the world.) Christ resists the blandishments of Satan, but Satan does not suffer a realistic defeat—not the kind of defeat common in epics and romances. God had waited through many generations of suffering men before he had sent a Messiah to put a stop to Satan's depredations. And yet here is this Messiah come and gone, and Satan left intact to continue his enterprise, having only been threatened with an indefinite second coming which might prove more fatal to him.

The fact is, unfortunately, that Satan in his true function of benevolent Demigod pretending to be the God was far from having been put out of business by his encounter with Christ. For he has won some grand triumphs since then, and the most extensive of all was the setting up on earth of the vast historic polity which we may describe as Occidentalism —the polity by which men have assumed self-sufficiency, and undertaken to effect the conquest of nature by their sciences. Even within the religion that names itself Christian this has come about. The Man-God who subordinated himself to the true God has been represented as claiming to be that God. In the Arian controversy this issue took the form: Did Christ repeat in his own person the precise essence of the Father? Most Christians would answer today, far more emphatically than the Council of Nicaea once did, that Christ is the very essence and identity of the Father. They have reversed the rôle of Christ. So there is now thought to be, not a plurality of Gods in a Godhead, but one God, and that simply the Man-God Christ. His intentions, humane; his technique, scientific—and also negotiable, or capable of being borrowed by the beneficiaries and employed for the sake of supplementing and hastening the God's good works. The God to whom the Man-God subordinated himself has been superseded.

Leaving Milton now, I would like to indicate a few of the more specific doctrines of the New Testament which look important for the history of our civilization. I am afraid that sometimes their importance has been in their misapplication as much as in their application.

(1) Christ came offering a reform of the law. The Mosaic code now seemed insufficient as a practical code, and

Christ gave a new commandment: "Love your enemies." There was a new hope contained there—just as there is hope of human welfare contained in every wise ethical prescription. To those expecting a Messiah who would bring about revolution in the political order, Christ offered a rule of conduct which was indeed revolutionary, but in a most unexpected direction. Its consequence was a new sociology with altruism as its principle; a new internationalism; a new science of social adaptations. "Society" in the modern sense could not have come into existence without it.

In this respect Christ *was* a sort of Messiah. He offered a rule which would work. It was simple, revolutionary, highly effective. It must have looked like a tremendous innovation, and it was: yet it was a perfectly secular prescription. It advised men to stick together, to pursue their joint enterprise in common, to put the social welfare above the individual. It was a very fine teaching—but not necessarily a religious one.

The new commandment was not meant to replace the old ones. But the trouble has been that the Christian communities have taken it as sufficient by itself, without remembering the code to which it was supplementary. In particular, they do not remember the four Mosaic commandments which defined the man-to-God relation. Christ himself said: "Thou shalt love the Lord thy God . . . and thy neighbor as thyself," indicating that the social ethic was not meant to stand alone.

The Christians, however, Westernizing more and more flagrantly, have come to the conclusion that Christian socialism is the essence of their faith: they have substituted Christian ethics for the Christian religion.

(2) For a second doctrine I will set down, as close as possible to the first one, the limiting one which I have already referred to: "Thou shalt love the Lord thy God"

Jesus was a loyal Jew, learned in the rabbinical wisdom, and not proposing in the least to overturn the religion of his people. Christ was a sort of Messiah to the extent that he brought an effective reform in secular society, but did not claim to be the God. For he did not expect that even Christian socialism would put man in firm possession of this world and solve all his difficulties.

Did he think at all about the limits of scientific power? What did he think about the Tree of Knowledge, of whose fruit Adam and Eve had partaken in the ingenuous hope that it would make Gods of them?

The Christian myth is a little bit cryptic on this point. Only when we study John's Gospel of Christ as the Logos or Word, and observe the interpretation which the Greeks and the Hellenized Jews of the Dispersion proceeded to give to the term—only then do we catch the grateful idea that Christ represented science, just like Prometheus and Satan. The modern religious scientists would like to think he represented it a great deal more successfully than these had done! But they would hardly think to find much about that in so many words in the New Testament. They suppose, rather vaguely, that Christ, though himself not a scientist—except that he was a "great sociologist," and possibly "the first Rotarian"—would have approved their sciences. He would have said, "Go ahead, study and possess nature, invent machines, produce goods: I bless you: I require only that you *distribute* your goods according to my law of charity." So they confirm themselves in their devotion to the secular enterprise of production and undertake—at best—to keep themselves spotless by giving thought to the morality of the social distribution.

The result in modern society is a strange one—a set of interests and attitudes unheard-of before. The new God, the adapted Christ, is such a perfect embodiment of secular human enterprise that in this capacity he requires no attention and fades quite out of the scientific consciousness. But he comes back into it again as the author and patron of a social morality which still requires a great effort of the will, and about which we continue to have a very acute awareness. We perform mighty works with our sciences, feeling no qualm about it, and then we go to our Christianity to get our social ideal.

This peculiar combination is reflected in our literature. The classical, Oriental, and early modern European literatures dealt, when they were serious, chiefly with the issue Man *versus* Nature, or Man *versus* God. They defined for individual or generic man his private economy, letting him take the best course he might with a nature over which he had better not think his rights were supreme. They showed him the error of pride and *hybris*. They bade him remember God. But modern Western literature, most of our literature since Milton, has presented in the main only one single issue Man *versus* Man, or Man *versus* Society. Dramatists like Ibsen and Shaw work on that issue; novelists like Tolstoi and Eliot—not like Hardy, of course; and even many poets like Tennyson and sometimes Browning. This literature is marked by the absence of metaphysical interest. It has no God. Discussing only the social problems, it seems perfectly confident that society has justified its aggressive scientific program, and that the only problem remaining to be decided is that of the reciprocal relations of persons within that society.

When we look at the older human communities, like that one which obeyed the Mosaic code, we see how a society might assist the private individual to keep his attention on Man-*versus*-Nature, and hold himself back from an unthinking belligerence against nature that might prove embarrassing. Such a society is one which governs itself with an orthodox religious code. But when we look at our modern

ommunities we see how a society may have a different and
nore baleful effect upon its members. It may quite blind
hem to the metaphysical problems. It may, by a technique
f herd-morale, encourage them in their aggressions against
ature, and persuade them unthinkingly to commit them-
elves to a war which can have no ending. The effect of so-
iety today with us is not what it was for its members in
gypt, nor in Judaea, nor in Greece, and not what it is
enerally for the Orientals today. The effect of society to-
ay is mainly to produce the city-mind, whose environment
 artificial, and whose difficulties are imagined to be ex-
lusively difficulties of personal relation. As for having trou-
le with nature, the city itself is the answer to that enemy!
ehind the massive fact of the physical city and all the prod-
ce of modern industralism it is too difficult to see that na-
ure still waits, unconquerable, unintelligible, and contingent.
his is a philosophical wisdom that is denied the citizens.

Modern societies have proved their collective omnipotence
oo entirely to their own satisfaction, and in so doing re-
oved the ancient God from their sight.

(3) As if he knew that his new sociology would work im-
rovement on earth, but would not suffice, Christ proclaimed
nother doctrine: "The kingdom of God is within you." That
 to say, happiness does not lie in material and physical
ell-being but in the disposition of the mind: be happy
herefore in your tribulations as well as in your prosperity.

Of course this is deeply religious doctrine. It possesses a
roper realism, for it knows that evil is everywhere and in
ny given crisis is very likely to prevail. But it requires the
eliever to entertain it without excessive repining and bit-
rness; to persist in his own virtue without expecting that
rosperity will necessarily be its reward; to make his adap-
ation to a world which does not devote itself conspicuously

to humane objectives; and not to try to hold God to respon
sibility for his acts. It is the same lesson that comes out of
the book of Job.

But this dogma may be misapplied, and with considerable
show of logic: for evidently it may lend itself to the sup
port of Christian Science. It may be taken to mean that evi
is a figment of the imagination, though a powerful one, and
that a sufficient discipline of the mind produces a perfect and
blissful comfort. Christian Science is a variety of subjectiv
ism, a solipsism. It is anything but in keeping with the
concrete realism of the Christ of the New Testament. The
Christian Solipsists are perhaps not quite pathological cases
but they seem to be really an inverted species of materi
alists. They have a fear, a phobia. Originally they are con
cerned immensely with physical evil, with sickness and pain
which they regard as the product of a savage material nature
They do not expect to control this material nature. They
cannot even face it; so they take refuge in denying it. Their
contribution to our age is a technique of anesthesia, or in
sensibility.

(4) A fourth doctrine was: "I go to prepare a place for
you." This doctrine is one of the most difficult possible from
my point of view—one that is almost certain to lead the
religionist wrong. It is not an Old Testament doctrine. It
is a piece of Platonism, taken at the point where Platonism
was most hopeful and least realistic, and it is acceptable only
with some stern reservations: for it has something to say
about the life of the virtuous after death. Of course the vir
tuous immediately seized upon it with wonderful relish. It
suited all of the contemporary world who were tormented by
the Roman yoke. And persecuted and suffering Christians of
all ages have wished to see in it a second Paradise reserved
for them after their journey through this vale of tears. But
by that construction this doctrine has left the actual world, in

which we live by the body, in its old condition of injustice and unreason, and relies upon a hope which realism is powerless to support.

But we can say of Christ's promise of immortality that he attempted to secure it from too crude an interpretation. In Heaven there would be neither marrying nor giving in marriage. His disciple John in the Apocalyptic visions saw Heaven under very fantastic forms, which were obviously symbolic. Perhaps none of the Scriptural authors expected it to be the restoration of a Garden of Eden existence in the flesh. It was a precarious fancy which they did not dare reduce to too tangible a shape.

And the doctrine of a Heavenly reward is balanced, even in the teachings ascribed to Christ, by the doctrine of damnation in Hell. The one is wrong without the other. The orthodox faith has made full use of these associated doctrines. Given the idea of a life hereafter, the Church did not pretend that it was necessarily bliss; that would not have been realistic, it would have been too great a departure from the manner of this life; and so Hell served a salutary purpose in the Christian economy. Now and then a human society has been founded very largely on these two doctrines: they were the sanctions that enforced its code of morals. There was something a little bit cheap in the religious thinking of such a society. But it was earnest and effective.

It is only latterly that we have had believers constituted so sentimentally as to maintain that their God would never under any circumstances send his creatures to Hell. They do not like the doctrine; therefore they cancel it. But if they do that, we must ask them with the very same stroke to cancel Heaven too.

(5) Saint Paul and the early fathers took the Christian doctrines, and finally there was established a Christian orthodoxy—with local variations, such as there must be. The doc-

trine I name now was owing to Christ's disciples rather than to Christ, so far as we have any words of his to show. It is Predestination.

Ethically, or as a matter of practical science, the Church emphasized the new sociology. But in the absence of any hundred-per-cent or even fifty-one-per-cent resulting happiness, they also elaborated the doctrine of the life hereafter in compensation for the shortcomings of this.

Even so, as realists, they were obliged to entertain certain misgivings. Let us observe how realism made its effective entry into the otherwise over-sanguine expectations of Christian theology. Saint Paul immediately following Christ, Saint Augustine four centuries later, and John Calvin eleven centuries later still, were all greatly concerned to know with what assurance men, even if they were obedient to the commands of the faith, could hope for Heaven rather than Hell. Clearly Heaven was a divine dispensation, a city not made with hands, and only God possessed the keys of admission. Would he admit all men? *Would he admit even all righteous men?* Realistic minds found little to make them think so; it would be a departure from the usual sort of thing if he did. In the ninth chapter of the Epistle to the Romans, Paul sets forth his fears, which had Old Testament authority behind them, and which were in turn to become a textual authority for Augustinianism and Calvinism. Paul says that the fate of the children is predestined in the most arbitrary manner before they are born: "For the children not yet being born, neither have done any good or evil, that the purpose of God according to election might stand, not of works, but of him that calleth." He quotes again: "It is written, Jacob have I loved, but Esau have I hated." And he reminds the believers that God had said unto Moses: "I will have mercy on whom I will have mercy, and I will have compassion on whom I will have compassion."

The associated doctrines of predestination, grace, and election were among the features of the late Christian orthodoxy which modernism has most ostentatiously canceled. Nothing could be more obnoxious to the modern temper. They are too realistic, too baldly unethical. They were agreeable only to a constituency which considered that the way to justify God's ways to man was not to gloze them, but to set them out frankly and let man make the most of them.

For an orthodox Christianity that qualified its hope with a fear called Predestination or Election, as for a Jewry that depended on its Old Testament exclusively, God remained inscrutable, and human welfare in this life or another was an event too doubtful to guarantee. The Christian like the Jew was forced to make an adaptation to this world which was respectful and submissive, and not merely an adaptation which was possessive and egotistical. The Christian could hardly conceive himself in the favored position of a profiteer on the universe.

Calvinism was a doctrine which, within its given setting, I find myself admiring greatly. Its service was to inform with realistic misgivings some religious communities which had otherwise made themselves at home in Zion. The Presbyterians might have made Christ supreme, and the way he prescribed to the Christians quite too easy and profitable —if they had not been instructed by Calvin that this way was not exactly free and open to all who sought it. For there was the inscrutable will of God which had first to accept them, and this will even Christ himself was powerless to command. The Will of God to a Calvinist is as stern as Fate, or Destiny, or the Greek Ananke: the symbol of pure contingency: an excellent article of faith.

I suppose it will be generally agreed that Calvinism is now, to all intents and purposes, dead. And I should not think it was particularly needed except as a corrective doctrine to go along with a doctrine of physical salvation after death; if this latter doctrine is gone now, Calvinism also is able to be spared. But where this doctrine survives it is a pity if there should be no Calvinism, as an extremely effective if homely check upon a plan of salvation that seemed to promise to take effect without a single casualty.

These are among the details of Christian doctrine that are not hard to consider and estimate as separate details. But I wish to go back to the central meaning of the Christ-myth, the one that Milton had in mind, the one that occupied a whole world of gifted religionists immediately following upon the origin of that myth.

Christ was a Logos, or Word. That is John's contribution to the myth, and that is the thing in it which chiefly interested a certain public, very expert in doctrine, to whom it was addressed. But the term is a Hellenism, and in effect a Platonism. The writers of the New Testament used Greek, and John especially was versed in Greek thought. His idea of Christ makes contact with the Greek circles which were still carrying on the Platonic tradition in their metaphysical speculations.

Milton understood this. (He had Aristotle's metaphysic, Plato's Gnosticism, and the Fundamentalism of an orthodox Christian.) He had equated Satan with the Greek Prometheus, and played upon the name Satan had borne in Heaven: Lucifer, the Light-bearer, the Morning Star. It was excellent in Milton's view to be a Light-bearer: excellent at least until the Light-bearer assumed the God. No reproach had attached to Lucifer before his fall—he had been perhaps the chiefest of the Sons of God, and wise and powerful within his limits. There was nothing in fact wrong with Lucifer until he had become Satan: that is, the Adversary, claiming to be the God and deceitfully inducing men to worship him. And now in the "Paradise Regained" Christ speaks (I, 294) and Milton says of him, even of Christ: "So spake our Morning Star then in his rise."

Christ as the Logos is the Patron of Science; the Reason which governs the universe so far as the universe is amenable to science; in modern terms, the Uniformity of Nature, upon which scientists lean so heavily. The Logos is the Platonic Idea, for the Platonists of the Christian era had substituted the one word for the other. We see the meaning of Logos best in its modern derivatives: the word *logic,* and the suffix *-logy* in the names of the sciences, like biology, bacteriology, meteorology, theology, and Soteriology. It is a divine Logos which makes the "manifold of nature" fall somewhat into classification and system and present itself as intelligible to the human mind.

But what an unlikely milieu to produce a Christ, a God of Rationality, a Man-God, a Patron of Science, a Friend of Secularism! The intellectual society in which Jesus and John moved had no secular power: abject politically; not advanced in scientific theory; unacquainted with applied science in anything like its modern sense. The religionists of the time, even though philosophically they were savants like John, and Paul, and Philo, and Irenaeus, and Clement, and Origen, were scientifically as babes. Mr. Millikan today might well tell us of the good sense of having a God defined as a Logos. It is by having such a God that he can talk so confidently about working on a nature that can be "depended upon." But how did the Fathers fall so neatly into this language? Nobody could look at first sight much less like the spiritual ancestor of Mr. Millikan than one of those same bearded, early-Christian, Oriental *enthusiasts.* And yet they founded the dogma to which he subscribes.

It is evidently a hard historical and psychological problem, how to find a relation between the specific background and the idea which emerged from it of a God who was Logos. The setting in general looks most unpropitious. Was the

Logos only a wish-fulfillment, improvised in a place and a period that were desperately and unusually unhappy?

Religion is the system of myths which gives a working definition to the relation of man to nature. It always has to join together in some fashion two quite different views of this relation. The first is that of nature as usable and intelligible for man: nature as a humane order, devoted to man's welfare, created by a benevolent God for the purpose of man's service. The second is that of nature as unintelligible and contingent, and therefore alien and unusable for man: nature as an order that is not the humane or ethical order. Occidentals are impressed with the first view, and inclined not to be quite sensitive to the second. Orientals prefer the second view and, in their hatred for science as a vanity, ignore the truth that is in the first view. It is evident that Occidentals need more of the Oriental humility, and it is of course from that assumption that I am offering all these remarks. (I am not undertaking to preach to the Orient.) But on the other hand, the world is not such a bitter habitation as it is made to appear to Orientals who do not dare to turn a hand in their own interests, and put no faith in the Human Goodness of its Author and Ruler. The most valuable service of a sound religion for Orientals might well be its emphasis on a Logos.

The most appealing words that could be spoken to people thoroughly defeated and sitting down in their impotence would be the sayings—which abound in the story of Christ —on this order: "Come unto me, all ye that labor and are heavy-laden, and I will give you rest." Or on this order: "Are not two sparrows sold for a farthing? and one of them shall not fall on the ground without your Father. But the very hairs of your head are all numbered. Fear ye not therefore, ye are of more value than many sparrows." Of course these sayings might produce only a Christian Science: a feeling of communion with the God, a confidence that evil is illusory, and that all God's works are really humane in their intention; and an uncritical rest, or state of inaction, in that confidence. But on the other hand it might produce the grand and tireless secular project of the West, which is also based on the faith that the world-order is a moral order, and that human enterprises have the right of way and must prevail. The Occident with its Logos, who has given such a good public account of himself, offers, to say the least, some refutation of the defeatism of Oriental religion.

So I would not be so bold as to say that there was no "revelation" of God's nature in the person of Christ the Logos. He revealed and emphasized an aspect of God that was very much in order. God became warmly and tenderly human under the Christian dispensation: showing a side of his being that had almost disappeared since the days when he had led his people into prosperity and happiness on earth.

And this will hold good, even if the thing that led the first Christians to find humanity in the God was after all a piece of *a priori* theory, or else just an irrational impulse; for they were not in a position to *see* much of this property being manifested. At best it was a hope and a faith—a great irrational frenzied leap of faith. The universe *must* be intelligible—it *would be* sooner or later understood—God *was* a true Father to his children, and one day all the world would bear witness to his good providence. These thoughts were rather wild and whirling, with a sort of temperamental urgency behind them. They represented a perfectly native mood in man which it was right to express, and which it was dangerous to express only if it monopolized his consciousness and inhibited other moods. The hope was as imperious as it was precarious. It is not strange if confusion has always attended its detailed promises. Were the Christians to expect prosperity in this life? Or a day of judgment when justice would be done on earth in the near future? Or a physical resurrection and translation for each man in a sort of private transaction? Or a life hereafter in which there would be compensation for the spirit only, in some sense not yet understood?

But for all our low opinion of the scientific status of the early Christians, and for all the triumphs of the Western sciences since, it is probably still safe to say: We have little better ground for the faith than they had at the time of its foundation. The Reign of Logos to which we aspire is about as far off as ever—and is imaged with just as much confusion with respect to its time and its place and its manner of operation. It is difficult to see how we have any great advantage over Abraham in knowing how to adapt ourselves to our total environment, which is nature. The principle of nature is certainly nothing so simple as a Logos: nature is not a system which combines a scientific technique with a benevolent intention to become a Humanistic Régime.

In the next general section of this book we shall have to consider the extent to which we have actually made the Logos prevail on earth after nineteen hundred years—to see whether science, in the words of Mr. Ayres' book, is not a "false Messiah."

The most winning recent exposition I have seen of Christ in the sense of Logos, outside the more professional writings released by the Churchly theologians, is Mr. Paul Elmer More's book, "Christ the Word." This work is entirely upon the metaphysical meaning borne by the founder of Christianity; and therefore upon the subject of this chapter.

I have a great respect for Mr. More's learning. But I will name two objections which even a lay order of hard thinking must bring against his argument.

The first is that Mr. More is not quite frank in maintaining the point of view from which he undertakes to write. He leads us to think that he approaches the subject altogether as a metaphysician, or as a psychologist of thought, analyzing Christian dogma in explicit terms as an act of mind performed by the believer. But suddenly at the critical moment he abandons this point of view and falls back upon the professional language of the priest.

The Christian revelation! That is a proper term to use within the congregation of the believers. It is a proper term for a human society to adopt officially, and in a unified society it may always be effectively used to indicate to an unbeliever the social sanction behind orthodoxy. But our own society has, by tacit consent at least, repudiated its religious unity quite thoroughly, and the term "revelation" has lost it coercive power and become an anachronism.

It is my feeling that now the intelligent non-believers must be treated as both intelligent and unbelieving, and that any religion will have to address itself convincingly to their minds by the frankest sort of intellectual persuasion. And that is the position which Mr. More seems generally to have taken. He does not pretend that miracles ordinarily are facts, or that myths are natural history. Yet when he comes to the incarnation, as the base of all the Christian dogma, he reverts to the idea of divine revelation—he assumes God as an objective Agent acting to bring about a specific fact in secular history.

He says of the early Christian philosophers: "Against this worldwide movement it was necessary to show (1) that Christianity was not one myth among many, but a divine revelation opposed to a swarm of superstitions." This flat assertion will hardly contribute much to the persuasion of modern Western minds trained in their skepticism.

In another passage Mr. More seems to be sensible of the doubtfulness of this policy even while he declines to modify it:

To some critics it will appear—as I confess it seemed, or almost seemed, to myself at one time—that the first step . . . would be to go back to the method of philosophy, taking pure intuition as the starting point of religion, and allowing mythology to come in at the end as a more or less serious play of the imagination. Does it not for the modern mind, such critics would say, endanger the very possibility of religion to demand that its foundation shall be a belief in some supernatural event of long ago? And the implied answer is in harmony with the present wide-spread desire to obtain the benefits of faith through a sort of vague theism without any definite content of dogma. But I am sure that this would not have been the answer of Plato himself, could the question have been proposed to him in such a form. He would have felt that this myth of Christianity gave precisely the one thing, the *unum necessarium*, for which he had been searching all his life, and that the compulsion it had laid upon him was evidence of its veracity. He was ready, he says in that conversation which he imagines to have taken place between Socrates and the young Phaedrus on the banks of the Ilissus—he was ready, if he could find any man so much as able to discern "a One and a Many in nature," to walk in his footsteps as though he were a god. Suppose it could have been told him that after six hundred years a student of his works would be applying these words to a person who did not discern, but in himself claimed to be, the One and the Many! Would not Plato have said, "My Lord and My God"?

Mr. More's argument here is a strange one. This is just as if Mr. More had written for the benefit of the modern unbeliever:

You won't believe me and the other Christians, but wouldn't you believe Plato if he could speak to the question? I tell you that Plato would have accepted the incarnation at once as a divine revelation.

Probably the unbeliever would answer without much hesitation that he does not believe Plato would have done any such thing. Plato had a wonderful grasp of principles, and also a certain poetic indecision of character. He knew scores of beautiful myths already, and he made some new ones of his own that were just as beautiful—always remembering that they were myths. He was in spirit like those Gnostics of the early Christian era whom Mr. More writes about. They enjoyed their myths, but would not commit themselves exclusively to any one, and so they stopped short of religion: they failed at the point where the Christians began.

But who knows? Mr. More may understand his Plato better than most of us. If Plato had had the opportunity, he might have become a Christian, and burned his bridges behind him. In that case the only thing for Mr. More to say would be: that Plato would have *legislated* his Logos into the authoritative position of a God but could not have found him with his senses as a pure historic fact.

So Mr. More would deceive the unbeliever a little there, and perhaps he would even deceive himself. But in saying this I seem to be quarreling only about the technique of his exposition. There is a deeper issue.

Mr. More wants his Logos worse than I do. He is like the modern scientist, very like Mr. Millikan. He wishes to see the world rational and benevolent; so he decrees that it be so. He would like to redeem the God from the odium he has borne for being too stern and inscrutable; so he says God, being Logos, is Love. This is only another version, with more show of learning, of Mr. Millikan's pleasant and popular faith in a "nature to be depended upon." This is the substitution of Christ the Logos for the whole of the Godhead. It is a piece of thinking in which a wish has been father to the thought.

Of course one knows that the immense reputation of Mr. More is not founded on any determined defense of science that he has ever been moved to make: he has not made any. Indeed, he is only revolted by the stress that moderns lay upon their applied sciences, and the furious and rather painful secular régime which is called industrialism. Mr. More is fastidious. But while he does not take his benefits quick and gross, he evidently does want to feel at home in the world; he does not want to see humanity set down against an alien nature; he is not satisfied with the human position unless it is of the highest conceivable dignity.

Mr. More considers that Christ's function in our religious history was to represent the Logos as supreme. It is my feeling, quite to the contrary, that this was the function of Satan. The function of Christ was to represent the Logos as partial and subordinate within the greatness of God.

Part Two

THE NEW GOD'S LIMITS

CHAPTER EIGHT

WHAT CAN HE DO?

O UR NEW religion is the worship of the Demigod, the Christ-God, or the Logos. It not only reflects a certain view of the universe, but it reënforces and helps to produce that view. When we compare it with the old orthodoxy we see its limitations quickly. Scientists are behind the new religion: a meeker breed of men was behind the old. The new God is limited as the author of good only, and our sense of evil has suffered an almost total amnesia. I cannot see how this can be counted a good thing.

Evil exists, the scientists would probably say. They would add, or at least they would think, that this evil is a function of human ignorance. But ignorance is temporary and remediable. The human intelligence has established its capacity for overcoming ignorance and acquiring science; and in the reign of science over us in this century evil is being defeated more and more decisively every day, and now begins definitely to disappear. God has willed this event, and man is assisting him. Having acquired God's sciences and "coördinators," we have no more use for such obscurantic doctrines as Adam's curse, predestination, a contingent universe, and essential evil, and with a great flourish of decision we have canceled these. We now confidently seek the improvement of human happiness.

Innumerable are the shouts of triumph that attend this

progress. "What hath God wrought!" said the first message that came over the Atlantic cable. Man had wanted quick communication; therefore God had wanted it too; and assisted by Morse and his confederates he had brought it to pass. Today we may do without the cable, and get the communication by radio. And likewise with many other aspirations, once the fabulous matter of dreams.

But contrary to the optimistic spirit of our times, reactionary, and in the nature of a reversion to the old stern realism, is Mr. C. E. Ayres' deliberate conviction that the new Messiah of science is a false Messiah, whose benefits are illusory. It is bound to be disquieting to those who had hoped too unguardedly. His book, "Science: a False Messiah," appeared, ironically enough—one might almost say it appeared providentially—in the same year as Mr. Pupin's complacent book, "The New Reformation."

Mr. Ayres' thesis is about like this: So far as we may judge the future of science by what it has already accomplished, there is no reason to expect that it will ever bring about any revolutionary improvement in human welfare. What has science done? Mostly, science has constructed machines for man to use, increased man's power, and increased still more his illusion of power. But the difficulty is that man with the machine can only do the kind of thing that the machine is capable of doing; and the goods which the machine produces may not be precisely the things that man wants. Man is reduced to being the tender of machines, whereas his happiest labor hardly consists in tending machines; and to using the machine products, which may not give him his highest satisfactions.

For instance, we now have easy communication; we may communicate by telephone, postal service, telegraph, radio, printing press, or educational establishment; but are we to look for happiness in a career of communicating, or of receiving communications? The principal thing about a communication is the thing that is communicated, and about that the machine has no judgment whatever. Let there be communication! But what has that to do with lightening some inner darkness, or satisfying some specific and difficult desire?

So with rapid locomotion. We may travel fast through space by many ingenious methods. But why should we? Perhaps we do not need to, as compared with the way we need to do some other things—and it is just possible that we may not want to. We will find that if we intend to enjoy the blessings of science, it will have to be by using the machines and machine-products that modern science has placed at our disposal, and then our existence will be mechanized, but not necessarily filled, not made more intelligent: we will have to spend much of it in doing what the machines dictate we should do.

There never was a civilization so "productive" as this one of the modern West; never a civilization that performed such massive transformations of nature, and stamped so many natural objects with the image of its desires. And that fact is certainly the consequence of a religious faith: it is due to the worship of a Logos. It is not a mere coincidence that our age is distinct from others in two things at the same time: first, in that it has applied its sciences to an extent never before attempted; second, in that its religion is the worship of the Man-God Christ, the closest approach to pure secularism that a religion has ever made. These two things are respectively cause and effect, or else effect and cause. It may be put either way.

A religion has to justify itself as an economy that makes for human happiness. Let us see where this proposition leads us.

Our new religion is thought to justify itself immediately because, as the man in the street says, "Just look at our prosperity!" America has taken the new God more seriously than Europe has, and worshiped him harder, and therefore America is inclined to say, "Look at our superior prosperity." This prosperity is easy to behold, though evidently rather difficult for the humanist to analyze in terms of its ultimate psychic values. Prosperity is thought to be indicated by facts that are hard, specific, and abstract, and that are supposed never to lie: by figures. There are the figures of our volume of production, and per capita production; of our volume of consumption, and per capita consumption; of our foreign trade; of our bank clearings; of our taxable wealth; of our volume of insurance in force; and many other such figures. And it is true that figures do not lie. But what is it that figures say? These figures say, quite accurately no doubt, what are the volumes of our production, consumption, foreign trade, and the like, just as they claim to do. But behind the figures is always the question of the human values they stand for—for we cannot live by figures alone. The popular idea of prosperity, as the general human condition that is proved by such figures, is not an idea that means anything precisely; but what it does mean to us ordinarily is not flattering to our mentality. It is vaguely supposed that the prosperity which the figures prove is a state in which no serious evil can befall a race.[1] If anything is more absurd, it is to suppose that the same sort of prosperity can ever belong to an individual.

In this and the following chapter I will try to make these assertions good, so far as I can do so briefly.

Of course they would hardly be questioned anyway by a certain section of American public opinion—and by a rather larger section of European opinion. Europe is doubtless being Americanized, but over a very powerful native resistance, which knows all about the fallacy of prosperity. I may there-

---

[1] Mr. Stuart Chase's admirable little book deals with this topic very persuasively, and in the direction that I am taking: "Prosperity: Fact or Myth?"

fore be laboring a point which does not need laboring with a great many people. But it evidently deserves to be advertised all the same, in view of the fact that the application of science goes on with increasing rather than abating fury. The figures of prosperity become more and more colossal, while the fact of prosperity becomes more and more dubious.

Science is ordinarily classified as having three grand divisions, which consist in the physical sciences, the biological sciences, and the social or psychic sciences. Let us think for a moment what these sciences, in their order, have produced for us. They are, as it were, the three benevolent activities of the God that we worship.

First as to the physical or mechanical sciences. It is particularly as the false Messiah of machinery that Mr. Ayres has exposed the new God. But it is certain that the wonders he performs in this field are by far the most spectacular of all. Nowhere else is he such a great and impressive God. In his other aspects he has not in the least held to the pace he sets as a physical scientist.

The modern mechanical marvels are much too numerous to catalogue here. They are such as new foods, new fuels, articles of dress, roads, skyscrapers and apartments and wonderful habitations, methods of heating and cooling and lighting, devices for communication, devices for locomotion at high speed, power machines, artillery and engines of destruction, appliances and "conveniences" of a thousand kinds. They are so numerous and so ingenious that we are tempted to think that our sciences can do anything we want done in the mechanical kind.

But this is hardly so. Nature is infinitely subtle, and we with our sciences are simple. We always tend to overestimate the triumphs we celebrate over nature. With all the physical goods that have been produced, there are deeply desired

goods not yet realized. Among these are the means of order-
ing our geological and climatic environment on a large scale
—so that we may no longer go in peril of floods, storms,
droughts, and earthquakes. Cannot physics give us a weather
guaranteed not to kill, even if it cannot give us one that is
comfortable? Among them also are the means of really con-
trolling the products which we have already learned to create
and enjoy. Our actual control is most imperfect. Otherwise
we should not be so endangered by the disintegration and
chemical change within them, producing wear and tear,
the collapse of buildings and bridges, explosions, poisonous
gases, the breakage of water mains and power circuits, and
fires. Our artificial environment serves us with many com-
forts, and also exposes us to many perils of its own.

The practical achievements of physical science are the
fruit of the greatest ingenuity and devotion, and they are
very considerable. We are able to transform environment
today to a degree that is marvelous. So it is not the hand-
somest point to make, for it sounds ungrateful; yet self-
respect will inspire the critic to remark that he is not so gullible as to think that physical science has yet mastered the infinite contingency of nature.

But there is another consideration, a hideous and depress-
ing one, which is not quite so obvious. As the grateful beneficiary of physical science looks over its multitude of clean,
shining, effective products, and sees their uses incontestably
demonstrated, a strange thought will occur to him: *For most
of them he has not consciously felt any particular need.*
He is forced to the conclusion that science, listing all these
products to its credit as products that fulfill desires, has been
faking some of the desires. The prospect of owning them
does not ravish him. On the contrary, he is appalled to think
of the responsibility that is imposed upon him as a regular
consumer to purchase them and make use of them. The

manifest destiny which is gently borne in upon him as the patron of science is that he must labor the harder in order to avail himself of an ever-increasing variety of scientific utilities that he doesn't really want. The most curious feature of our industrialism is illustrated just here: it is the fact that the production inevitably exceeds the demand.

For what it fails to give us, mechanical science would like to make up by giving us plenty of things that we do not want. Science is like a benevolent small boy who has heard us say that we wanted to conquer nature, and proceeds to bring us such a series of instruments for that purpose that we become sorry we ever said it.

A machine or a machine product that we possess and use without having any real need of it is nothing but a toy. And in this respect science is a Santa Claus, filling our stockings with objects of this sort. If science had never produced one device that was useful, it might still have a busy vocation producing its toys—just as Santa Claus would continue to be one of the major saints in the calendar though he brought nothing to minister to our grievous needs, but only ingenious playthings and balls of tinsel. So it is part of the rôle of the physical sciences to supply us with toys—in which part there is something that is good and pleasing, and something that is very tiresome.

In the carnival atmosphere of the scientific Christmas there will be plenty of people who will feel spiritually comforted by any pretty mechanical device whatever, such as confetti, rattles, horns, firecrackers, balloons, and jacks-in-boxes. Or they may be scornful of such cheap pleasures, and then be taken in by more elaborate entertainments like the new car and the radio. But there will also be those—I should think they are older mentally, but they might be simply more bilious of temperament—who will quite fail to register pleasure in these things.

People like this will spoil the Christmas spirit if they are in sufficient numbers. They are such harsh critics that I feel a little embarrassment in defending them. They are the permanent opposition to the works of mechanical science considered as the true source of delight. Fortunately for science, they have been for several centuries in a steadily diminishing minority among the patrons. Unfortunately for science, there are signs that their numbers, after falling very low, are now on the point of rising again, and that they will prove in the future more of an encumbrance to scientific promoters.

The rejecters of mechanical toys—the chief contribution of practical science after certain primitive needs have been supplied—are those who may be said to seek their pleasures on an esthetic basis. This is a basis which science is constitutionally unable to furnish them.

What is the pleasure of amusement or entertainment anyway? We do not expect it when we are in the throes of some urgent drive, such as to catch a train, to close a trade, or to relieve our hunger. In the accomplishment of our furious natural desires everybody is likely to be as scientific as he can. What we require then is satisfaction, and we seek it by the most efficient technique possible, using all the machinery available. Amusement, on the other hand, is something expected from our leisure, during the interval between desires. And how does science enable us to secure it? Science directs us to amuse ourselves, between desires, *by simulating and putting through another desire-process*. This is a remarkable answer; it is the only one that science can think of. Science can furnish us with some clever process, or contrivance, or machine, which is wonderfully successful at fulfilling a certain desire, and the idea is that we will find pleasure in working it whether or not we have the desire.

For example, here is a speed device, a piece of efficient machinery. Never mind whether we want to go anywhere. In fact, we probably don't know just where we do want to

go, though we are determined eventually to get back to exactly where we started. But it is supposed to be fun to drive
the machine anyway, and to realize the great speed or efficiency of which it is capable.

This is clearly a pleasure that goes with the sense of
power. The fun consists in our proving to ourselves that we
can control nature. We may not at the moment need to, but
we are aware that often in the future we shall, and our
success for the present promises well. It is like the flattery
of the man who flatters us on general principles. It does not
assist us towards any given objective, but pleases us with the
impression that we have wonderful powers, and are destined
to succeed. And that is why we tend to hail every new mechanical achievement with joy, and with a joy which is quite
regardless of whether the achievement confers upon us any
specific benefit. At the least it proves to us the power of the
species to which we belong.

But the sense of power that comes from the operation of
machinery is to be distinguished from esthetic pleasure. This
latter does not come to us till we have abandoned the desire-
process. The mark of the esthetic experience is its desireless-
ness—this is the character in which authorities like Kant and
Schopenhauer have celebrated it. The esthetic attitude is the
most objective and the most innocent attitude in which we
can look upon the world, and it is possible only when we
neither desire the world nor pretend to control it. Our pleasure in this attitude probably lies in a feeling of communion
or *rapport* with environment which is fundamental in our
human requirements—but which is sternly discouraged in
the mind that has the scientific habit.

I should say the esthetic attitude is definable with fair accuracy in the simple and almost sentimental terms: the love
of nature.

Consider the attitude of the speeding driver, for example,
by way of contrast; it is one variety of attitude that we may

take towards nature; in this case, towards a rural landscape. The driver's attitude is one of maximum indifference: he values his machine in precisely the degree that its speed can obliterate the landscape, which is an endless distraction, and achieve a pure transit. This is not the attitude of the lover of nature, whose wish is to receive its detail as fully as he can.

The machines, and the mechanical amusements, which are nothing but so many pursuits and drives after play-objectives, have the purpose of making us indifferent to the sensible infinity which constitutes the landscape of our world.

And unfortunately the mechanical entertainments in an age committed to progress are progressive: they must grow more pretentious all the time. Nobody knows the limits of magnificence to which the scientific imagination will go in devising them; nor the extent of the tyranny by which they will be imposed upon us for our enjoyment as entertainments that have the sanction of society behind them. They have as their function to minister to our pride of power and our scorn of nature, and they are all but features of the ritual of the Logos.

The toys which science showers upon us are therefore amusements just a little more than innocent; for they flatter us and quiet our apprehensions: they are anodynes. The speeding driver in the car cannot afford to observe the infinite variety of nature, he must confirm his sense of power. He is deliberately practicing a technique of anesthesia.

It is in this respect that science as a habit of mind is a true cousin to Christian Science.

Let us assume a man in trouble. (Such an event is still not very difficult to imagine.) What sort of trouble? A bereavement by death; an unrequited love; the failure of a cause to which he has devoted himself; the final breakdown of a personal project; the ingratitude of a public for what he has done; a crash in business; an irremediable physical afflic-

tion; even—for our griefs may have all sorts of origins—
his failure to find him a God and profess to a religion; his
metaphysical or epistemological difficulties. These troubles
arise from our inability, in spite of the aids of our sciences,
to manage our material and social environments. They may
be quite devastating. I am far from suggesting that sometimes a man in this situation may not need an anodyne: the
psychotherapist might well prescribe one if the patient is in
bad enough shape, just as the doctor would prescribe an
opiate for a man in intolerable pain. Let the patient take up
golf, and hit the ball as hard as he can, where his power
will produce its results. Let him get a car and drive it fast.
Let him work at something where he will be impressed by
his own effectiveness. Give him a position of responsibility
where his commands will be obeyed. All such measures
would improve his state of mind by restoring his courage.

Technically, they would remove his attention from the
field in which he cannot help being conscious of his own impotence, and direct it upon a field where his force is visible
and certain.

The common name of this technique is work. It is supposed to cure all our troubles. The homely practical precept
which the scientists never tire of pronouncing is, Work,
and work hard. They do not ask that we will always calculate the object which work will produce for us, and make
sure we desire it: the work which they advise is a furious
play-process, an occupation intended only to use up our energies and leave none over, a way of forgetting, and an escape.
When the youth in "Sartor Resartus" is beset with problems greater than he can solve, and griefs greater than he
can bear, Carlyle would bid him simply betake himself to
Work, which will serve him for a religion and a faith—
Work, with a capital W.

There is always a field in which we can demonstrate
our effectiveness if we must. Science is an economy of effort,

a concentration of attention, which will get results, and ther
is always a place where we can practice it with obvious suc
cess. We can dig up the ground if necessary, and admire th
mark we have made in the world. Baffled on one line, w
may always find another line on which we will certainly suc
ceed.

But as the physical sciences are the most effective, th
tendency is always for us to forsake the higher endeavor i
favor of the lower. The tendency is to substitute materia
successes for biological and social failures, and to lead a lif
which is outwardly successful, yet not so advanced in its com
plexity. One man cannot realize a happy domestic life bu
he can make money: therefore he throws himself more an
more into his business. Another man is a failure in his chose
profession because it is difficult: so he steps down and make
a success in a lower one. Many a creative artist of indifferer
success is driven to become an applied scientist out of shee
desperation, and lest he lose his morale altogether. The mod
ern behaviorists are probably a case in point. Originally the
were perhaps just ordinary psychologists doing the best the
could in a hard field; were baffled by the slipperiness an
the fullness of their psychic phenomena; abandoned the psy
chic project and took to studying objective behavior-patterr
and the chemistry of nervous tissue; and found there som
precise physical phenomena with which they could mak
quite a show of science and success.

So Christian Science and secular science are close kir
Christian Science says to the man in trouble: Don't notic
your failure—it is illusory—believe you are successful—Go
is on your side—there is not really any evil. But secula
science says to the same man: Don't meditate your failur
here but go to work where you can get results—anywher
—the field of opportunity is wide open. Both of them evad
the problem of evil.

It is as a sort of corollary to this doctrine that collectiv modern science advises us all, for our own good, to be large consumers of its products. The commodities it brings us are all so brilliantly successful and practicable, so flattering to the user, so appropriate for typical Occidental or American citizens; but the real desires of our hearts are so likely to be vain and impracticable. Science instructs us very carefully in what we ought to want, indicating always the things that it knows how to furnish.

Work, Power, Activity, Business, Industry, Production—these are the great words of an age of applied science. They do beautifully for those who need them badly enough, and who are willing to abandon their deepest personal interests. They reflect power on those who cannot bear the sense of impotence. They are deeply Occidental—and they are quite scorned by Orientals, who insist upon their contemplation and their freest inner development regardless of what *impasses* they may find waiting for them on that road.

Mr. Calvin Coolidge in a recent address before the Agency Directors of the New York Life Insurance Company had his interesting passage:

It is in our economic life that progress has been most astounding. The productive capacity of our people has proved to be beyond comprehension. Recently the press stated that a scientific investigator reported that the United States, with 1/16 of the population of the world, does about 1/2 of the work of the world. That is the efficiency of a free people.

Upon a little study of these figures, we observe that our /16 of the world's population performs 8/16 of the world's work, which is just 8 times our share of it, and just 15 times s much work as the rest of the world's population is performing proportionately. It cannot be denied that these figres betoken an efficient people, and it may be assumed that our efficiency is attended with the usual benefits: a sense of occupation, for example, and a general illusion of personal and collective power. The latter is a thing which every flattering public speaker likes to play upon.

But I am far from sure that these figures betoken a free people. It is much too likely that they betoken a defeated and escapist people—a people which is afraid of the fullness of the inner life and prefers to rush into violent action— a people that takes its work as an anesthetic—an impotent people building up a legend of power. The only escape from that reasoning is in the assumption that we have unduly protracted our period of youth, and not yet come to try the inner life on any general scale. But that again is a disaparagement which it is not pleasant to utter: for on those terms we are unduly prolonging our childhood, we are exhibiting a certain infantilism, in the bad or pathological sense.

Now for the other sciences and their achievements. Evil manifests itself largely in our failure, as living beings, to keep up an unimpeded activity; that is, in disease and death. Undoubtedly the new God exhibits some strenuous enterprises when considered under his second phase, which is as the God of the biological sciences. It is too bad that these sciences are less scientific, or less capable of calculation, prediction, and management, than are the physical sciences. It is true, of course, that we have a modern materia medica, a modern dietetic, a modern surgery, and modern disinfection and sanitation. It is also true that we still have disease and bodily pain, and we still have decay and death. We shall doubtless continue to have them; and by the same token we shall continue to have careers, heroic projects, romances, that no sooner bloom than they are cut short by the brutal contingencies that issue in mortality. I call them contingencies because they are compounded of subtle materials that forever escape human understanding and control. Pru-

lence might suggest that we would do well to prepare our-
elves for these contingencies. The religion that ignores
hem, and sets up a God that does not authorize them or
anction them, but only vainly if hopefully wars upon them,
s hardly a competent religion.

And besides the physical and the biological sciences we
have the psychological and social sciences. The new God in
his third aspect is a Social Scientist, and our own social scien-
ists are in his service. But the social sciences fail even more
egregiously than do the biological sciences of being competent
nstruments of prediction and control. They study such com-
plexes as the forces of production, the distribution of wealth,
he arrangements for sex and childhood and education, the
penal and moral codes of conduct, and the organization of
political communities as they function both interiorly and in
foreign affairs. In this field the biggest talker will be the
biggest authority. The materials of study are the common property of all observers; nor are there such esoteric
and technical methods of penetration as to yield to the expert any spectacular results like those that are attained by
he difficult methods of the physical sciences. The social
ciences exhibit many contrivances intended to insure success
n social relations of all sorts, but they are generally marked
"very theoretical": they are not the sure-fire utilities that
might serve us against the wars of nations, the economic
competition of individuals, the grief that proceeds from sex,
envy, and unkindness. For of such as these are our social
evils. And what is the status of that God whose ablest and
best worshipers, borrowing of his own secrets, quite fail to
put a stop to them, or even pretend that they do not exist?

We cannot keep evil out of the body, and out of society.
Nevertheless, there are plenty of schemes and processes
offered to us for that purpose by the biological and social

sciences for what they are worth—for that much at the least
The man with bodily ailments and difficulties of persona
relationship will contemplate them with proper gratitude
but probably he will also feel the same misgivings tha
attacked him when he regarded the multitude of mechanical commodities that the physical sciences showered upor
him. The beneficial product of the biological sciences is a
medical treatment or a hygiene, and that of the social science
is a scheme of education or a social organization of some sort
Their effectiveness ranges very widely between 100 per cen
and nothing, but it is in their number that they appall him
He can never try all the good things offered him in these
departments! In his own poor person he can never get round
to all the physiological treatments and regimens freely put
at his disposal, and with the limited allotment of his years
he can never do his duty by all the good social movements
he has an opportunity to join. Here again, there are more
goods than he has ever wanted, and he is embarrassed by
the obligation that he feels as a loyal patron of these sciences
to save his body and his soul according to all the prescriptions.

The products of these sciences are not too welcome to the
person with esthetic gifts, for a reason that we have seen
they submerge his sensibility in their intensely practical and
exclusive processes. Life seems to lose its dignity if it has to
be lived with so much fuss.

But of course they are perfectly welcome to the man who
wants his anodyne. This again is according to our argument.
It is wonderful to be occupied with a practical formula for
health that takes our attention entirely, or with participation
in societies whose members regard them seriously and in
whose service they find a busy career. A very large fraction
of our total occupation in this age is with organizing, and
then with elaborating and perpetuating the organization.

A European said to me: "Wherever three or more Amer-

cans meet in one place for as much as fifteen minutes, they
will write a constitution and found a new organization."
So far as there is truth in this, it is because we have discovered that in organizing we seem to be accomplishing something, and that is the very thing we want most to do. This
is the gospel of work again; the illusion of power. The col-
legians of my acquaintance have almost an obsession for
taking part in organizations. It seems to them a more effective kind of action than working at problems that cannot be
solved. It permits them to feel that they belong without
waiting any longer to the ranks of the world's most productive race and are bringing into existence objects that were not
here before. If the volume of our production should be
figured solely with respect to the production of new societies and cults, one may well imagine that our rating would
be just as high as Mr. Coolidge found it to be in the production of material objects. Somebody might say of us a
second time: "This is the efficiency of a free people."

A terrible overproduction, in the view of esthetic and
Quietist persons; an inestimable boon, in the mind of people
who want the anodyne of action.

The history of our practical sciences is one of successes
and failures. We must not forget the failures. The purpose
which we would accomplish, through our careful scientific
formulation, is defeated by interferences which could not
be predicted, and which may therefore be called contingent.
We have constructed, for example, a bridge: but this bridge
for some surprising reason does not bear the strain which
the best of calculation said it would bear. Its hard stone dis-
integrates, or its steel suffers a crystallization, or an enemy
undermines it, or a geological cataclysm loosens its foundations. But a moral code is also a scientific construct, of even
more importance than a bridge—and of even more precarious standing. This moral code gets itself faithfully em-

bodied in a person's life, but it does not prove to be quite effective. It is not good enough after all, whether for inner reasons (the unsuspected tragic "flaw" of character) or because of outward circumstance that hits him when and where he could not anticipate. So a bridge and a hero will collapse alike.

Science is a calculation which leads from one step to another by a theoretical necessity, and there are people who cannot see why a perfect efficiency is not its goal. But really the bridge it raises or the personal character it forms is enveloped in a contingency that may at any time choke it up. The practical processes are like a thin stream of history whose materials seem perfectly under control. But the materials after all are not fully understood, and in any case the stream flows through an indifferent universe whose irruption may at any moment shatter its continuity.

Of course this is not a highly contemporary sort of doctrine. We have abandoned the religion that would have prepared us to receive the lesson of tragedy and failure. We perform wonderful feats in the laboratory and we live in cities made marvelously with hands; we are able to gloze certain facts very obvious to more primitive societies which have never lost contact with earth and the elements, or to more religious societies who have been instructed by many defeats. Under these circumstances the Genius Loci declines rather flatly to hear of disagreeable realities.

But if our new God is a very different being from the God of Israel, we may remember that the America which recently celebrated its sesqui-centennial anniversary has had as yet no history so instructive as that of Israel between Abraham and Malachi. That is a very honorable excuse for us; it is the best one we have.

The friends of science, the worshipers of the Logos, are very busily celebrating their triumphs. Physical science has done much to talk about, and the other sciences have done enough to talk about. But nature, the total environment which we have to manage, is still the Djinn of the fairy tale, and science is only the golden-haired boy who pursues him. The young prince is armed with a bottle and a stopper. It is his intention to get the Djinn into the bottle and then put in the stopper. Perhaps he will set the bottle on his laboratory shelf and, by letting the Djinn's power out through a control-valve, perform wonders of safe magic. The sympathy of the public goes out rather whole-heartedly to the brave young prince. But there must be some hard-headed realists to whom his undertaking seems a little bit absurd.

Shelley was the prophet of the new God, who anticipated the religious attitude of our leaders of today with remarkable precision. He undertook, in his drama, to unbind Prometheus, the spirit of science, from his rock. Aeschylus had left him bound to the rock; at least the play which he wrote to unbind him had perished. In his "Prometheus Unbound," Shelley gives an ecstatic but by no means Aeschylean picture of the millennium. Prometheus is now free to work his wonders, and they are largely in the mechanical and physical kind. But he is also the spirit of love, and therein he represents the new sociology in its latest and boldest—and let us hope its most effective—manifestation. Equipped with sciences both material and social, Prometheus goes forth to deliver a world held in the bondage of darkness and suffering. The passages in which the prospect is celebrated are astonishing. Prometheus solves the hidden mysteries of nature to such an extent that nature cries out:

> The lightning is his slave; heaven's utmost deep
> Gives up her stars, and like a flock of sheep
> They pass before his eyes, are numbered, and roll on!
> The tempest is his steed, he strides the air;

And the abyss shouts from her depth laid bare,
Heaven, hast thou secrets? Man unveils me; I have
  none.

This is the very language of the moderns talking about
the triumphs of their science; but it is terribly juvenile. As
a matter of fact, Shelley was young, and it was not in him to
grow much older.

The only reservation which Shelley made was in not
dating the unbinding of Prometheus. The millennium of his
vision was still indefinitely in the future.

Nowadays there are those who think that Prometheus
has already been unbound, and that the millennium is here.
They are not the men whose judgment I respect.

CHAPTER NINE

WE HIS POOR FOLLOWERS

INDUSTRIALISM, a régime which governs our whole manner of life, is the kind of expression which we have
now given to our Occidental humanity. It seems a miserable fate for any people to suffer; but it is one which we
have invited upon ourselves with our worship of the God of
Science; and one which we will hardly get rid of till we
shift our whole view of the universe and once more reduce
the Demigod to his place of subordination within the Godhead.

If a religion is of no importance in the life of men, it is
strange that there should be such perfect fitness between this
practical turn that we have given to conduct and the new religion that little by little has been winning its way with us.
Industrialism is the effect of a Christianity that has elevated
the Man-God to the throne of Jehovah, and made of Christ
the temporal Messiah that he intended not to be.

There is a paradox here with which we must reckon: The
greater we make God, the less responsibility we put upon
man; and the more we subtract from God's dominion, the
more we add to man's burden and discomfort. So long as we
left the understanding and the governance of the world very
largely to our God's inscrutable purposes, we undertook as
men only a modest career that was practicable and easy. But
when we conceived God in the image of a Scientist, whose

purposes and technique we as little scientists could understand and emulate, we undertook to play a part which was
beyond us. In attempting to sustain it we have been far too
heroic, and have spoiled the happiness of which we were
capable. Under industrialism, which we conceive to be our
divinely appointed mission, we scourge ourselves like true
fanatics.

So, when we attack the industrialism which now prevails
in the West, and especially in America, it is not quite as if
we were attacking an ordinary institution, like the Society for
the Prevention of Cruelty to Animals, or the Republican
Party. These institutions will have to look to their credentials. But industrialism has a sanctitude of its own: it is the
practical life which men lead in obedience to their religion.
If the animating principle of the universe is Logos, then we
as men must possess it and employ it without ceasing, and it
is a duty as well as a privilege. Industrialism is something
practiced and defended by the adherents of a faith: they
consider it not only expedient but right.

Doubtless there are a great many of its spokesmen who
do not yet fancy the rôle of openly defending industrialism.
It is still new, and it has come up from below so far as the
social scale is concerned. It may seem to them to require a
profession of faith which is yet a little underbred. Many
of the actual forms which industrialism takes are quite distasteful. So even in this generation it takes a bold man or else
a slightly obtuse man to be willing to go before the public
as an apologist of pure industrialism. Mr. Millikan and Mr.
Pupin do it, and I take it they fall within the first class.
They see with ineluctable logic that there is no use believing in the Logos of a universe unless you are going to perform his works. They draw the moral of their faith relent-
lessly. They come out on behalf of industrialism more
roundly than anybody else of equal importance in the world

of thought, and they are the most advanced prophets of their time.

The less courageous, or the more fastidious, of the believers, do not talk much about industrialism, however they may be compelled to approve it—but content themselves with saying fine things about Science. Industrialism is simply the economic consequence of the faith or the cult whose name is Science. So they do a service, they advance the cause of righteousness on earth, even if they only talk about the Spirit of Science. For if the Spirit of Science is holy then the works of the Spirit are holy too, and if we believe stoutly enough in Science-in-the-Abstract then we shall necessarily believe in the applied sciences. Industrialism is nothing but science applied—applied persistently, in whatever place it can be applied, commercially, on the grand scale, uncritically, religiously, without a single reservation, and as the one means of salvation.

The Europeans are not such industrialists as we are, and that is not hard to explain. It is not that they are too pusillanimous, and lack the courage of their convictions: it is rather that they are not yet quite convinced. Science as a cult is something of an Americanism. It is not yet quite regularized as a European thing, it is only making rapid progress in that direction.

There is a large body of critical doctrine in circulation at the expense of science as theory: but where did it come from? It is a blasphemy almost wholly of European origin. For instance, there are in English the writings of Mr. Russell, Mr. Eddington, Lord Balfour, Mr. J. S. Haldane, and Mr. Whitehead. So far as I can see, there are simply no important American writers comparable with these that represent the same point of view: men who know their science and yet bring metaphysical criticisms to bear against it, men who tell of its limitations as a knowledge and a practice. Until these great skeptics and all their camp are destroyed, or else converted to the Logos, the British community cannot be solid in the support of the faith, and the Kingdom of Logos will not prevail on British ground; which is to say that British industrialism will not be so fast, so furious, and so whole-souled as ours.

I will try to define the meaning of human life in the barest possible terms as we are led to conceive it under industrialism.

Industrialism assumes that man is merely a creature of instincts. That is, he is essentially an animal with native appetites that he must satisfy at the expense of his environment. His life consists entirely in the satisfaction of his appetites. But he differs from the other animals in one glorious particular: he has a reason. And what is its function? His reason is a superior cunning that enables him to get the objects of appetite out of nature faster, in greater purity, and in more abundance than they can. His reason is his science, and its characteristic act is to supply him with a process or with a tool which will wrest from nature with ridiculous ease the objects of his desire. In other words, man is an animal, but with a reason which permits him to live a life more animal than that of animals. For his reason serves his instinct, and concentrates and brutalizes the usual process of desire and satisfaction.

That is human life in brief, according to the theory of industrialism. I may also indicate briefly another theory about the meaning of human life—an old-fashioned theory which, before it is done, becomes a pointed criticism of industrialism and bids us halt the industrial progress. If this were an age of orthodoxy, I would name it simply as the religious theory of life; but heresy is becoming orthodox and I cannot. I will call it then an esthetic theory of life.

Reason, in the sense of science, is of great service to man

with his animal constitution, and makes him a very superior animal. But man distinguishes himself from the animals not only by the effectiveness of his animal purposes but also by the unique manner in which he chooses to proceed with these purposes. *Man not only lives his animal life but enjoys it.* And that is by the exercise of a faculty that animals possess just as little as they possess his reason: by sensibility. By pure reason man would hasten and brutalize his animal processes, but by his free sensibility he elects to observe them, complicate them, and furnish them with background and accessory detail that cannot enter into the exclusive animal consciousness. As an animal merely, man would simply partake of the banquet of nature as he required. As an animal with reason, he would only gorge himself the more greedily upon it and have more of it to gorge upon. But as an animal with sensibility, he becomes fastidious, and makes of his meal a rich, free and delicate esthetic experience.

Eating is one of the two great symbols of the life of appetite. Sex is the other. The manners of man at his feasting distinguish him sufficiently from the beasts. But his manners in love confer upon him an even greater distinction.

The sexual life which animals know is the life of lust. And man is thoroughly capable of it. He with his science is able, if he wishes it, to gratify his lusts more abundantly, more cheaply, and more safely than they can. It is true that lust is such a natural function that he cannot quite delegate it to a machine to accomplish for him. But he can greatly assist it in finding its occasion.

Quite unexpectedly, however, so far as the theory is concerned which sees man only as an animal equipped with a science, man does not elect to keep his sexual life on the instinctive or brute level. He transforms it, turns it into romance, and converts lust into love. The technique of love is not the technique of a science but the technique of an art.

The lover is the man who opposes and stops the drive of his lust in order to enrich and solidify the experience. He has sensibility. Instead of concentrating upon the act he plays with his free mind upon the objective nature with which he is concerned: upon the beloved one, and not merely her person but her history and all the circumstance that expresses her; upon the whole immediate world in which his love is to be consummated, its earth, sky, flora and fauna; and upon all the kindred detail of his life which memory cares to associate with the present moment. Operating on this scale, he makes his simple instinctive act into a massive experience; but he does not owe it to his reason.

Industrialists will never be able to account for so peculiar an experience as romantic love—all their emphasis is on effectiveness and action.

Nor will some of the Humanists themselves be able to account for it, without revising their doctrines. Mr. Babbitt, for example, is far from being the man who would advocate lust in preference to love. Yet he is an expositor of reason, and a mighty hater of sensibility. Apparently he does not see that the cult of reason leads him straight into the cult of science, where he is in the exact middle, the very headquarters, of the camp of the industrialists, committed as they are necessarily to the rule of the most effective action. In order to be human, we have to have something which will stop action, and this something cannot possibly be reason in its narrow sense. I would call it sensibility.

From this point of view let us see the meaning of our industrialism in more regular economic terms. An industrial age is an age of machines, and an industrialist must defend the machines. Mr. Millikan and Mr. Pupin do this very flatly and confidently—and with a simplicity which is not that of profundity.

Their argument is the common one to this effect: A machine is a labor-saving device; therefore it is automatically beneficial, and the benefit is exactly equivalent to the labor that is saved.

But I would suggest an alternative theory about that: A machine is a labor-saving device; therefore its benefit is doubtful, and depends on how far it is advisable that labor should be saved.

The assumption which Mr. Millikan and Mr. Pupin make is of course the one which industrialists and professional "economists" all make likewise. It simply regards labor as an evil, which industrialism would obviate: "Let the machine do it." But if labor is an evil, what is the good? The industrialists would answer, surprised probably at the question, that the good is the end, the object of desire to which the labor leads; and that the labor is justified only in the sense that the end justifies the means. That is to say, they define a man as a bundle of appetites, and propose to endow him with the maximum efficiency in gratifying them.

This much can be said for such a doctrine, that it is indeed the end of labor rather than the labor for itself which is really imperative, and that the instinctive desire of the end constitutes the original mainspring of our action. Primarily, we hunt and fish and till the soil in order that we may eat, and eating is a necessity that we are driven to by reason of our animal constitution. And if food is scarce and difficult to secure from nature, the labor is grievous, and science is invaluable in offering us relief through its efficient technique. Lacking science, we might have to labor without ceasing, and under painful hardships, in order to support our life. Life would then be a sorry thing: it would be, as Hobbes put it, "solitary, poor, nasty, brutish, and short."

But fortunately, a little science will go a long way, and nature is not nearly so implacable as this account of her might indicate. Even under primitive conditions, and even in such an elemental pursuit as that of food, men find the fullness of living complicated immensely beyond the simplicity that science attributes to it. (The simplicity attaches not to life but to the scientific view of life.) For how do primitive men partake of their food when they have got it? Ordinarily they do not gobble it raw, nor yet snatch it from the pot and gobble it, as if eating were a mere instinctive function. Actually they introduce into it a certain fastidiousness, or luxury, which is not instinctive at all. For they prolong the moment of satisfaction, and develop a rite of eating, a decorum, a studied leisure, and an art. But what is much more astonishing, and unaccountable from the industrial point of view, is that they introduce the same features into the labor of securing their food. For the manner of hunting, fishing, and tilling the soil develops likewise into an art and a luxury. Labor ceases to be a mere means and a necessary evil, and becomes also an end in itself, so that you cannot tell whether men are practicing it for the sake of the object or for its own sake, you cannot draw the line between the labor which is evil and the end which is good. In other words, there arises to delay and complicate the process of instinct a process of enjoyment, which instinct knows nothing about.

Let us consider first this human complication as it enters into our labor, or into that department of our life which is known to economics as production. Then we may observe the complication that attaches to our satisfactions, or to that department which is known to economics as consumption.

It cannot be said that the enjoyment of labor precludes all scientific efficiency of effort and makes our labor unproductive. On the contrary, the enjoyment of labor cannot come till there is economic security, or a feeling of certainty about the main satisfactions. The hungry belly must be filled. But that is easily done; especially is it easily done with the aid of a little scientific equipment. It is so easily done that it might as well be done with enjoyment. If we are wise, we will achieve not only enjoyment but happiness, which is a continuous state of enjoyment. That is a rare and splendid destiny, and only possible when we have by a scientific economy made our instinctive ends secure, and then formed the habit of transforming every cycle of animal instinct by importing enjoyment into it. To be happy, we must have learned how to enrich the simplicity of all our instinctive actions.

The applied sciences aim at a maximum efficiency and a minimum duration of labor, and therefore they have a purpose which is destructive of enjoyment. They could not have proposed the saving of labor as their objective if they were familiar with the enjoyment of labor. They divest labor of its dignity and make it servile. So they have set up the modern industrial system: a system which may be defined outwardly as producing goods as fast as possible, and inwardly as deliberately sacrificing the enjoyment of labor. The characteristic tempo of industrial labor is too fast for enjoyment. If it isn't now it soon will be: it is accelerating. And its forms make little effort to be agreeable. It is logical that the labors of a labor-saving generation should be performed in factories, in cities, in houses, in artificial surroundings of excessive simplicity and drabness as compared with a natural environment. For otherwise how could the laborers defend themselves against the incessant stimulants to sensibility?

I am led to a thought which once was trite, but now has gone so out of fashion that it sounds perhaps like a great novelty. All labor should be effective without being arduous; and with that general proviso the best labor is the one which provides the best field for the exercise of sensibility—it is clearly some form of pastoral or agrarian labor. Agriculture has always held the primacy as a form of labor. At least it has until recently, when it began to be mechanized, hurried, and degraded. Farm labor cannot quite be routinized like factory labor, though the industrialists have done their best to do it in recent years. The infinite variety of nature makes it impossible for one day's farming to repeat another's, or for two rows to be plowed alike. Routine or servile labor never comes to the farm unless under certain monstrous conditions: unless the farmer is a slave working under the lash; or is a regular industrialist working for a "money crop"; or has been totally corrupted by the arrogant modern doctrine which says that man must "perfect his control over nature," and consequently hates nature and all her works. Farmers work inevitably at a leisurely gait. You cannot make a farmer increase the tempo unless you insist that he ride a machine.

But all labors might be like agriculture in their leisure and enjoyment if they would. In agrarian societies, as they were called, agriculture was not necessarily the only labor, but agriculture was the most respected of the forms of labor, and its example affected all the other forms. Then there was no curse on labor.

After production, consumption. One process invites the exercise of intelligence just as much as the other.

The importance of consumption at this time is indicated when we observe the large fact that we have been producing at such a rate that we now have on hand a surplus of products for which there seems to be no consumption available. This fact is marked in countries like Britain, where consumers are stubborn in their resistance, and where many industries have had to slow up their operation or stop it altogether, with consequent stagnation of capital and unemployment, and only the faintest prospect of improvement. But overproduction obtains in all advanced industrial societies. It begins to be a fearful phenomenon even in America; and this in spite of certain great advantages which our industries possess, among them the possession of a home market with a youthful and almost indiscriminate appetite for consumption of all kinds. Overproduction is almost our chronic condition.

The main concern of industrialists just now is to tempt the consumers into further consumption. They have no theories about what is proper consumption, and no compunctions about the private happiness of the consumers. In order to seduce them, they advertise and solicit orders. The development of advertising—along with that of its twin, personal salesmanship—is an alarming feature of modern industrialism. It is the attempt of an unsound economics to approve itself before men. Without it the rate of production could not possibly be maintained. To bait the hook for the consumer, advertising divests itself easily of scruple and dignity; it is obliged to go behind his spontaneous wants and persuade him to want the goods which industry has undertaken to produce. And still it falls short always of its goal, still it fails to bring the volume of consumption up to the volume of possible production.

But why should the consumer consume all that is displayed before him? And does the average man as consumer really want the goods which the average man as producer has offered him?

If anything is more monstrous than a labor which is not enjoyed, it is an act of pleasure which is only formal and not inspired by actual desire. In the field of sex this is the act performed by the prostitute. Intelligent consumption must have an actual instinctive want to start with, not a hypothetical one; and its business is, while gratifying that want effectively, to complicate it and make it massive and important by the exercise of sensibility.

When the machines and the processes shorten the time of our labor, on the ground that labor is evil, they are creating for us a new problem: the problem of leisure. What shall we do with the time we have saved? We are left without a proper career and a natural occupation. I suppose that the industrialists would say at once that we must spend our surplus time on increased consumption, and ought to be glad to do it! And they offer us, as we have seen, more goods to consume as well as more time in which to consume them. But unfortunately, we as mere men have a very puny natural equipment for fitting into that pretty program. We are not Grandgousier. Our bellies have just so much capacity, and our other appetites are far too backward to do credit to their opportunities. They have a certain elasticity, but it will not stretch very far.

If this means anything, it means that modern man has simply made the mistake of applying more science than he had any use for.

He says to himself periodically, Labor is over now. It is not yet time to sleep, and no appetites seem to be stirring. Shall I drink some draughts, or nibble at sweets, or take a fast drive, or play a furious game? Shall I dance, or shall I drowse, to the music of the radio? Or shall I pass the time provisionally with a book, a movie, a seat in the park, in the hope that by and by some sort of provocation—preferably sexual—may arise to excite me? For modern man, having saved his labors so well, finds himself hour after hour with nothing on earth that he feels powerfully drawn to do. It is a position of great discomfort. He has failed miserably in trying to flagellate his backward appetites to the extent of living up to his modern advantages.

And here is a fact which offers an ironical comment on the eagerness with which we set out to save the time of our labor. We have made an enormous achievement in the saving of labor: but it has not taken anything like a proportionate effect in diminishing the actual hours that we work. The schedule of professional labor now calls for only 20 per cent less working time than it did forty years ago, says Mr. Millikan; only 18 per cent less working time than it did thirty years ago, says another writer. I interpret this to mean that we have indeed saved a great fraction of our necessary working hours; but have then found ourselves incapable of disposing of the saved time by increased consumption; and have been actually driven back to labor again for pure pastime.

At any rate, it is certain that the labor which is saved in any particular industry by the introduction of new machines and processes goes almost immediately and almost entirely into manning new industries and producing new commodities. It never is given back to the workmen in the original industry in full. They probably would not know what to do with it if they had it.

The sublimest and most ridiculous application of labor-saving I have yet heard of does not come from Mr. Millikan, but from his confreres in science, the biologists; among them, from the younger Mr. Haldane, who eagerly looked forward to it in his "Daedalus, or the Future of Science," where he prophesied the mechanical triumphs of science. This particular triumph was to be ektogenesis: the extraction of the human egg from the body of the mother and its incubation externally without the pains of labor—that is, without labor in the specific sense as well as the general. To what use would the biologists put the time and attention thus saved to the woman? One would think that the substantial function of carrying and delivering the infant might be construed as a constitutional and inalienable right, like other forms of natural occupation. One would be apprehensive that, if such functions were one by one to be removed from the human being, and handed over to machines, he or she might cease to be human, and be left without any special rôle at all.

I must not slander the industrialists. I observe that many of them have ceased to brag about the new leisure in terms of the extra volume and variety of physical satisfactions it permits—seeing how soon the human appetite reaches the state of satiety—and are proposing now quite a new program. This program is the acquisition of "culture"—of learning, of manners, of esthetic understanding, of the amenities of life.

This proposal falls on grateful ears, as a matter of course, with those whose profession is to disseminate culture: such as Chautauquas, lecturers, travel bureaus, publishers, and authors and artists. Industrialism is so kind! These gladly accept the patronage offered them, but, even with the best of motives, they play into the hands of the industrial system and do not accomplish the good they intend. It is true that no one but a misanthrope can wish such a program anything but success. No one can deny that an industrial world needs culture.

But this sort of program is far too limited in its prospect of being of service. For a very simple reason: the amenities of life are sacrificed whenever a generation commits itself to industrialism; and before long they are lost to that generation irrecoverably, no matter how badly conscience pricks it to recover them. Those who are in earnest about the amenities can best show it by proposing to cancel the industrial ideal and give the amenities a chance to develop spontaneously.

Culture consists essentially in having and defending a delicate sensibility even while we are engaged upon the stern drive of the practical life. Lovers betray their sensibility and become roués, desperately unhappy because they are enslaved by instinct beyond hope of release. Industrialists betray it and become producers, to whom the enjoyment of life is only a melancholy memory. If they have aged in the service of industrialism, they will never acquire culture. But if they want to save culture to the young, they must, in all logic, wish and plan for the industrial engine to perish with themselves, and not be handed down as a curse to their successors.

The education acquired in schools is greatly overestimated as a means of acquiring culture. Unless it teaches young men and women how to live, it is a vain affectation, and in teaching them how to live it will teach them not to go out and plunge into industrialism with their fathers and uncles. The industrialists who contribute magnificent sums for "higher education" should understand that; but it is doubtful if they do.

The advantages of travel and of cultured society and of wide reading are misunderstood in the same way. They mean nothing if they do not inspire in those who partake of them the courage to live simply and with sensibility. There may easily be more true culture in circumscribing one field with a plow than in the Grand Tour itself as it is sometimes conducted in these days. Culture, in other words, is not a material commodity to be bought and consumed, but the by-product of a humane kind of life.

Culture is something which will have to be trusted, like the grace of God, to come of its own accord, but will never come unless the right sort of living invites it.

The industrial revolution has come much too fast not to have upset the historic economy of human life. It eliminated the leisure from man's labor, and shortened and concentrated it in forms that did not permit the old enjoyment. It gave him time for consumption greater than he had any natural aptitude for. But it also gave him so many goods to consume that he had to hurry to get through them. And he knew how to hurry—he had learned this lesson as an industrial laborer, and it had carried over into his life of consumption. So there is little to choose between the indignities of modern man as a laborer and as a consumer. He is simply, either way, a new man: he was not known as a historical inhabitant of this planet until lately.

That is bad, but it is not the worst. It is conceivable that many persons—of impaired tastes, as most of us now are— might elect to put up with the industrialism that is already in effect, and count themselves sufficiently happy; without thinking of a revolution which would involve sabotage and destruction, and tear down the industrial establishment that exists. They might yet make themselves comfortable—comfortable at their present forms of labor, comfortable even at their present rate of consumption. At both of these they might yet learn to loaf and invite the soul. Hamlet noticed that even grave-diggers could sing at their trade, and was informed: "Custom hath made it in them a property of easiness." Possibly no occupation however industrial, or no schedule of consumption however greedy, is quite hopeless as the source of enjoyment. But its hopefulness is on the assumption that it will stay defined for a while just as it is. There must be such a sense of security behind the industry that the workmen may learn the comfortable and easy ways of laboring at it, and not risk their positions if they seem to be doing less than it is humanly possible for them to do. The consumers in their turn must be delivered from the constant coercion put upon them to buy new commodities, while they learn to make an intelligent use of those they have already undertaken to patronize.

But just there is the trouble. Those who are optimistic, though they may be deeply concerned, about our high-speed industrial order are not reckoning on one thing: industrialization does not intend to stop where it is today. *This is not merely an age of machines but an age of progressive machinery.* We have capitalized the industries, but at the same time we have capitalized the laboratories and inventors, and promised to employ all the machines and labor-saving processes which they may invent. There is not a big industrialist now operating who can consider the present economic basis of his industry as permanent, without running the risk of ruin. There is not a citizen at large who may be assured that he will not always be attacked by the salesmen of new commodities. There is no economic stability. There is progress.

Mr. Millikan is not insensitive to the perils of our rapid changes. In his most recent book he writes:

> I refer to the craze for the new regardless of the true, to the demand for change for the sake of change without reference to the consequences, to the present-day wide-spread worship of the bizarre, to the cheap extravagance and sensationalism that surround us, as evidenced by our newspapers, our magazines, our novels, our drama, our art in most of its forms, our advertising, even our education.

This is tolerably realistic. But it is evident from the context of this passage that Mr. Millikan is not a diagnostician. He names some distressing symptoms, and has an idea there is some sort of disease in the body politic, without having much idea of what it is. It is not the disease of "change for the sake of change," exactly—that is not quite the name of a disease which you can treat. I would suggest that we are suffering from the effects of a bad religion.

Mr. Millikan himself is one of those who are responsible for the new religion and all its consequences. He is the prophet of a God who is both scientific and progressive. From another context I can show how deep is Mr. Millikan's responsibility.

He did a thing which I deplored at the time, and which I would invite him to notice that he too must now deplore, if he has become fearful of the spirit of change for the sake of change. He published in 1928 a little book, "Evolution in

Science and Religion." In this work he undertook to distinguish modern civilization from ancient in respect to their basic ideas.

One basic idea had to do with the question, What is the natural state of bodies on the earth? The Greek physicists answered, The natural state of bodies is a state of rest. But Galileo was not content with this answer.

> He proved conclusively that the natural state of a body is not one of rest, but that it is rather a state of rest *or of motion in a straight line;* and that force or effort is proportional, not to motion, but to the rate of change of motion. In other words, he got the idea that is expressed in the famous equation of motion of Newton's, $f = m\,a$.

The *a* here is for acceleration, or rate of change: the distinctive concept of modern physical science.

> Not a single dynamical machine in existence today can be designed without its aid, not a steam engine, not an automobile, not a dynamo, not a motor, not an aeroplane—not a machine or device of any sort for the transformation of work or the utilization of power. Subtract merely the result $f = m\,a$ from modern civilization and that civilization collapses like a house of cards, and mankind reverts at once to the mode of life existing in ancient times, a life well equipped with statics, such as are involved in building processes, but wholly wanting in dynamics.

The concept of acceleration is of course perfectly innocent as a concept with which to build machines. Unfortunately, Mr. Millikan found in it a new and determining concept of God, of the active spirit of the universe, and of human destiny. It supplied him with a variety of progress all his own. He has much to say about the stern duty of man o get his private life oriented according to the spirit of modern physical science.

We ourselves may be vital agents in the march of things.

The peculiar use of "things" in this saying was probably un-onscious, but it was revealing. It meant that Mr. Millikan wants us to base our lives upon the mechanical laws of things, and cultivate the same acceleration which they do. This may sound rather amusing than otherwise, but ac-ually the doctrine has proved to be a cruel one: people have believed it, and undertaken to go by it. I suppose it did not originate with Mr. Millikan—it could hardly have traveled o widely since his pronouncement. It is so wide-spread that t is quite a commonplace in the church and in the college chapel to hear that men must put their lives on the "dy-amic" basis. As if the machines were not bad enough to keep s servants, and far more expensive in that capacity than we an afford, we are being instructed to take them as our pat-erns. Our God accelerates like a machine, and we must do likewise. This is without any question one of the most fan-astic of the world's religions. This God for monstrosity and ruelty compares favorably with Moloch.

The God of Machines is one variety of the God of Prog-ess. A similar variety, not quite so bad perhaps, is the God of Evolution. This one is due to the instance of the biolo-gists. For they too have conspired against human dignity and private happiness. The biologists of the last century, doubt-ess for very good reasons, came to hold opinions about the onstitutional modifications that the human species had un-ergone in the presumptive course of aeons. Then they be-an to declare that individuals must "consciously hasten" hese modifications in their own poor persons, and thus undertake in private a responsibility which at best had only rested on the broad and unfeeling shoulders of the species. This hastening process they offered as their own contribution to the meaning of progress: it was certainly a contribution that reflected their own special interests.

The biologists were quite religious about this: they talked about the God whose process was evolutionary. And they did not forget to formulate his commandments unto men. For instance, that private persons must cultivate their intellectual development at any expense, and regardless of the resistance of the physical constitution, since progress was to take that direction. Or again, that private persons must become completely selfless and social-minded, and toil for certain abstract social objectives in lieu of their own private happiness. The evolutionary moralists, in fact, were ready to abandon private happiness as perfectly unworthy and to substitute the happiness of the species—which was not demonstrably the happiness of anybody on earth. All this was simply the imposition of the law of species upon the conduct of private life.

But then, as we have seen, came Mr. Millikan, a physicist, with an even more far-fetched proposal. What he would impose upon the conduct of private life is the law of machines. Progress, to Mr. H. G. Wells and the biologists, meant only Evolution. Progress to Mr. Millikan means Dynamics, or Acceleration. I think it is clear that his form of progress is capable of producing more change than theirs, more hurry, and more mischief.

The Greek physicists evidently knew much less than we do about the possibilities of acceleration in machines. But they would have had too much humanity to have welcomed Mr. Millikan's peculiarly modern assumption as to the advantage of accelerating human life. They had a significant legend about Ixion, who for his presumption against the Gods was bound to an ever-turning wheel. Evidently they saw that a development which did very well for a piece of metal would not necessarily do for a piece of flesh. The Greek physiologists would have objected to Mr. Millikan's plan on behalf of the body, and perhaps the psychologists would also have objected on behalf of the soul.

The old God would never have involved our lives in such painful business as this. He was the God whose ways were fairly inscrutable—who had not imparted the secrets of his universe. It was his function to operate the universe in his own way, it was man's function to live modestly and therefore comfortably within it. But the modern scientists defined God as Science; and immediately they began to define him in detail according to the terms of the sciences which they happened to favor; the evolutionists giving him an evolutionary cast, and Mr. Millikan giving him a dynamic one. They conferred upon man the grievous responsibility of being God-like in the sense of practicing evolution or practicing acceleration. And such doctrines as these are the causes and the aggravations of our present distress.

CHAPTER TEN

WHAT DOES HE KNOW?

THE new God is Logos, the great Scientist. We have just examined his practical or productive power, his attempt to make the world more habitable and more possessable for his dutiful creatures. It is now in order to be a little more technical or theoretical, and ask: What is the nature of his knowledge? What are its limits? For we have done our God the doubtful honor of defining his omniscience as science. And we can tell, without researches that are painfully deep, what are the limits of science as a way of knowledge.

Mr. Eddington the astronomer has recently made some alarming revelations about the precariousness of scientific knowledge as he has found it in a particular field. Mr. Whitehead the mathematician had been doing it for some time. In this connection one thinks also of the names of Mr. J. S. Haldane the physiologist, Mr. Bertrand Russell the mathematician, Mr. McDougall the psychologist—and possibly Lord Balfour the statesman. These are British names. They are the names of capable scientists, or at least of men who know their sciences; and they are the names of critics of science who, even within their own professional fields, have resisted the delusions under which scientists often labor.

But where are the corresponding figures in American

cience? Evidently they do not exist here. We have our
minent scientists—two of them have been honored with a
Nobel Prize award in physics—but they must be immersed
n their scientific projects, incapable of detachment, unpro-
ided with a critical equipment. Scientific knowledge enjoys
 peculiar immunity in America, a sort of divine right. It
;oes uncriticized. It is supposed to be final and absolute,
unless at some local point where an issue or two is still being
lisputed between the scientists. There at least do not appear
o scientists to be any major defects in the system of knowl-
dge that science has constructed. Our science basks tropi-
ally in the sunshine of universal veneration, but, just as we
night expect, it is spiritually not too hardy.

Oddly enough, though we are short on critical theory, we
re beginning to develop at home a rather powerful economic
nd practical opposition to science. Practically, our sciences
re heavily capitalized, and turned into great producers:
heir total effort constitutes that formidable thing known as
he American industrial system. The American public has
een completely sold on the benefits of applied science, and
as set in to realize them on a scale never heard of before,
ssuming that the more of them the better. But the ensuing
happiness has not been quite proportionate to the effort, and
Mr. Ayres, Mr. Chase, Mr. Borsodi, and Mr. Adams think
he effort may have been greatly overdone. So that we are in
 fair way to convince ourselves shortly by actual experience
bout the practical limits of our sciences.

But what I have in mind here is the limits of science
s a way of knowledge. It is another question altogether,
nd theoretical rather than practical.

It is quite simple for the poet, or the person of sensibility,
o tell what is the matter with science in this respect. The
ame thing is the matter with theoretical science that was

just now the matter with applied science: *It drives too har*
after its objectives, and pays no attention to the setting.

This is a difference between seeing the abstract and seein
the concrete. We might call our awareness of the concrete
through the exercise of our sensibility, by the term: ap
preciation. Then we may say, roughly, that there are tw
kinds of knowledge, and science is only one of them: th
other knowledge is appreciation, and science unfortunatel
has no acquaintance with it.

This difference may be easily illustrated. Here is a geo
metrical figure which science values very highly—but her
again is a painting which represents a landscape. It woul
be rather ridiculous to say that either one is better than th
other, but it is necessary to say that neither one will sub
stitute for the other. The geometrical figure never becomes
painting, unless a painter takes hold of it and works on it
and then he has to submerge its pure outlines in detail whic
is not at all geometrical. The painting on the other han
never becomes a geometrical figure; though the scientis
might conceivably discover a geometrical pattern conceale
under it, he would have to erase the detail that covers it up
and then it would no longer be a painting.

We will not disparage either the scientist or the painter
Sometimes we require geometry, and sometimes we requir
landscape. I am only pointing out that science is not appre
ciation, and that is a limitation that it can never overcom
so long as it remains science.

Instinct and enjoyment are the corresponding terms tha
we used in examining the practical life. We saw there tha
science serves instinct if we let it alone, and shortens an
concentrates the drive of desire by making it efficient. Bu
one of our human necessities is sometimes to halt our science
delay the drive of appetite, and simply enjoy the worl
upon which we are practicing. It is because industrialism
gives an undue encouragement to science, and too muc

ight of way to appetite, that we have to take the position
hat industrialism is far too dangerous a thing for us to in-
lulge in. But for a similar reason we have to oppose the cult
·f science on its purely theoretical side when it tries to mo-
iopolize our intellectual life.

Nowadays we live in a scientific climate, and it is a cli-
natic change that we need.

Scientific knowledge is always crystal clear—like a geomet-
ical pattern. It is hard and logical—as it must be in order
ɔ serve the Logos. *But it is too restricted in its detail.* That
; the observation which the poet, or person of acute sensibil-
·y, will pass upon it without hesitation. It never cares to
otice the detail which is contingent, outside of expecta-
ion and prediction, irrelevant to the pattern, and distract-
ng. Nothing in fact is so contrary to the intention of
cience as to be distracted, or drawn outside the path of its
worn commitments. But there is nothing which as human
eings we must insist upon more strongly than the obligation
f suffering this distraction. Knowledge is incompetent if it
retends that there really isn't any distracting detail there.
Ve do not make a sufficient contact with the world when we
lect to be exclusively scientific, because that means blind-
ess: that is the intellectual variety of anesthesia.

The worship of the Logos plays us false equally when
· dictates our practical conduct and when it dictates the
·hole form of our knowledge.

The above general criticism of science will do for a be-
inning: it is the criticism of the amateur who is outraged
y the usurpations of science and puts his objections in an
nmediate and not very technical form.

But there is no need to improvise any critical canons with
·hich to investigate the limitations of scientific knowledge.
he criticism of science is presumably about as old as science
:. Our modern science is fairly young, and the so-called

Critical Philosophy which undertook to deal with it was named by Immanuel Kant, but was started before Kant by the British philosophers. I should say that the critical or skeptical principles which modern philosophy has advanced are mainly two: one which goes back to David Hume, now a century and a half in his Edinburgh grave; and one which has been most powerfully urged by our own contemporary, M. Bergson.

Let us look at Hume's principle first.

Hume was a "sensationalist" in the technical sense. He held that knowledge orginates in the evidence of the senses. What we call fact is the sensible phenomenon, either experienced by us or certified to us. But an object which is entertained by the mind but which is not accessible to the senses is something else than fact. It is hypothetical, inferential, fabulous, or fictitious. Hume observed that scientists very generally confused their facts and their fictions. That is the substance of Hume's criticism.

His argument I will render rather freely. One phenomenon is succeeded by another one. In certain cases the scientist says that the first is the cause of the second. But we add nothing to the demonstrable or factual content of the first when we call it the cause of the second. (Nor to the demonstrable or factual content of the second when we call it the effect of the first.) Nevertheless we repeat the phrase lovingly, along with many equivalent phrases which Hume listed: "power, force, energy, necessity, connection, or productive quality." Soon we are likely to imagine that we are witnessing a new quality that is not there. We think we see in it not only the factual qualities, but also an organization of some kind that might conceivably bring about the second phenomenon. We begin to specify the nature of this organization. The first phenomenon by itself was a fact, but when we have invested it with this gratuitous organization it becomes a fiction. It is but too easy to supplement observa-

ion in this way with imagination, and never know we are
loing it.

I will quote a little of Hume's characteristic argument,
hough it will be a little difficult out of its proper context.

> When we talk of any being, whether of a superior or
> inferior nature, as endowed with a power or force,
> proportioned to any effect; when we speak of a neces-
> sary connection betwixt objects, and suppose that this
> connection depends upon an efficacy or energy, with
> which any of these objects are endowed; in all the ex-
> pressions, *so applied,* we have really no distinct mean-
> ing, and make use only of common words, without any
> clear and determinate ideas.

And again:

> Suppose two objects to be presented to us, of which the
> one is the cause and the other the effect; it is plain that,
> from the simple consideration of one or both these ob-
> jects, we never shall perceive the tie by which they are
> united, or be able certainly to pronounce, that there is
> a connection betwixt them.

In answer to this damaging piece of skepticism, it might
be claimed by the scientists that cause-and-effect is not discovered between two objects merely, but between the respective members of a great number of similar pairs of objects:
not between A and B alone, but between the *a* and *b* of
similar couples everywhere. But Hume foresaw this, and is
quite ready with his answer. It makes no difference to his
skepticism:

> But it is evident, in the first place, that the repetition
> of like objects in like relations of succession and con-
> tiguity, *discovers* nothing new in any one of them. . . .
> Secondly, it is certain that this repetition of similar

objects in similar situations, *produces* nothing new either in these objects, or in any external body. For it will readily be allowed, that the several instances we have of the conjunction of resembling causes and effects, are in themselves entirely independent, and that the communication of motion, which I see result at present from the shock of two billiard balls, is totally distinct from that which I saw result from such an impulse a twelvemonth ago. These impulses have no influence on each other. They are entirely divided by time and place; and the one might have existed and communicated motion, though the other had never been in being.

There is, then, nothing new either discovered or produced in any objects by their constant conjunction, and by the uninterrupted resemblance of their relations of succession and contiguity. But it is from this resemblance that the ideas of necessity, of power, and of efficacy, are derived. These ideas, therefore, represent not anything that does or can belong to the objects which are constantly conjoined. This is an argument which, in every view we can examine it, will be found perfectly unanswerable.

And now to enlarge on Hume a little. The gratuitous organization that we confer upon the object—to represent its "power" or its "efficacy"—and to make it a cause—may be quite loose and wavering. Sometimes we improvise some machinery in the object. Sometimes we give it some personality, likening the object to a human person as an effective agent.

Let us look at some of the fictions employed by the sciences. In physical science, we are constantly arriving by mathematical inference at objects that cannot be witnessed by the senses. Generally a sensible phenomenon is crude and massive. A quantity of sodium and a quantity of chlorine become the material cause of a quantity of table salt. But that is a wholesale process. We call for the precise minimum or unit of action, and by mathematical analysis we obtain it. The unit process is the formation of the molecule·NaCl out of the atom Na and the atom Cl; or, Na + Cl = NaCl. Unfortunately, we cannot observe the atoms, or their process, or even the resulting molecule. They are infrasensible. So we have to imagine about them, and what we imagine is imaginary.

It is likewise with the supra-sensible objects, such as the universe, obtained by mathematical synthesis. The quasi-sensible properties we give to this will be fictitious also.

Mr. Eddington reminds us that there never was such a stir and turmoil within the scientific ranks as at this very moment. Theories are changing, and nobody knows just what theories the physicists are going to adopt officially when they think they have solved their new problems sufficiently. He gives the "prying philosophers" some very good advice: they had better not rush to criticize the new theories of atomic constitution and the many-dimensioned universe— for nobody yet knows just what these theories are going to be before they take their final form. The situation is just as if the temple of science were in the hands of its carpenters, with a large sign posted over the door: "No admittance except on business—alterations in progress."

But it is not to be dreamed by anybody that the new and definitive science, when it is completed, will have found a way to get rid of its fictions. The new theory of light, or of gravitation, if it is to have the least bit of content, will have to be fictitious—because the infra-sensible constitution of light or of gravitation will be shown as sensible. So with a new representation of the supra-sensible universe, even if it is not entirely a Euclidean one, and therefore not so pictorial as the old ones. There may be contemplated no new representation of the molecule as a combination of atoms, but the forthcoming representation of the atom as an arrangement of electrons will be a fiction de luxe.

These are mechanical fictions, such as are favored by the physical scientist. A physical scientist is one who prefers his fictions in the shape of machines. But some other scientists prefer theirs in the form of persons, just as religionists do.[1] Consider the meaning of such terms as Life, Evolution, Vitalism, Élan Vital. They look like poorly disguised versions of personality. The person may not be so called, he may go disguised as a Principle, or Guiding Force, or Impersonal Intelligence: but these explanations are dodges: look hard and they stand for a person. He may be kept preferably in a dark room where the skeptic cannot look at him too closely; but whatever is made out of him is something other than a machine.

Then, nearer home, there is the State: a supra-sensible object pictured as having the psychic apparatus to feel and know and will with, and a long arm to enforce its will, the whole person gallantly conceived as a lady. And there is Liberty: a lady clothed in the Greek style, bearing a torch. We hear also of plenty of Movements and Tendencies: spirits that inhabit racial, political, economic, social, military, literary, and many other regions. Much of science is busy with exhibiting spirits of one kind or another.

The spiritual atmosphere may indeed be so thick as to make the visitor rub his eyes to see if he is not attending upon a religious exhibition. For science is often very spiritual,

[1] There is probably no essential difference between the fiction of a machine and the fiction of a personality as the explanation of phenomena. A machine implies a mechanic—who is a person; and a purpose—which brings us into teleology. Mechanistic explanations inevitably reduce to personalistic ones if we linger on them a little. Mr. Pupin has an essay in which he defends the machines of industrialism on the ground that the universe itself is a big machine full of little machines: but now and then he drops into the language of personality as he thinks of what these machines are for, and what good they do, and how they got assembled and started to running.

and comes close to being religious. A sure sign of this mood is to be found in the scientific habit of capitalizing some of its polysyllabic objects. Thus learning unites with imagination to produce those formidable but elusive spirits which fulfill for science the functions that used to be fulfilled by the honest old anthropomorphic deities.

All these fictions are apparent to the modern Humist, who can easily derive them. They are meant to serve for causal explanations. But they have too little visibility, or sensible quality; and in order to be dwelt upon, felt, and experienced in full, they have been stuffed out with fabulous properties.

Hume, then, brought forward this critical method for the examination of science. It penetrated: it made its way even into the physical sciences (having found the other sciences quite too easy), where it showed that a good deal which passed for fact was really fiction.

In leaving Hume, it is necessary to make mention of Kant, if only for the sake of saying that he did not destroy Hume's criticism, but elaborated it. The popular idea of Kant's accomplishment is contained in the saying, "Kant answered Hume." But just how did he answer Hume? I will have to oversimplify Kant's answer, as I have oversimplified Hume's argument which he answered.

Most of the body of scientific knowledge, as Hume had contended, was a mixed tissue of facts and fictions. For example, the causes, the forces, the powers, and all their kind, which bulked large in their scientific importance, were only fictions, so far as there was anything objective and demonstrable which corresponded to them. Kant confirmed this claim entirely; but he added, "They are necessary fictions, which it is according to the constitution of our minds to compose." Kant humanized, regularized, and classified—and in that sense justified—the fictions. If all men as men were

obliged to think in some manner of A as the cause of B, then
the proposition that A was the cause of B had a universality
it was valid for the mind everywhere.

But Kant did not bother to look with a very curious psychology at the precise content that we assume in A as a
cause. How do we see cause there, in what form, doing
what? These questions he did not ask. Unquestionably every
man, if he tarries on a cause, fills it up in his own way: he
cannot keep the image of it from forming in his mind, but
it may not be a fully conscious one. It is safe to invite every
man to construe his causes to suit himself, and then to tell
him that they are certainly quite fantastic and improbable

Kant classified the fictions under categories, which are
simply the leading types of fictions that the universal mind
imposes upon the barren facts. They are the *principles* which
the mind assumes as underlying the facts. Kant established
beyond question the human necessity of assuming principles
in our science. But he pointed out painfully, and reiterated
it a thousand times, that the principles are subjective, have
no basis in fact, are not of the same kind of knowledge as
the sensible facts.

I have interpolated between Hume and Bergson this in-
adequate section about Kant only to show that he did not
deny Hume's critical doctrine, nor yet added another critical doctrine. He built up Hume's doctrine in systematic
style.

It remained for Bergson, as I see it, to name a quite different critical doctrine.

The skepticism of Bergson takes off in a different direction
from Hume's. To many of the objects of our science Hume
would be crying, Fiction! But Bergson always, for his peculiar criticism, cries, Abstraction! According to Hume, science
is given to seeing in a situation a little more machinery or
a little more personality that it can ever demonstrate. But

according to Bergson science is careful not to see in a situation all the sensible facts that are there. It is Hume's view that science tells more than the truth, it is Bergson's view that science tells less than the truth.

Both views are justified, but in different contexts.

To get Bergson's view, let us think not so much of the sensible images that science employs to represent the hidden operations of nature, as of those formulas and definitions that provide the scientific rules for our positive action. Scientific knowledge in the practical sense is a vast system of classifications, generalizations, and directions. Science tells us how to dispose of any particular thing for the sake of our systematic knowledge, and the method is surprisingly simple: Give the thing its classification and go on to the next thing. But the trouble is that the particular thing will not stay where it is put. The particular always exceeds the class in the variety of its quality, and can never be contained within the class definition. If we look observantly at it, it comes out of its classification and exhibits a vigorous and various individuality all its own. As the old books of logic used to say, you can define man but not Socrates. It is the limitation of science that it has no technique for apprehending Socrates, and has to remain blind to his existence.

And this is just the criticism that I represented the ordinary amateur in philosophy as passing on science, at the beginning of the chapter. Every poet, every religionist, everybody with a touch of Oriental mentality, every sensitive person, every person with the beginnings of philosophical wisdom, would offer just this criticism—which it is right to call Bergsonian, because Bergson made the argument with so much force that it cannot be dissociated from his name. All these people would see at once that science with its abstract types and patterns disposed too brutally and quickly of the particulars which it encountered, and that it really had no use for particularity, and no sense of it. Science is an ab-

stract way of knowledge, but there is also a concrete way
This is a very serious limitation upon the validity of science

M. Bergson has not been specially interested, I am sorry
to say, in defending the particularity of physical objects. He
has devoted himself to defending the particularity of living
organisms, and of states of mind. There his labors have been
very telling. He has shown that consciousness is free, in the
sense that science cannot predict or determine a conscious
state, which in its fullness exceeds definition. He has fought
and triumphed on behalf of that apparently lost cause, Free
Will, indicating the irreducible wholeness of the mind at
each moment. And with respect to the biological forms or
species, he has shown that their emergence always presents
novelties which were not included in any knowledge of the
parent forms. This is a gospel of Indeterminateness, or Contingency, which he regards as entering constitutionally, and
fatally so far as predictive science is concerned, into the
working world. But this gospel is for the salvation of living
organism and psyche only.

For example Bergson refers to the way scientists are wont
to assert that some conscious state is determined in some very
simple manner which they can indicate:

> It is only an inaccurate psychology, misled by language,
> which will show us the soul determined by sympathy,
> aversion, or hate, as though by so many forces pressing
> upon it. These feelings, provided they go deep enough,
> each make up the whole soul, since the whole content of
> the soul is reflected in each of them. To say the soul is
> determined under the influence of any one of these feel-
> ings is thus to recognize that it is self-determined.

"The whole content of the soul is reflected in each one
of them." It is common enough for science to single out
some favorite aspect, something simple, as the "essence" of

a whole and to throw the rest away—that is the way to build up a systematic knowledge. But sensibility, reviewing the situation, recovers its wholeness. The "essential" aspect by which science defines the whole becomes again just one of many aspects, and presently we have, not an essence, but a particular in its fullness. Bergson recovers to consciousness the dignity of its particularity.

But he might just as well, I should think, have saved the inorganic objects too. It may be more gratifying to us that living beings like ourselves should be set free than that things should be set free, and one may be willing, if sure of one's own emancipation, to abandon the things to complete mechanical determination. But we need not if we do not wish. The things too are whole and free if we look closely enough—that is, they are free enough to baffle any determination that the sciences would like to impose upon them. For example I will cite the first pebble that we can pick up on going out of the room in which we are sitting now. Let us challenge the geometer to define for us the configuration of the pebble. The gallant pebble will defy the geometer, for its configuration is not a matter of regular or geometrical surfaces, and the geometer after great effort will only succeed in producing a rough approximate description. But this is true of things always. Being particular, a thing is of inexhaustible qualitative variety and its concrete energy will never submit to determination.

So here are Charybdis and Scylla, the Whirlpool of the Fabulous and the barren Rock of the Abstract, the alternate perils between which the fastidious thinker would like to steer his course. It seems unlikely that he will manage to avoid either peril. On the one side he will find himself drifting out of the stream into a monstrous world of deep waters, where he whirls till he grows dizzy with uncertainty, and does not know whether he sees objects or hallucinations. But again on the other side in due time he will find himself driving furiously on errands so simple and exclusive that he is soon out of the living water altogether, stranded high and dry, and not a sailor any more. Man as Thinker or as Scientist must wreck himself, one way or the other, again and again. His obvious immortality will keep him from perishing, and get him back into the current.

Can science avoid Charybdis? Not all the scientists fail to see this peril: they may know very well when they are dealing in fictions. Mr. Eddington knows, and he always confesses handsomely. Other European scientists confess often; American scientists less often. But the Positivists think it is quite possible to write science without using any fictions at all, just sticking to pure facts. I suggest that somebody who is competent take Mr. Eddington's book, "The Nature of the Physical World," and examine it with an expert psychology, in order to determine just what is left of the story when every mathematical object there has been pared of those sensible properties that cling to it in our stubborn associations, but are not actually demonstrable. It is my idea that the story that remained would not be intelligible at all. But I am even more confident that the stories written by the biologist and the human historian would not survive this test.

But there is a good joke here at somebody's expense, which has not had half the circulation it deserved. (The Positivists do not like to hear it.) It was perpetrated by David Hume, who amused his superior mind not a little with the frailties of his contemporaries in the world of thought. Almost from time immemorial the scientists had perceived and exposed the fictions current in theological circles. They had visited the religious establishment and made disparaging remarks. For example, the God who spoke Hebrew to Moses' ears, begat his Son of a virgin, and indulged in alternating moods of favoritism and vindictiveness—this God was too fictitious for the scientists of Hume's day. Indeed, no homely anthropomorphic God would suit them, in the absence of sensible evidence that could be historically attested. Their skepticism was a damaging one to apply against religionists who said they saw and heard and felt their God; though it rather fell to the ground so far as it touched those religionists who said they only thought their God. But then came David Hume with their own precise form of skepticism, but applying it against their own objects of science. He did not hunt down the simple religionists, he found his game among the enlightened scientists. They were thinking or imagining their objects, often enough, which could never be demonstrated or placed on the level of actual reality. Hume's delicious pastime was to hoist the engineer with his own petard.

But at any rate science cannot possibly dodge Scylla. The nature of its professional business requires it to steer to the right. Bergson put his finger on the essential weakness when he showed how science is obliged to deal entirely with universals. All logic is an exercise in universals. Particulars are delightful things to contemplate, as the painter contemplates his landscape, or the lover his beloved, but science is practical and purposive and must deal strictly with some selected aspect of the particulars which it encounters.

A heavy penalty must be paid for every decisive action, whether it is an action of our hands or of our minds, that we take in order to dispose of an objective situation. The object acted upon, even if it is only acted upon by the mind in the definitive way of science, immediately conceals its particularity and vanishes into thin air. This would seem to furnish an excellent reason why we should not indulge in more action than is needful. The Orientals know all about such matters.

If M. Bergson had defended the freedom of inorganic as well as of organic objects, he might readily have become the great champion of the arts, for the freedom of their objects is precisely what they are devoted to. The artistic representation of a particular is itself particular—infinite in its wealth of quality, though doubtless an abridgment of the infinity of the original. Art celebrates the concrete, the richly sensible, and M. Bergson as the exponent of the free will was in a position to expound also the freedom of the artistic object. But he did go so far as to make one generous motion on behalf of art when he wrote his little book on laughter— an important chapter for esthetic theory.

And M. Bergson might easily have defended orthodoxy in religion. He has not come to this point, though many religionists have taken comfort from his doctrines, and M. Chevalier, his Roman Catholic disciple, has undertaken to show the favorable implication that they have for orthodoxy. The Bergsonian point of view here is the same as that of a Hebrew poet: The earth is the Lord's and the fullness thereof. Emphasis on the fullness. But the deity whom scientists worship preferably is not very full nor representative. They enthrone him as the one who is to determine the world under the finite qualifications that they can name and classify. They refer to him in such a phrase as the Uniformity of Nature. They mean that he does not desire in his world any particularity or contingency, but only uniform or indifferent instances of type. Their wish is father to their thought, for they want to believe that he has simplified the world so that it may fall completely into their possession. The truth is, of course, that it never does.

The Logos is only a Demigod. He exists, properly enough, in the sense that our sciences are possible. But he is not the whole God, in sense that the sciences render so much less than a complete account of the world. They have their limitations: and he, as their patron, has his.

CHAPTER ELEVEN

A TABLE AND A GEOGRAPHICAL MACHINE

I F so simple a statement of them did not spoil them, those were the two criticisms which Hume and Bergson had brought to bear upon science as a form of knowledge: Hume showing the illusions or fictions in it, and Bergson showing its abstractness, non-particularity, or incompleteness.

The remarkable activity which is now going on in physical science has evidently inspired hopes that these defects, or any others that might once have been imputed to science, are going to be overcome. There are those who actually believe that through physics we are about to secure a fairly complete and perfectly competent knowledge of the universe. This is a separate chapter in honor of physics alone.

Mr. Eddington the physicist—who has certainly a good store of metaphysical genius too—is not ordinarily a comfort to those who entertain such hope, and in fact his influence as a general thing is quite in the opposite sense. I do not like to cite him as a source of error. But if he has unguardedly committed error upon an occasion or so, he is all the more valuable as an exhibit of what the powerful temptations of science will do to even a very critical mind.

Mr. Russell the mathematician and philosopher is one of the most ruthless thinkers of this generation. But he too is fascinated by the positive achievements of science and he commits what, to my way of thinking, are errors. He has passages which seem to lend support to the false hope which I have mentioned.

Mr. Eddington has talked about his study table in what I consider to be deceptive terms, and Mr. Russell has been even more explicitly in error in talking about a certain imaginary geographical machine. The Eddington table and the Russell geographical machine come to exactly the same thing in the way they lead us to estimate the value of the physical sciences. If we look rather closely at them they will serve us beautifully in seeing the revolutionary expectations popularly held for the new science.

Both the table and the geographical machine are entirely subject to the invincible criticism which Hume and Bergson have put into our hands if we want it. Mr. Eddington and Mr. Russell have installed in their contrivances no patent features which give them immunity against skeptics of either of those usual orders. And therefore, if I put in here a chapter about them, it will serve as illustrative matter for the principles stated in the previous chapter.

But furthermore: the table and the machine, as we shall inspect them, will suggest still another principle of criticism which does not seem to be either Humian or Bergsonian. This will be a third principle—not comparable perhaps in importance with those two principles, and not so spectacular, but nevertheless worth noticing. And in that respect this will be a new chapter.

It is in the Introduction to his "Nature of the Physical World" that Mr. Eddington exhibits his table. He sits down to write his book, and he has a choice of two tables on which to rest his manuscript. One is the ordinary study table that we would see him at if we looked. The other is the table

that a physicist would find in it or under it. It is the latter
table that Mr. Eddington seems at the moment to prefer.

The first table needs no comment—none from me, at
least, and none to the ordinary kind of reader. It is the
common or parlor variety of table: it is not mysterious and
repulsive to anybody but a physicist. Its principal quality is
that it is solid or *substantial*. But this is the very quality
which the new order of physicists will not put up with.
Here is their table:

Table No. 2 is my scientific table. It is a more recent
acquaintance and I do not feel so familiar with it. It
does not belong to the world previously mentioned—
that world which spontaneously appears around me
when I open my eyes, though how much of it is objective and how much subjective I do not here consider.
It is a part of a world which in more devious ways has
forced itself on my attention. My scientific table is
mostly emptiness. Sparsely scattered in that emptiness
are numerous electric charges rushing about with great
speed; but their combined bulk amounts to less than
a billionth [1] of the bulk of the table itself. Notwith-
standing its strange construction it turns out to be an entirely efficient table. It supports my writing paper as
satisfactorily as Table No. 1; for when I lay the paper
on it the little electric particles with their headlong
speed keep on hitting the underside, so that the paper
is maintained in shuttlecock fashion at a nearly steady
level. If I lean upon this table I shall not go through;
or, to be strictly accurate, the chance of my scientific
elbow going through my scientific table is so excessively
small that it can be neglected in practical life. Review-

[1] To get the full force of this I will quote a sentence from Mr. Eddington's Preface: "It may be necessary to remind the American reader that our
nomenclature for large numbers differs from his, so that a billion here means
a million million."

ing their properties one by one, there seems to be nothing to choose between the two tables for ordinary purposes; but when abnormal circumstances befall, then my scientific table shows to advantage. If the house catches fire my scientific table will dissolve into scientific smoke, whereas my familiar table undergoes a metamorphosis of its substantial nature which I can only regard as miraculous.

There is nothing *substantial* about my second table. It is nearly all empty space—space pervaded, it is true, by fields of force, but these are assigned to the category of "influences," not of "things." Even in the minute part which is not empty we must not transfer the old notion of substance. In dissecting matter into electric charges we have traveled far from that picture of it which first gave rise to the conception of substance, and the meaning of that conception—if it ever had any— has been lost by the way. The whole trend of modern scientific views is to break down the separate categories of "things," "influences," "forms," etc., and to substitute a common background of all experience.

Then follows Mr. Eddington's commitment as a physicist to Table No. 2:

I need not tell you that modern physics has by delicate test and remorseless logic assured me that my second scientific table is the only one which is really there—wherever "there" may be. On the other hand I need not tell you that modern physics will never succeed in exorcising that first table—strange compound of external nature, mental imagery and inherited prejudice—which lies visible to my eyes and tangible to my grasp. We must bid good-by to it for the present, for we are about to turn from the familiar world to the scientific world revealed by physics. This is, or is intended to be, a wholly external world.

This is a sniffish language to use at the expense of Table No. 1—our kind of table. But Mr. Eddington goes on to say, in effect, that physics now cannot use tables that are made out of wood, or other common substances:

> The physicist used to borrow the raw material of his world from the familiar world, but he does so no longer. His raw materials are aether, electrons, quanta, potentials, Hamiltonian functions, etc.

Reality, or externality—these are Mr. Eddington's own terms—attaches exclusively, then, to tables built out of electrons, and such raw materials. The common table is false and subjective. And this is a very flat statement, I believe, of the physicist's ordinary and professional attitude.

But it is not worthy of Mr. Eddington.

It is not quite the point of view which Mr. Eddington observes for the most part through his book. If it were, his book would hardly have been hailed as such an unprofessional interpretation of physics as a form of knowledge.

He swings back toward the opposite point of view almost immediately, while still in his Introduction. It occurs to him now that the electrons, and such other raw materials as the physicists fancy, are merely shadows—that they have lost all life and content.

> The external world of physics has thus become a a world of shadows. In removing our illusions we have removed the substance, for indeed we have seen that substance is one of the greatest of our illusions. Later perhaps we may inquire whether in our zeal to cut out all that is unreal we may not have used the knife too ruthlessly. Perhaps, indeed, reality is a child which

cannot survive without its nurse illusion. But if so, that
is of little concern to the scientist, who has good and
sufficient reasons for pursuing his investigations in the
world of shadows and is content to leave to the philosopher the determination of its exact status in regard to
reality. In the world of physics we watch a shadow-
graph performance of the drama of familiar life. The
shadow of my elbow rests on the shadow table as the
shadow ink flows over the shadow paper. It is all symbolic, and as a symbol the physicist leaves it. Then comes
the alchemist Mind who transmutes the symbols. The
sparsely spread nuclei of electric force become a tangible solid; their restless agitation becomes the warmth
of summer; the octave of aethereal vibrations becomes
a gorgeous rainbow. Nor does the alchemy stop here.
In the transmuted world new significances arise which
are scarcely to be traced in the world of symbols; so that
it becomes a world of beauty and purpose—and, alas,
suffering and evil.

Mr. Eddington is a sound man who reveals his humanity
here. He does not care to leave the ordinary world altogether and become the ascetic of the physical laboratory.
But his philosophy, with these contradictions in it, is a hard
one to make out. His oscillation of attitudes indicates that he
is not quite decided about some things.

Mr. Eddington said some things which were too good for
his Table No. 2. Both Hume and Bergson could have taken
hold of that table and punctured it, in spite of the shuttlecock energy of its electric particles resisting foreign invasion, and in spite of all the physicists could do.

Hume would have got through easily. He would have
asked the physicists to *show* him their table. They would
have had to reply that it was invisible and insensible, and

that they had not found it but *constructed* it out of Table No. 1; to which he would have replied, "Is the object which you infer any less fictitious than the object from which you infer it?"

Hume would have been assisted (especially for bringing conviction on this point to philosophers who want their terms a little more technical) by his successor Kant. For Kant would have shown that the physicists simply apply to the phenomena of sense their professional forms of thinking, which are a matter of subjective constitution, in order to produce their table; and that their forms of thinking, with respect to external reality, are not a bit better than the forms of thinking which the rest of us apply in order to compose our table.

And Hume would have been assisted also by Mr. Eddington himself, at many points of his book—by Mr. Eddington *passim*. For Mr. Eddington in this book is by no means a loyal professional physicist. He lays bare the assumptions of physics now and again as subjective and arbitrary. His description of the physical world is doubtless the most remarkable exposure of the subjectivism of physics that any physicist has ever written.

And as for Bergson, Table No. 2 offers no difficulties greater than many others which he has successfully overcome in the past. Years ago, M. Bergson broke down, in his "Matter and Memory," the claims of psycho-physics. This was a European school of thought which was one of the spiritual ancestors of modern American behaviorism. Here were psychologists who could not manipulate the data of consciousness to their satisfaction, and therefore decided to reduce them to data of chemistry and physics. The physical data were comparatively precise, hard, and measurable: the psychic data were comparatively massive, loose, and imponderable. A passion for control led them to abandon the difficult field for the easy one—the higher for the lower. But the same passion operates everywhere in the intellectual world. Science is always neater, more mathematical, and more efficient as it goes down the scale of phenomena from higher to lower; so scientists are always tending to take that direction. This is what happens when a scientist, for example, is unwilling to take the rich complex of color as a finality, but reduces it into a measured location on the spectrum, or else into a numerical vibration-frequency. At the latter point the color may be said to disappear: there is too little of it left to be worthy of the name. It is not to be denied that the vibration-frequency is within the complex of the color, but it is certain that the color is not in the vibration-frequency. The net result is that the scientist has elected *to abstract something from the color which he can manage*. I do not mean to say that there is anything unnatural or criminal in that.

The usual limitation of science is symbolized perfectly in defining the color by the vibration-frequency, which is to substitute the part for the whole.

The physicists have no warrant for saying that Table No. 2 contains all that is real in Table No. 1, the rest of it having been illusory. They mean simply that Table No. 2 contains all that they want of Table No. 1. They have an immense interest in Table No. 2; but this interest is only a partiality or an interest which is exclusive, arbitrary, and perfectly selfish.

Table No. 2 fills us of course with admiration—it is a difficult and ingenious construction, a marvel of science. But I would look at it now from a new point of view. It is a pragmatic point of view. Just what do the scientists want with that table? What does it give them? Why on earth do they abandon the homely and solid qualities that attach to Table No. 1 and are the ground of all the sentimental associations that any table can ever have, in favor of so strange and apparently useless a thing as Table No. 2? The answer is that it is not useless: they expect it to be extremely useful, and so does nearly everybody else just now. Table No. 2 is not a mere scientific amusement. It represents an imposing and ambitious undertaking that science has just now in charge; a revolution in scientific technique will be brought about if it succeeds; and in short it is either the most dazzling project that science ever broached, or it is one of the most dazzling projects. Mr. Eddington scarcely treats this matter at all, except by a give-away phrase or so. He is interested in showing what his scientific table *is*, not what it *is for*. So I will have to guess.

It is my guess, in brief, that the scientists, with their Tables No. 2, hope to have, in the first place, *a means of predicting Tables No. 1;* and in the second place, *a means of producing Tables No. 1.* They have their eye on the origins of being, and they mean to take a hand in those origins in a marvelous way. In Table No. 2 they seem to have found something like the philosopher's stone.

Physical science has a new raw material, and wants to know what can be made of it. Table No. 2 is evidently regarded as the "makings" of Table No. 1. It is a test case which is worth our examination. In what sense is Table No. 1 made out of Table No. 2? For if tables—tables of our sort, the practical tables that cost money—can be made out of this new material, so can other valuable things. That is the importance of Table No. 2. Otherwise why does it lead Mr. Eddington into talking about breaking down the separate categories and substituting a "common background of all experience"?

Everybody knows that our table (No. 1) is made out of something: everybody sees that it is a good thing to know what. Ordinarily we will find, let us say, that it is made out of slabs of oak wook, and through a process understood by the cabinet-maker. But what is oak wood made out of? We consider that oak wood simply grows, with a little encouragement perhaps, and as long as we had plenty of oak wood we would not bother to ask that question. But suppose we ran out of oak wood, and began to think of a substitute, or a synthetic oak wood? Then we would have to refer the question to the chemist. The chemist would find that oak wood is an aggregate of homogeneous units or molecules, and each characteristic molecule is made out of elemental atoms, so many of each kind. He knows where the elemental atoms are to be secured, and it is his business to arrange for their combination into suitable molecules. *The chemist prepares the material for the cabinet-maker.*

But what are the elemental atoms made out of? The ordinary chemist stops there. The atoms he has regarded as atoms; that is, as units of material which could not be further divided, and which were of some ninety-two different kinds. But now comes the modern physicist, who refuses to consider the atom an atom, but analyzes it into its parts. The constituent parts are electrons, plus a few protons. And all the electrons are of one single kind, for he can transmute one kind of atom into another kind simply by recombining the electrons. Just here is the promise of the physicist's usefulness. If the simple chemist runs out of the right kind of atoms, the physicist will take the atoms that are available and turn them into the right kind. *He controls the source of materials for the chemist.*

But to supply the original material is one thing, and to determine the final product is another. Before the assemblage of electrons becomes our sensible table, it has to become an assemblage of atoms. That is what the physicist will be peculiarly the one to predict and to effect. But there his usefulness ends, there the matter passes out of his hands.

For then the assemblage of atoms has to undergo a re-assemblage and become an assemblage of oaken molecules: that process is under the direction of the chemist. Then the oak wood has to be assembled into the table, and that is work for the cabinet-maker.

The physicist cannot go from his electrons direct to the table. Knowing only his electrons, he knows, as a matter of fact, nothing about a table. Mr. Eddington has referred to his electrons as raw material, and that is all they are; they are very raw indeed; *they are not ready to go into anything so far along in the series of processes as a table.*

Table No. 2, therefore, which the scientist thinks he has in his possession, is something, and it may prove to be something valuable, but it is not a table. It will never compete with Table No. 1, and Table No. 1 is safe. So much for Mr. Eddington's two tables.

From this point of view let us now take a look at Mr. Russell's geographical machine. It is constructed with the same ideas in mind, only much more frankly.

This machine is not yet actualized, of course; and in the absence of any very detailed specifications probably nobody has yet attempted its construction in fact. But it is "theoretically" possible, according to Mr. Russell, who describes it in his little book, "What I Believe," where he briefly reviews the recent accomplishments of science.

I have not seen any discussion which the geographical machine may have provoked. It was proposed some five years ago, and indicated the hopes which were then rising high wherever the wonders of the new science were being talked about. Perhaps Mr. Russell's readers did not think the prospect he outlined particularly extravagant. They would hardly have counted it as in the same class, for improbability, with a perpetual-motion machine. There were certainly plenty of people then, as there would be plenty now, who took it rather as a matter of course.

Here it is:

> Physical science is thus approaching the stage when it will be complete. . . . Given the laws governing the motion of electrons and protons, the rest is merely geography—a collection of particular facts telling their distribution throughout some portion of the world's history. The total number of facts of geography required to determine the world's history is probably finite; theoretically, they could all be written down in a big book to be kept at Somerset House, with a calculating machine attached, which, by turning a handle, would enable the inquirer to find out the facts at other times than those recorded.

From this we are to understand that physical science, knowing the electrons, knows everything else, and is theoretically capable of setting up and operating a prediction-machine which, from the plot of the electrons at a given moment, will reveal all the future events into which they will enter. It is well known, to be sure, that physical science has been wasting no time in the feverish activities of its recent years. The geographical machine which Mr. Russell proposes is his idea of the result that physical science has accomplished, and we can see that it is the very goal toward which the ambition of physicists has long, and more or less consciously, been tending. It is a fairly widespread belief that a knowledge of the geography and habits of electrons, and of such-like "raw materials" of the new science, provides a knowledge of everything in the world.

It must be admitted that Mr. Russell himself, and also Mr. Eddington, would make the reservation: everything in the physical world, but not everything in the world of consciousness. But many other scientists would scorn that or any other reservation as unworthy of the glorious destiny of science.

But the skeptical mind, however amiable it may be, will think up all too easily the objections to Mr. Russell's machine. It won't work. If the critic knows his Hume and his Bergson, the appropriate objections will appear at once; and perhaps his common sense will suggest still others. I will list some of the difficulties in order as they occur to my unscientific mind.

(1) There is one difficulty that Mr. Eddington in writings later than Mr. Russell's, and undoubtedly Mr. Russell too by this time, is well aware of. And that is the difficulty of charting the elusive electrons. Mr. Russell was a little premature; the electrons have not behaved as nicely as was once expected of them. This is a practical difficulty, and it seems to be this difficulty rather than any theoretical considerations which has caused Mr. Eddington to break with his fellow scientists, and to dash their hopes by refuting the general idea that physics is a flourishing example of a truly determinate science. Mr. Eddington has seen it tried, and it simply isn't. He gives testimony on the issue of the fact.

The more the electrons are studied, even under the most favorable possible conditions in the laboratory, the harder they become to define with respect to their location and material nature. Every process that handles them must treat them in great multitudes. They are not isolable. They are in fabulously rapid motion. Their geographical arrangement within any single atom, even the simplest, is at the present time purely inferential or fictitious. The physicists have scarcely begun as yet to agree upon the official fiction, which is not going to be less fictitious for being official. And therefore any map of the electrons in a region, so far as the pres-

ent state of the science enables us to tell, is going to be
largely fraudulent, or else given to vagueness and indecision in a manner unusual for self-respecting cartography

(2) Another objection is close kin to the first one. It would
seem to be expected by Mr. Russell that the physicist, by
knowing the electrons, will now be able to accomplish what
many other scientists hitherto have only piously aimed at
complete prediction. But how will he manage that? I believe it is in Mr. Russell's mind to answer: by possessing the
chart of *all* the electrons. How to secure this all in his acquaintance with the electrons is the problem.

A geologist makes a feeble effort, let us imagine, at predicting earthquakes. However, he has an excellent alibi: he
cannot get enough of the subterranean data that he needs
The region he is concerned with is not entirely accessible to
the geologist. But is it accessible to the physicist? It seems to
be assumed that the physicist will be able to chart the electrons in regions where the geologist and other scientists cannot chart even their much grosser molecular or mineral substances. "The number of facts required to determine the
world's history is probably finite," says Mr. Russell in an
off-hand manner. But it is at least very large. And the question is whether the physicist is going to be able to get at the
electronic facts any more fully than other scientists can get
at much cruder and more massive facts. Is the cartographer
who supplies his machine going to be furnished with an
electron-detector?

It is unfortunate that, at present, the order in which electrons are found and charted is evidently just the reverse
at present the chemical material is the given, and within
that—within very small portions of that, indeed—the electrons are hunted for—and partly discovered and partly improvised there. So that the machine will probably have to
start with a good deal less than all the electrons in some

regions about which information is sought, and it will have to base its predictions there upon only *some*. In which case it will have no special advantages in respect to completeness over the machinery of prediction already in effect—and that is not much to say for it.

(3) The electrons are in size something less than minute, and accordingly the map, and the attached machine, will have to be something more than large. An ordinary molecule is small enough to elude a powerful miscroscope. An atom is perhaps smaller. But small as is the diameter of an atom, it is said to be 50,000 times the diameter of an electron. It follows that a map which just managed to chart all the atoms in a region—and a good-sized map that would be—would have to have its scale magnified 50,000 times to chart the electrons.   Most maps are reductions.   The ordnance maps which I once used in artillery training, for instance, were on the scale of 1 to 20,000. An architect's plan for a house might well be on the scale of 1 to 24. But the proposed map is no ordinary map, because it is an enlargement, not a reduction. The scale will therefore have to be inverted—24 to 1, or 20,000 to 1. Or rather, Mr. Russell's map, if its notations are to be visible at all, will have to be many millions of times as large as the region it is charting.

How then could Somerset House hold the map which showed the "facts of geography required to determine the world's history," even though the number of facts were "probably finite"? The area of Britain would not contain the map of the electrons of Somerset House alone. Neither Britain nor Somerset House, nor any other area for that matter, would contain the map of its own electrons. And Somerset House could certainly not begin to contain the map of the electrons of Mr. Eddington's table. We might figure as to whether the finite universe now conceived by the physicists would be big enough to contain the map of the solar system, or even of this planet.

Mr. Russell does not speak exactly of a map, but of a book "recording" the geographical facts. The briefest record imaginable is their notation on a map, but of course this map need not be spread out all at once horizontally; it might be paged in a book, if the machine could use it in that way, and then the space required to hold it would be less formidable. But at least it is mathematically certain that the record, of whatever form it might be, would never be able to include the representation of itself. The best the machine could do in handling the geography of electrons would be to treat a tiny section of itself.

(4) The critic who knows his Bergson will now raise an objection which has proved damaging against all the machines that have ever been constructed hitherto, with the remark that he sees no reason why it should not once more prove so against Mr. Russell's machine. Machines never take into consideration the particularity of particulars: you feed a machine with homogeneous stuff, and you get back homogeneous stuff.

The new machine is to treat the facts furnished by a map, and unfortunately a map, though itself ordinarily a great abridgment of reality, will still deal with particular facts. Nothing is more particular than the relative position of a lot of natural objects. They do not assume those ideal configurations so highly fancied by the geometer. At least there is not any reason why they should, and if they do, it is an accident which has to be verified just as laboriously as if they were perfectly irregular. Exact scientists cannot define the contours of the nearest pebble, nor those of the most monotonous landscape. Cartographers do not try to define them: they try only to copy them. Maps at the best, however, do great violence to their objects. Generally they sacrifice the dimension of elevation and try to represent their objects as they might be vertically projected on a plane surface. But even the reduced display on the plane surface is still highly particular, and cannot safely be generalized, or machined. It does not matter whether the display is of lands, seas, grains of sand, drops of water, molecules, atoms, or electrons.

But when the operator turns the big crank of Mr. Russell's geographical machine, the particular facts will have their particularity well rubbed off them. The prediction which follows will be like the usual one: simple, gross, and lacking in specifications. The logic of universals—the only basis that a machine can be constructed on—leads to the prediction of universals but never to the prediction of a single whole particular. "Given the laws governing the motions," says Mr. Russell in his premise—but the laws govern only universals, not events in the whole of their qualitative variety. It has always been felt by competent observers, and Bergson reassures them if they lacked any confidence in their observation, that *an event in its fullness can never be predicted.*

What would a complete act of prediction be like? "I see an island formed in a stream," our oracle would say, consulting his record of electrons. The critic will call for details. Will the oracle give a true map of it? May not a map generate another map as particular as itself? Hardly: that is against the rules. But on second thought this persistent critic even wants an image of the island that is psychically complete, not merely a map, that he can explore with all his senses, and know as if it were present before him. At this point the oracle will fall into a deep silence. Obviously a map cannot generate a landscape.

These are some of the logical objections to incline us against putting much faith in Mr. Russell's prediction-machine. If it is ever constructed and put on exhibition, it will have to have met and answered each one of them, and the critic will be there to see it done. But there is at least one other objection. The critic takes exception to a certain claim, not one which Mr. Russell makes in so many words, but one which he thinks Mr. Russell has in the back of his mind. And not only Mr. Russell. Even Mr. Eddington seems to have it in his mind. But whether or not Mr. Russell and Mr. Eddington are counting on the machine for this peculiar benefit, there are a great many people who are; and here it is.

(5) It is assumed that physics, with its hard-won electrons, is going to dispense with the other sciences and predict finished events, such as tables, directly, immediately. Here is one of the most revolutionary advantages seen in the new physics. The other sciences are rather expected to bow themselves out in favor of this key-science. This is the day of physics.

But we have seen in what sense the electrons are the "makings" of the table: by no means directly. The table is made out of a molecular substance by a carpenter, the molecular substance is made out of atomic elements by a chemist, and the atomic elements are made out of electrons by a physicist. But no chemist can make the table out of atomic elements, and no physicist can make it out of electrons.

And as for prediction, Mr. Russell's geographical machine presumably will know its electrons, but what can it predict from them? Only the things that are made out of electrons. A field of electrons may generate some electricity, or some atomic elements. But that is all.

There is a progression in the stages of composition which is fixed by nature, and which forbids skipping. This progression operates just the same whether in prediction or in production. Substitute for the table a natural object such as a tree. If you care to predict a tree, you must do it as a botanist, you cannot do it as a chemist, and still less as a physicist.

And this is what I meant in saying there was a principle needed which neither the skeptical Hume nor the skeptical Bergson had exactly propounded. I see it is not a highly technical or difficult principle, being rather a principle of the ordinary "common sense" variety. But I think a good many false hopes might have been avoided if it had been written out and pinned over the desk as a reminder to all the writers on contemporary science. I will try to phrase it properly:

The material facts in the analysis of an object have to do with the material parts which compose it immediately, and the more ultimate facts revealed by an analysis of the parts are not material to the object but only to the parts.

There are many sciences, even many physical sciences. Their laws are ordinarily the formulas of composition which relate the facts material to the prediction or the production of objects and events. In order either to predict or to effect the objects and events, you have to know their material causes—not the causes of the causes. It is vain to talk about discovering causes unless you mean material or immediate causes.

There is no limit to the number of types of objects and events, whether the natural ones we try to predict or the artificial ones we manufacture. For every type there is a science (or sub-science) or a technique, which is expert in its material causes. That is what science is for. Each science has a monopoly on the special materials it studies and the recipes for compounding them. There is no short-cut single science which can do the work for all. The miller handles the wheat but he cannot bake the bread, nor even predict what bread will be baked out of it. Still less can the farmer who grows the wheat in his field. The cook stands between the miller and the bread, and the cook and the miller both stand between the farmer and the bread.

As a matter of fact, the objects and events are far more various than even the great number of the sciences would ever indicate—each one being unique or particular, and never duplicating another one. For the critic in his most militant mood there are too few sciences rather than too many, though as a practical man he is disposed to concede that a science is obliged to deal grossly with general types or sets of objects and processes. But at least the sciences that there are cannot possibly be reduced in their number and still get their work done.

But now the world, or at least some of it, is disposed to think that, when the new physics shall have consolidated its conquests, all the materials will have been safely comprised within the first or rawest materials, and all the objects and events will be open to the observation and manipulation of a master-science. It is a grand idea but a poor one. The new physics has taken the analysis of materials one step further back towards rawness. But it knows nothing about the eventual disposition of the raw stuff.

In order to predict eventual objects, the physicist will require the services of that very same corps of brother scientists who now do the predicting.

The consequence is that the geographical machine will have to be far more complicated than any machine that has yet been constructed. It will have to contain a distinct mechanism for every physical science, for every branch of a physical science, and for every single physical law. Only then will it be in a position to furnish the desired information about future events. The future event may be astronomical, seismological, oceanic, dynamical, thermo-dynamical, chemical, electrical, visual, phonic—or have one of many other still more special physical aspects. These are aspects of the event in its physical nature purely, and say nothing about its aspects for biology and psychology. The machine will have to be equipped to pursue the assemblage of electrons through the successive material organizations of every sort which they can possibly take, till it comes to the aspect about which information is sought. The machine will have to embody not only the difficult geography of the electrons, but also a perfectly exhaustive compendium of universal knowledge.

I cannot think Mr. Russell contemplated such an elaborate machine as this when he sketched it in a cavalier fashion, however "theoretical" he conceived it to be. If he had any serious meaning behind it at all, I believe he was really though half-consciously thinking of a sort of magical machine, whose magic virtue would consist precisely in short-cutting the usual laborious scientific processes. The owner and operator of this machine must have seemed to him like the latest scientific version of the old-fashioned fortune-teller who could foretell events by the cards, or the old-fashioned palmist who could foretell them by the lines in the hand, without condescending to know a single thing that was really material to the events.

The lack of mechanical specifications in Mr. Russell's description of his machine is too suspicious.

There has been, then, a new revelation of the God of Science, and it is the revelation of God the Physicist. In this aspect God thinks Einsteinian or space-time thoughts, for one thing; and for another, he understands electrons, and other such forms of a natural material which is the material of all materials, or at least a material more ultimate than his previous revelations have ever made known.

It is about this last of his activities that I have written this chapter. For, once more, his followers have been led to entertain estimates of his omnipotence which are too flattering.

For example, he may have just the right number of electrons, and in just the right place, to go into a table, which is a valuable thing; but his electrons do not compose the table; he cannot see them as a table or predict a table out of them; he will not know a table is there until he has forgot to be a physicist, and taken stock of it with his senses. And as for his productive power, he will not be able to make the electrons into a table until he has taken his coat off and applied himself in the old-fashioned way as a chemist and as a carpenter.

So the last and most imposing version of the Logos is not much better than the old ones. The Logos is not the whole of the Godhead, and we are deluded if we permit ourselves to think he is.

Part Three

GHOSTS: INCLUDING THE HOLY

CHAPTER TWELVE

FINITE GHOSTS

IN THE two earlier sections of this book I have made a good deal of mention of myths, the fabulous, fictions, metaphysical assumptions, Gods, hypotheses, and the like. So do any other writers who discuss the issue between science and religion. But in this section I propose to discuss these objects a little more systematically than I have done, and I do it under a name which may at first appear strange: Ghosts.

It is good if this is now a strange term for a sober discussion. It insures to the discussion a certain curiosity on the part of the reader, and a hearing. I must recall the fact that ghost is historically one of the most reputable names that has ever been borne by the class of objects named above.

It is a reputable name, with this reservation: ghosts have no great public standing at this moment—that is, in an age which is so firmly convinced of its own enlightenment that it inclines to be intolerant of anything that has conspicuously defied its knowledge. But once ghosts had a status of great privilege. Once not only were there many ghosts that walked, but there was the Holy Ghost himself: against whom any man was wary of committing the sin of disrespect lest he run the risk of receiving the crown of infamy.

Evidently the times have changed. But I wish it were possible to revive the ancient prestige of the ghosts. They

are as good for our logic today as ever. Our minds could wel
afford to offer their hospitality to ghosts, or at least to certair
particular ghosts; for the ghosts are in our minds whethei
we invite them or not, it is unhandsome of us to pretend to
have hunted them out, and it only makes us slightly ridiculous.

A ghost is a *Geist*, an anima, a psyche, a spirit, a soul.
Some of these old-fashioned terms have considerable vogue
in religious literature still, and it is science which has regarded them with an increasing professional disdain. Demonology, as a science of ghosts of a certain sort, has fallen
into entire disrepute. Theology itself, whose name implies
the possession of some scientific character— *-logy* means
"science of"—does not have a ticket of membership in any
of the associations of allied sciences today; its considerations
are apparently too fabulous to suit the ruling temper of
science.

Ghosts are not only fabulous but, as they are reckoned
in scientific circles, too pallid and anemic. But this idea of
them is fallacious, and shows that the critic does not understand his ghosts. The truth about ghosts is just the contrary:
they are the sensible, flesh and blood, substantial beings,
evoked to take the place of entities too thin and empty.

It seems to be necessary that we should believe in ghosts.
At any rate, we all do, which comes to the same thing.
Professional scientists do it like the rest of us. They are inclined to dub their ghosts with polysyllabic titles, such as
Evolution, or Electro-Magnetic Energy, under which titles
they may look a little less ghastly and those who see them
may the better escape the charge of superstition. But when
the scientists write these terms with capitals they show that
they mean them to have a little more than ordinary strength,
and in fact to be the names of ghosts. The principal difference is that the scientists believe in ghosts rather surrepti-

tiously, and in their capacity as men rather than as scientists. But it is their right to be men if they will, and it is certainly a winning, if occasional, weakness.

We need a ghost, and if we are not too strict we will indulge in a ghost, whenever the object we are considering is too poor in its actual attributes. We are accustomed to good, rich, substantial objects which gratify many senses at once. But suddenly we encounter an object with little or no sensible quality. So we make up a ghost to fill out this unsatisfactory object, and we indulge our senses slyly in this ghost when they would have been inhibited if we had stuck to the pure original.

But it is important to state a qualification which may or may not enhance the reputation of the ghost before the general public: The ghost is not only a hypothetical or supplied object: *the ghost is also an unhistorical, mythical, or miraculous object*. In this sense a ghost is to be distinguished from most of the objects evoked in our daily experience, as objects whose fullness is not present before us but is capable of being inferred. For example, over the telephone wire comes to us a voice which we recognize: that is, we envelope that voice, a lonely sense-datum, with a body and bodily attributes which seem as certain to us as if they were present, but which nevertheless are not present, and have something less than the validity of present sensible bodies. And we may be mistaken; the voice may belong to another body than the one we suppose. But generally we prove to be right. And anyhow we have assumed for the voice a kind of body which is historical, and which awaits our investigation without fear. When we resort to a ghost, on the other hand, we assume an unhistorical kind of body which we never expect to validate; and we assume it deliberately, knowing it to be unhistorical, and for the very reason that the lean datum which we have encountered, and by which we are oppressed, seems to be all that history is going to offer us.

Suppose that we are sequestered in the country, and dis
quieted over a mysterious midnight rapping upon the bed
room wall. This sound is an object of a qualitative simplicity
such as is unusual in our experience. It is not associated like
most sounds with any visible or palpable body. The scientifi
members of our household say there is a body there, of his
torical kind if it could only be made out, that it has managed
somehow to elude our inspection, that it will yet be discovered. But after waiting vainly for this event, or in the mean
time, we improvise a ghost to embody the manifestation
Let this sound, we say, be the sound made by the spirit of
a man who once was murdered in this room. By premedita-
tion we make the ghost miraculous or unhistorical, on the
theory that historical evidence quite fails us here and that
super-history is required. Yet this ghost satisfies us, to the
extent that in his quasi-sensible way he offers himself to the
inspection of our senses, which can partake of him in imagination if not actually. Ghosts are the imagined objects that
we resort to for the sake of sensible experience when we are
baffled by the historical objects.

It is safe to say that no ghost ever walked unless there
was a situation that required him: a situation of which the
senses could not take their fill as they desired.

How inconsiderate therefore is the person who would
keep us from indulging in our ghosts! when we have created
them upon our own responsibility for the express purpose of
enjoying them. And how mistaken is the person who says
that either the ghost is there or he is not there, and lies in
wait to catch him, or else to expose him as a sham. The
former person is a grim moralist. The latter person is a
scientist, carries a notebook, and "wears a green, naturalistic
look." He will not find the ghost; we could have told him
that in the beginning.

A kind friend has just sent me the account of a dear old

lady who lived out her days trying to catch a ghost in the act, and never succeeded. I will quote from the account as it is furnished me:

Aunt Nan was a hunter of ghosts her whole life but she differed from others of that profession in her neighborhood in this way: after working you up to such a pitch over her preparations for catching the ha'nt, and after filling you with rumors concerning the supernatural visitation, her stories invariably had one ending: she looked grimly into the fireplace, set her strong jaw, and said:

"But not a thing in the world did I see."

A list of her investigations would be lengthy. She would get the elderly people to sit up with her on the night of a certain moon following death, and wait vainly for the apparition. This practice she had started as a girl, when she once spent all night in the empty cabin where a woman had died. She waited and waited, but "not a thing, not a single thing," did she see.

She spent nights by the grave of the Yankee soldier buried in the hollow—a place well known to be beset by devils—but not a thing did she see.

The home of her husband's father in Kentucky was so ha'nted by strange lights that not a tenant would rent the place, and the house stood unoccupied. Her daughter tells us how Aunt Nan investigated it. "Mammy and Pa were walking home late at night and they had to pass that house. Pa looked up. 'There, look! Nan, the light!' Then Pa ran for the thicket in the other direction—Mammy always accused Pa of being a coward."

"Did Aunt Nan see the light?" we ask at this point.

"No. She walked up to the window and put her hands above her eyes to peer the harder. But she couldn't see a thing. Pa said afterwards that the light moved to the other side of the house just as Mammy went up."

Aunt Nan had always heard that children, and other relatives long dead, come back sometimes to visit a person on his deathbed. So Aunt Nan's time came, and her mind was the same clear mind it had been all through her long life. She asked the nurse if anybody had ever told her how it felt to be dying. Well, Aunt Nan told. She described her cold feet and hands, her difficulty in breathing, and other sensations. But she kept watching to see her dead relatives appear to her. She was conscious almost to the end, but once more—not a thing did she see.

Aunt Nan's most important son belongs to the Society of Psychic Research.

Evidently this son favors the mother in his scientific disposition. But let us hope that his luck is better than hers.

As scientists we are loath to indulge in hypothetical objects of an unhistorical nature, though we incessantly infer, on the strength of a very few data, the sensible or historical objects with which we are familiar. And yet there is at least one hypothesis, created in the very heart of scientific territory and enjoyed by scientists of unimpeachable standing, though a perfect ghost: the ether. The ether is the substantial ghost evoked in order to give quasi-sensibility to the meager datum of light. Its history is something like this. Evidently light came off an object and hit the eye. How did this happen? In its progress it would come through glass, and other transparent substances; or through a vacuum. The physicists decided to imagine a new substance as its carrier—the ether. It was present everywhere, in the transparent substances, in the vacuum, and the motion beginning at the object could communicate itself to it as a wave, and travel through it till it reached the eye. But no sensible evidence whatever supported this notion—the ether was only a ghost which gave a certain amount of comfort. According to the psychologists, a muscular sensation attends every image of motion that we entertain. We figure a motion just as we have experienced our own motions: as overcoming a material resistance. But here there is no material resistance, there is nothing material to offer resistance. The facts are too bare to be endured. Hence the ether. In contemplating the ghostly ether we seem to be sensible of light as an object shouldering its way, with rich detail of feeling, through a resistant medium. This is a scandalous traffic with ghosts to have gone on unrebuked in science.

But this is not the ordinary variety of the scientific ghost. Much more common is the ghost that is evoked to take care of the supersensible magnitudes of science. A census is taken, and we learn that a hundred and twenty millions of people inhabit within a given area. We do not think of questioning that datum, 120,000,000 persons. It is given indubitably as a mathematical synthesis. But it is wholly beyond the reach of our senses, and as such we cannot endure it. Its name is the United States of America, and we make of it a quasi-historical entity, or a super-person. This is Columbia. This is America. It has a will and a long arm, a disposition to protect us and the physical capacity to do it. Preferably, it is a woman, and the occasion of romantic emotional responses from us. But at any rate it is a very lively ghost, though naturally one that will not bear too detailed an investigation.

And just there a new light is thrown upon the genesis of our ghosts. We resort to ghosts by a gesture of revulsion, *in which we repudiate objects that are very precise as to quantity but too barren of quality.* We invest these quantities quickly and vigorously with a substantial qualitative background, though we never hope to establish the background in history. It is an improvisation for the enjoyment of our inhibited senses.

Of course the frustrate senses are quickly appeased by this concession. They have been offered in place of the inaccessible object a quasi-object in which they may participate. But they are probably more interested in the principle than in the fact: content to know that they may partake if they like, and not actually making too extensive a use of their privilege. They will not ordinarily push their exploration of the ghost into such detail as to commit us to some decisive and dangerous line of action. They remember that a ghost is only a ghost.

And which is better on the whole, to entertain a quantity or to entertain a ghost? As an organ simply—that is, when my mind identifies itself wholly with a single organ of knowledge and a single interest—I prefer the quantity. But as an integer, a household, an establishment—that is, when my mind remembers its political genius and wishes to provide all its members with a suitable life and expression—I prefer the ghost.

Evidently it is necessary to discuss the relation of quantity and quality. They imply each other. And first let us discuss the quantification of qualities.

A datum of knowledge, such as an odor or a color or a sound, often seems to us a final and irreducible thing: it seems to us an absolute. But this is a dangerous term. The color will doubtless maintain its absoluteness for a long time, in the sense that it will not consent easily to be compared with the odor. But its absoluteness disappears on short notice if we care to compare it with other colors. And the fact is that we ascribe to it its color only when we have made this very comparison.

If the data are of the same general kind—data of color,

or data of sound, or data of economic or political or moral behavior—they are not absolute but relative. For it happens that there is no such thing as a datum which does not imply a system of related data of the same kind.

And how are they related? They are quantities of the same quality, and as quantities they are comparative and commensurable. Objects might well be absolute if they did not have to exhibit, as they constantly do, a quality in common; but if they have a quality in common they are simply quantities of it, and their absoluteness is quite gone. Quantity is the intermediary between the objects. Quantity bridges the chasms that separate the objects.

It sounds strange at first, and monstrous—or Hegelian, which perhaps ranks as the same thing—to say that the apparently absolute sense-datum must renounce its absoluteness and become relative on pain of not being a datum of knowledge at all; and that a quality cannot possibly defend its self-existing purity, but must constantly *other* itself and become a quantity. But the logicians with great unanimity have reiterated this consideration. The discovery of a quality in an object is the discovery of a quality that is common to objects. Or, the discovery of an object as having a quality is the discovery of the object as one of a series of quantities. Thus with the qualities red, sweet, heavy, spherical, old, kind, or swift. No object possesses such a quality except by comparison with other objects. But *comparison means measurement*—even if not necessarily any special precision of measurement.

Scientific knowledge is that type of knowledge which occupies itself with exact comparisons and precise measurements. A science that has been perfected offers us a chart on which all the objects (of the kind affected by that science) appear as locations or quantities. All their separate qualities have become measurable variations of one common quality. It does not matter theoretically that not every science is an "exact" science. It is the intention of a science to be just as exact as its objects allow. A moral science, for example, must deal with very elusive and intractable objects, and yet its technique is a technique of measuring which involves as much mathematics as will apply. A man is brave as compared with other men if he carries out his purpose more quickly, or with less hesitation, in a hazardous situation; or if he takes more risks: the "more quickly," "less hesitation," "more risks," being quantitative terms. It seems perfectly possible to construct a sort of sliding scale of bravery, as Aristotle almost did, to compare men by.

It looks like a sound scientific method when theorists try to define the qualities of character, which seem peculiarly inaccessible to mathematics, by the physical and measurable distinctions exhibited in behavior; and this is evidently what the behaviorists are trying to do. They are psychologists who are envious of the precision of the exact sciences. So they refuse to handle the pure psychic data, which are incapable of such precision. They substitute the data of physical action, where mathematics can find a foothold. And along with these data, they pay a good deal of attention to brain tissue, and its data, which are also physical. They make it a point to translate psychic data, which are very rich but very mixed and insubordinate, into something more practicable that they can handle "scientifically."

So the scientist becomes, under this view, a sort of draughtsman who draws up the draughts or charts upon which may be located the objects of our knowledge. Given the ground of comparison, or the locus, which is the kind of the sense-datum, an object is capable of becoming a configuration or a numerical value. This is the method by which knowledge becomes systematic.

The most simple and inclusive of all possible draughts is the one which locates the various historical objects within the locus of space, and which is called a map; or the one which locates the various phases of one set of objects within the locus of time, and is called a chronology or a schedule. Modern physicists, of course, are now contemplating a very difficult feat which is admitted to be beyond the comprehension of ordinary men: a piece of draughtsmanship which will combine the space-chart and the time-chart into one chart, having space-time as its locus, and exhibiting at once both all the objects in the world and all their temporal sequences.

But this is very ambitious. So far as most of us are concerned, it is chimerical. Speaking more practically, there are many draughts, as the data are of many kinds, and each kind is the occasion of a new draught.

And of course some sciences are not exactly draughts, either; they are synoptic, or classificatory, or they offer a series of graduated formulae; they are only as mathematical as they can be; and they need not be graphic at all. But whether draughts or other systems, there are many of them. *There does not exist Science, exactly, but rather a great many sciences.*

And this is just the difficulty we encounter in our attempt to obtain a single harmonious and systematic knowledge. Let us take, for example, the geographical chart which exhibits a garden as one of its locations. Exploring that area on the chart, we suddenly encounter the notation: An ant-hill. With respect to its position in space, the location on the chart is sufficient and leaves no more to know. But if, by the guidance of the chart, we seek out the real ant-hill, it does not by any means consent to remain a mere area in the garden. There are data spontaneously suggested to us there and then that have no relevancy to the chart; among such data, there are ants. The discovery of ants suggests a new chart altogether; for example, the one that distinguishes the species or forms of the animal world for the biologist. Again, as we explore the garden, we encounter a leaf, and then, interested in its color, we begin to call for still other charts: for instance, the chart which shows the colors in the spectrum and locates the color in question; or a bio-chemical chart which shows systematically the pigmentation of plants. On any one of a number of charts the object we are considering receives a definitive valuation or a quantification.

But there is no single chart which will value it or quantify it for all its sensible data at once.

It is not enough that an object should have its precise place upon a draught which is drawn for one quality only. The same object, when we regard it attentively, wishes to be located on other draughts. *This is why a science can never give us an adequate knowledge of the concrete thing.* The concrete thing never capitulates to the scientific enterprise. The essence of the concrete thing is its *variety*. It may seem docile enough as it yields to some specific science, and is ticketed and disposed of very neatly. But all of a sudden we observe that the concrete thing is not really embodied in that science. Only one of its aspects is there. One by one it reveals other aspects, and challenges other sciences to take hold of it and embody it; and the other sciences undertake to do so, but it is inevitable that each one in its turn must fail in precisely the same manner.

What then can we do, in the interest of the scientific project, but sit down in sackcloth and ashes? It remains for us only to lament the lack of a science which will include all the sciences, and thus contain the perfect representation of the concrete thing; the lack of a super-draught which will include all the draughts; the lack of a book of knowledge which will codify all the books. What we actually have is only sciences and sciences, draughts and draughts, books and books.

When M. Bergson so vigorously attacks the competency of some science to give an account of the world, I wonder if his strategy is entirely correct. For he appears to be for the most part disputing science in respect to the validity of its quantitative comparisons—as if he cherished the view that there existed objects so sacred or so unique that they permitted no comparisons. He has talked now and then about the absoluteness of objects in this sense. But this view is not only contrary to the whole assumption of science, but contrary to all accepted logical thoery. Logic tells us that there is no percept without a concept; no datum without a ground; no difference without an identity; no quality that does not imply quantitative comparisons.

Objects are not unique in the sense that they are entirely out of relation with other objects; nor is any one of their qualities unique in this sense.

And yet, when M. Bergson defends some one of his revered objects—such as some state of mind—from spoliation at the hands of science, I seem to find that every time he is really defending it on the excellent ground that it is simply too full of qualities to suffer the usual disposition under a one-quality system. The object simply does not belong, or has not sold out, to any single science. This would mean in other words only that M. Bergson is annoyed because science proposes to disqualify his object of most of its quality. But that is the very point I have been making. *A scientific definition of the object is not false in the sense that it is not the truth, but only in the sense that it is not the whole truth.* It is not so bad that science is going to quantify the object, but that in doing so science will be obliged very largely to disqualify it. The object cannot deny its definition: it can only exceed it by inviting others.

It will be clear at this point what the subject of quantity has to do with ghosts. When objects have been defined strictly, they have been quantified; but when they have been quantified, they are mostly disqualified, and no longer the concrete objects they were. If we are sufficiently resentful on behalf of the objects, we will re-qualify them, and some-times this process involves the evocation of ghosts.

So any object as a quality is going to be quantified. That is how it becomes an item in a useful system of knowledge which is a science.

I would like to look rather closely at the question: What does a sensible object actually mean to us as we encounter it in the usual run of experience?

I do not refer to the difficult question of how we build up our knowledge as infants; but to the question of what the things mean to us as adults. We have our sciences at this stage, and we encounter a world which has been treated in vast detail by these sciences. We have an organized knowl-edge which is prepared to make a disposition of anything we may encounter. And how do we actually construe an object when we meet one? I believe there are three different con-structions which we may put upon it.

(a) The object possibly occurs to us first as a mere quan-tity within a draught or a system: that is, as a definition. This is the most practical view which we can take of the object. And being practical persons, and in haste, we probably stop with that meaning. "That is another bill coming in: ten dol-lars more." "There comes the postman: it just suits my schedule: give him the letter." These judgments make dis-position of their objects in very short order. The objects are assimilated into our existing schemes, and their existence at the moment consists only in occupying their places within the respective schemes. Practical people are gifted at passing these routine judgments and making these quick dispositions. Theirs is a gift for order, which implies always a set of positions upon a chart. But if we are curious, if we are sated with routine, if we have an untamed sensibility, we are far from ready to stop there.

(b) The object will occur to us also then, upon looking

twice, as having a second definition, or a location upon more draughts than one. We did the object an injustice when we stopped with the one as if that had exhausted its being. Regarded now more respectfully, it probably exerts a charm for us, for it becomes a concrete object. It offers qualities that imply the construction of fresh draughts, or at least that imply allocations upon other existing draughts, and this is pioneering work which the object as a novelty provides for us.

The gift for taking the second look, for refusing to make routine dispositions, is the esthetic gift. It is the property conspicuously of the artist, who will exhibit lovingly, in his portrait or in his landscape or in his poem, an object with which we thought we were familiar, but whose detail now strikes us with great astonishment, so that we study this representation of it as if it were a new object. And indeed we were familiar with it; and that was just the trouble. This gift, however, is not monopolized by the artist; it belongs to all people who can love romantically, whether the object of their affection is a person or a bit of nature. Love is peculiarly respectful of its object, which it does not propose simply to use, and therefore to reduce to that single aspect in which the object is useful.

So the concrete object reveals its various nature under proper observation, and we are charmed with it. Doubtless we have a perennial relish for novelty, being never completely monopolized or anesthetized by the simple and imperious projects upon which we are engaged practically.

(c) The object occurs to us in still another way. As a quantity it contains smaller quantities and is contained within larger ones; especially, so far as we are concerned, the former. The smaller or larger quantities, to which we are led when we consider the given object as a location upon a draught, may be of more interest than this one. So we find our way to them by the assistance of the draught and contemplate them instead of the original object. They appear to us, first, of course, as locations upon that draught, or in the capacity of *a* above. But then they also appear to us as inviting other draughts, or in the capacity of *b*.

In short, the sensible object is, in this third aspect, an area to be explored within for smaller objects, and a point of departure for the discovery of larger ones: the beginning of incursions and excursions. And this is a very important aspect of the object. Frequently we imagine that we are occupied with some object, when in fact we are occupied with the objects within it. For example, we decide to explore the country which stretches visibly and perhaps uninterestingly around us: we take it to be an area within which there may be some local excitements; or if we have the map of this country we detect in advance the local notations which attract us. Many an object would be insufferably barren in its quality if it did not have other objects within it which promise to gratify our senses.

There is no assignable end to the activities described under *b* and *c*. But the object may be at any time frozen in one of its single capacities as an *a*, if we become tired of regarding it.

As an *a* which carries the threat of becoming a *b* or a *c*, it may be said that the concrete object baffles formulation. This is an unequivocal statement, even if the way in which it baffles formulation is by being too formulable, or formulable in too many ways; that is, by being inexhaustible.

An object as a quality inevitably quantifies itself as we have seen. But we have also seen how a certain quantity within a system means a fresh qualitative object and a new system. And in this way *a quantity may qualify itself*. This is complementary to the other rule about the quantification of the qualities; this one is about the qualification of the quantities.

But for this latter rule, there would be no fertility in nature, and no point to our ordinary manufacturing processes. We form a new quantity when we put the materials together according to a quantitative formula. For example, a gasoline engine is compounded of metal parts, and its quantity is their total aggregate. But the new quantity has sensible properties which were not the properties of its components. The gasoline engine is not only a new quantity but a new qualitative object whose behavior is not the behavior of the other quantities. And so with other compounds or aggregates in quantity: a house, a synthetic drug, an Irish stew, a coat, a gun, an electric lamp. New quantitative arrangements of given qualitative materials produce objects with new qualities.

The principle is true also for the new quantities obtained by dividing, as well as for those obtained by compounding: they too are new qualitative objects. The human body is a quantity with its own qualitative behavior; but microscopic anatomists divide or dissect it, and study its parts, which are physico-chemical substances, and whose behavior is not qualitatively at all the same as the behavior of the whole. And in chemistry the compound which is one quantity can be resolved into components which are other quantities, and have their own distinct qualities.

But perhaps it will be said that in all these illustrations I am dealing with wholes made up of heterogeneous parts; and that it is not so very wonderful that the combination of quantities of different materials makes an aggregate of very novel qualities. But materials, as a matter of fact, are never quite homogeneous; and *different quantities of the same material offer new qualities*.

Homogeneity is the assumption we make whenever we perform a practical operation in mathematics, but it only works very crudely and within limits. If you add to a pile of material some more of the same material, you naturally give the pile a quite new configuration which the mathematics of addition says nothing about. But even if you re-arrange the new pile with the same configuration as the old one, you still have novelties: for instance, variation in the pressure and heat, and in the relation of volume to surface.

But most of the objects which we have to deal with practically come in rather fixed sizes, and when you put a number of them together their interactions are perfectly unaccountable. Fifty men weighing a hundred and fifty pounds each make an aggregate of 7500 pounds of man: they also make, under certain circumstances, a mob; or a written Constitution; or an Irish wake; or a platoon of soldiers.

There used to be an obscene guide in Windsor Castle who would point the American tourist to a famous painting showing "how to make English beef." He was a man whose sense of humor was tickled by the truth that qualitative novelties arise from the combination of certain "materials" in certain quantities; in this case, from the union of the male and the female of the animal species. The production of a third member of the species is a biological phenomenon which is perfectly surprising to the mathematical sense.

But these exceptional results must be allowed for in performing mathematical operations with all sorts of objects— objects in physics, objects in chemistry, objects wherever we are able to examine them in different quantitative arrangements. Homogeneity is one of the most precarious of ideals to hold up to a material whose quantity is going to be tampered with.

The Greek skeptic Aenesidemus perceived this principle, and accordingly attacked the idea of a schematic knowledge by showing that qualities differ according to the quantities. In illustration he remarked that the horn of a goat is black; but that small fragments of this horn are whitish.

The qualitative wealth of the world goes strictly along with the infinite componability and divisibility which it possesses as pure quantity. The qualities belong to the innumerable quantities, and are discovered by degrees as we pass from one quantity to another. In this respect, *concreteness may be regarded as something which is created incessantly out of the variations of quantity.*

The senses differ remarkably in the kinds of testimony which they report of their objects. But it is not always observed in this connection that their respective objects also differ greatly in magnitude. The senses are very unequal with respect to the magnitude of their appropriate objects. Taste, for example, is evidently one of the most local of the senses, and acquaints us with objects which are of very small dimensions: namely, objects which can be dissolved upon the tongue. But touch gives us a larger object. By touch we become acquainted with objects whose size is limited only by the area of skin that can make a simultaneous contact. Now taste is a very meek faculty, but if it had a cult and a fanatical following, its devotees would be outraged by the testimony of touch on its grand scale, and would ask in indignation, Where and what are these great magnitudes if they cannot be tasted?

The object which is thus accessible to touch but not to taste does not exist for the latter. *It is sensible for one sense but supersensible for the other.*

But exceeding the capacity of touch in its turn, or supersensible for touch, are objects with which still other senses are acquainted quite easily. I do not pretend that the senses may be arranged precisely in a progressive series, depending on the magnitudes of the objects with which they make contact, for too much depends on the arbitrary way we elect to define the minimum unit of sense-perception in our physiology. But theoretically, there might be some such formula as the following, where the sign $<$ stands for "is less than":

Smell < Taste < Hearing < Touch < Sight

The unequal senses, if we cared to listen to their quarrels, might well be in perpetual contention over issues that seemed to them of immense metaphysical importance. And I believe it is said by the Talmud that something like this is the meaning of strange passages in Scripture, like that in Genesis, xiv, where the four kings war with the five kings.

So it is common within the sensible world to find objects of different magnitudes existing for different senses. A garden has no taste when there is no gustatory apparatus capable of dissolving it. It has also no smell, though it may be said (probably not in strict accuracy) that peach-blossoms and honeysuckle have. It does not make a sound that we can hear, though out of its area we may hear birds, bees, and whistling gardeners. It is supersensible for all these senses. But it is quite sensible for vision, unless it is a very large garden.

The senses partake of unequal magnitudes, and discover within these the appropriate qualities. A material within one range of magnitudes will have no qualities or be supersensible for a given sense, while within another range of magnitudes it will have quality or be sensible for that sense.

Let us stop for a moment on the fullness of testimony offered by some one particular sense by itself. The best one for the purpose will be vision: it makes by far the subtlest discriminations, and offers much the largest variety of evidence. The point is that vision plays in succession upon different magnitudes and reports back with testimonies that are quite different in kind. Vision is but one sense: but so far as it operates upon a whole range of objective magnitudes it reports varieties of quality as if it were so many distinct senses.

The eye permits of many focuses, and each time it takes a fresh one it is like a new eye: where it finds new magnitudes it also finds new qualities. The ant-hill is a magnitude whose qualities are not the qualities of that other magnitude, the garden. As, for instance, it has ants.

Wide landscapes are real or witnessed objects with qualities all their own. But they cannot ordinarily possess any fauna or flora, which have to come in much smaller dimensions. When we go out to look at nature, we must make the decision whether to use our eyes like a landscape painter, or like a naturalist. Our experience will vary accordingly.

In general, we will have to choose between seeing the wood and seeing the trees. A wood as a sensible object is not a tree, nor is the tree a wood.

The qualitative difference between different quantities of the same material may possibly be indicated even better than this to the reader. The reader may look at the printed page as a whole, or he may look at that unit of the printed page which is a word. They are evidently very distinct magnitudes in a black-and-white material; but it would seem that they are even more startlingly distinct in quality.

One magnitude gives us the format of a printed page. Immediately, this qualitative dictum assumes its position in our schematic or quantified knowledge of printer's technique. We have made a scientific reference and disposition, but not a very important one.

The other magnitude, the word, is of more importance. It gives us, let us say, the passion of Othello: another kind of quality altogether. Of course we may quantify it too, or give it its value in a scheme of human passions. But the printed page was supra-sensible for the sense which reports words, and the word is infra-sensible for the sense which reports the printed page.

If somebody should be disposed to deny that new quantities exhibit new qualities, we might consider putting out his eyes. It is probable that the grievance he would feel mainly would be *that of his extreme localism:* he would mourn for his lost magnitudes, with which his other senses could not bring him into contact. Of course also, even in his reduced world, he would resent the qualitative poverty of his knowledge, the absence of quality that was not now presented to him. But as he mourned his lost landscapes, he would have to confess that certain qualities were as functions of certain quantities, since a great order of quantities and qualities had vanished together.

But the same confession might be obtained from him by less heroic measures. We might sentence him to wear constantly over his eyes artificial lenses for long-distance vision exclusively, or for near vision exclusively. In either case he would be deprived of a range of objective magnitudes which are the only magnitudes that could furnish him with some of the most precious qualitative phenomena in the world.

The same object may be sensible for one sense, but supersensible for another, and we are never to suppose that a sensible object is one in which all the senses must participate. Doubtless most sensible objects will be objects that are supersensible for some of the senses.

But there are other objects which are wholly supersensible, inasmuch as their magnitudes do not come within the survey of any senses at all. A sensible object is, for example, an apple, and a supersensible object is, for example, the area Pennsylvania. How do they differ?

The apple is both a defined object and a concrete object. It is a defined object when we take a routine knowledge of it as placed in some one system of values: as being worth five cents, for example. But it is a concrete object if we allow ourselves to observe that it offers other definitions, or if its insubordinate energy forces itself upon our attention in calling for other valuations: if we become interested in its colorful appearance, or if we are pained when it falls upon our head.

The area Pennsylvania is not like this. It exists only in the first of these ways. For it is a defined object, an area of the earth's surface; but it is nothing else; it cannot spontaneously offer fresh qualities and suggest other definitions.

An object of this sort is a work of synthesis. We have not found it, we have created it. We have put the parts together by mathematics but not by hand, we have no sensible experience of it, and we therefore cannot observe its behavior. It is a fresh quantity, and yet it does not present itself to us as having fresh quality; not at all analogous to H_2O as compared with the H and the O, a new quantity with new qualities also; not even analogous to the façade of some great building, which is the aggregate of all its component and homogeneous stones, and yet has a sensed quality which the stones did not possess. So that we are obliged to confess: *If it is true that a new quantity of any material exhibits new quality, this truth is good for sensible quantities but not for supersensible ones.*

We cannot convert a supersensible object into a sensible one either by claiming that it is sensible, or by behaving as if it were. It is in vain, so far as this possibility is concerned, that we give the object a name, even a proper name like Pennsylvania, or England, or the Roman Catholic Church, or the Nordic race, or the Crusades, or the Twentieth Century. In vain we celebrate it in ceremony and song; or feel intense emotions as we contemplate it; or even die for it. It is also in vain that we agree unanimously among ourselves about its sensible existence, sanctifying the agreement by treaty, compact, and oath. It remains a supersensible object and cannot be penetrated by the senses like a historical or sensible one.[1]

It is true that if we behave as if it were sensible, our behavior has consequences which return upon us, all the more

[1] I am trying here to stick to supersensible objects which are still finite, or capable of mathematical representation. I do not refer to infinites, like God, Energy, or 0.3333. . . . These will come in the next chapter.

spectacularly if our behavior participates in the common behavior of the community. These consequences may be very
rich and valuable, but they are not the manifestations of the
supersensible. The supersensible is not going to manifest
itself. It stays where it has started: a mathematical synthesis.
Prosperity or glory is not visited upon us by the State, acting in any capacity like a sensible object. Prosperity and glory
may be sensible blessings, but they are strictly contained
within the system of sensible objects. History does not support us if we claim them as the activities, however mysterious, of supersensible beings.

Supersensible objects are therefore not historical objects
—and yet it is generally understood that they have some
kind of historical status, or place in history. But history carries them in its records as pragmatic entities entirely: as
essentially ghosts: though as ghosts that communities of men
have agreed upon, discussed, and filled their minds and behaviors with. The supersensibles which history has treated
are those which have had a great name among men, in whose
name—but not by whom—great deeds have been done on
earth. With this meaning they might conceivably enter the
pages of some Gibbon, who would mock their hollow pre-
tensions with his ironical deference, or the pages of some
Buckle, who would permit himself to brand them rudely as
the objects of pure superstition.

The validity of a supersensible object like Pennsylvania
is not a historical validity, as of an object of which we have
had sensible witness, but a formal or mathematical one.
Given the areas of all the sensible parts, the total is Pennsylvania, about which we may know only that it is the true
aggregate of its sensible parts. Its existence is wholly con-
fined to being an area upon the draught, a within-which that
is pure locus, and that can never partake of concreteness.
(Neither does any other quantity upon the draught as such,
of course, even if it is of sensible dimensions; it is only the

object which is represented by the quantity that does that.) It is composed with singular purity of the genuine stuff of which the locus is made, the stuff that mediates between the sensible objects, but it is good for nothing else but mediation.

Naturally we are surprised and appalled to encounter upon the draught a location which has no correspondent off the draught, and can never be identified and observed. We are very likely to pretend that it has an actual correspondent; but this correspondent is only our ghost.

And here I come back to ghosts: to those fabulous objects which we make up for the satisfaction of our senses when they are defeated by the barrenness of certain objects.

It is not my intention to ridicule ghosts. The point of view is wholly respectful, regarding ghosts for the most part as wholesome fictions, of enormous frequency in our thinking, which it would be both unnatural and unnecessary to forswear. But it might seem in order, in spite of this point of view, to expose the ghostliness of ghosts when they are being enjoyed by scientists who maintain that they do not have anything to do with ghosts. If ghosts creep into the thinking of scientists without their knowing it, the fact seems to be worth showing. And besides, there are ghosts and ghosts, and the ghosts that infest the scientific mind are not necessarily the best ghosts. If this point can be made, we have made a modest contribution to scientific thinking.

Of course the humanistic or inexact sciences offer the most occasions for ghosts. These sciences concentrate their study upon objects admittedly of more sensible complexity, or more energetic concreteness, than the physical sciences do: persons being generally agreed to be fuller of quality than mechanical or chemical substances. These sciences are so used to wealth of quality that they are likely to put it into their objects when it is not really there. Thus the economists, statisticians, military writers, "scientific" historians, moralists, and even biologists and physicians have to make constant employment of supersensible objects, and very often they force them to bear more or less of a quasi-sensible meaning. For example: A nation; the wealth of a nation; a sum of money invested at interest; a corporation; a racial, or social, or national, or international "movement"; the day's market, as "bullish," "bearish," or "sluggish"; the average man, as the possessor of money, education, and character; the nineteenth century spirit; any other Zeitgeist; the electorate; the Democratic party; the ravages of a disease; geographical entities; the Church; the county, the state, or other political division; the law of the land; the will of the people. These terms and a vast number of similar terms constitute much of the great stock of terms in which we think and talk together. But we must ask of ourselves, or of those who use these terms, if we are capable of so much introspection, to analyze carefully what we mean when we employ them, in order to see if there is not very generally a great deal of imported sensible meaning there.

But the ghosts walk even in the mansions of the exact sciences, bringing with them properties which are enjoyed but not always confessed by those to whom they appear. The supersensibles of the physical sciences are both, and equally, the supra-sensible magnitudes too large for the senses, and the infra-sensible magnitudes too small for them. These magnitudes abound in physical science; but even physical scientists have senses that, though sternly disciplined, may resent frustration and require their exercise: so that they are made into ghosts. This is done satisfactorily when the supersensibles [1] are picturized for the senses, or given concrete representations with special properties that have not been historically attested. Ghostly properties inhere in such supersensible objects as the earth; the celestial economy; the

[1] I use the term supersensible to cover the more specific terms supra-sensible and infra-sensible.

molecule as described in stereo-chemistry, like the "benzene ring" devised by Kekulé; the macrocosm of the known universe or the microcosm of an atom; the force represented by a graph.

There appear to be but two alternatives open to us as we deal with supersensible objects. The first is to convert them frankly, according to our human requirements, into ghosts, give a factitious exercise to the starved senses, and be of peaceful mind. The second is to keep them strictly for supersensible objects, inhibit the senses, and be disquieted. Or is there some third choice?

It is well known that Immanuel Kant performed a novel and powerful work of analysis in offering his esthetic theory of the sublime. Here he was discussing this very problem of the mathematical supersensibles. He distinguishes the beautiful and the sublime substantially as follows.

Beautiful is the name of the effect enjoyed when we contemplate the sensible object in such a way that all our faculties work in harmony. But sublime is the name of the effect enjoyed when we contemplate a supersensible, or nearly supersensible, object, and are distressed because our faculties do not partake equally of it.[1] Our mathematical faculty takes perfectly good hold of an object when our senses cannot touch it or know it: therein lies their inequality, and the source of our disquiet.

Thus the spectacle of a mountain, or of a storm at sea. These great magnitudes suggest to the senses that the mathematical organ possesses objects which they cannot possibly reach. Of course, the mountain or the storm is still sensible for the eye, but barely so, and only at a certain focus, only

---

[1] I am not being quite accurate in citing Kant to this effect. He lumps all the supersensible objects together in his treatment as infinites. In strictness they are not necessarily infinite: mathematically they may be quite finite, while yet being beyond the grasp of the senses. So I must choose between bringing his contribution in here under "Finite Ghosts" or saving it to bring in under "Infinite Ghosts." I use it here as the first place it will apply.

as a vast landscape: it is a sensible magnitude taken just at the point where sensible is about to pass into supersensible. The feeling attending this experience is not a pleasant one. It is an epistemological event; yet Kant describes it with a good deal of feeling; it is not a dry event. It testifies that we are creatures of a knowledge which is hopelessly unequal in its features. It inclines us against any hope of a systematic knowledge.

But what are we to do about it? asks Kant. He will not tolerate ghosts; or at least he will not in the mood in which he writes the Critique of Judgment; for in this mood he is the Protestant, the Puritan, and the rationalist of sternest order. We imagine therefore as we read him that he will have to prepare his mind to be perpetually disquieted by his experience of the sublime. But it is not quite true: for he has a hope of a sort of third course which takes us wholly by surprise. He speaks confidently of the "supersensible destination" of the mind, as if it were the mind's destiny to strip off its senses and live wholly in the barren and simple world of the quantities. It is actually in this consideration that he takes comfort.

But this is to hope for a peace that is hardly to be distinguished from suicide, and not at all from mutilation. And even the fact that Kant himself proposed this hope need not deter us from believing that we must either defend the supersensibles in their purity, and suffer the consequences, or else convert them into ghosts, and satisfy this strangely assorted yet integral mind with a fiction.

For this mind is perfectly at home in history, where it lives and secures nourishment from sensible objects for its senses. But it can scarcely breathe in the rarer world of mathematics, and when it enters this world it must either suspend the most of its vital functions, or else take along for a sort of artificial respiration a supply of its comfortable native atmosphere.

CHAPTER THIRTEEN

INFINITE GHOSTS

PURE mathematics is at the base of the sciences; it is the basic science. It is a body of knowledge which applies very freely within the exact sciences and so far as it may within the others. By mathematics the sciences or systems of knowledge become possible.

But there are some defects in pure mathematics which keep it from becoming the perfect technique. Though all things seems numerable and measurable, this is not quite true, and the fact has considerable importance. For it is certain that any defects that exist in pure mathematics will also be carried over into applied mathematics, and that we must to that extent fail to possess the world as a precisely known system of objects.

The defects in mathematical technique come to light when we examine the mathematical infinites.

It is not a characteristic of the modern scientists to be enamored of infinites—that is, of modern scientists in their militant moods. The term infinite, to the lay mind, carries very chastening implications: it seems to mean that something has been attempted which cannot be accomplished: the moral of an infinite is that the mind must confess to its impotence, and rest in its humility. And it is to be expected that the term has much the same meaning for the most technical of scientists. They fear it, and they would do away with it. There is a pronounced disposition on the part of scientists to claim that the infinites have been overcome, and that the world has become finite for human knowledge.

For instance, Dr. Max Radin, of the University of California, in a paper delivered at the celebration of the two hundredth Mendelssohn anniversary at San Francisco, in 1929, is most outspoken on this point. Dr. Radin takes Job to task for his well-known opinion that the physical sciences could never accomplish a complete knowledge of the physical world; or in other words, for his antique and unworthy belief in infinites. On this subject Dr. Radin has his own opinion, which is as follows:

> Modern science has taken a new turn. I have no right to speak with authority on what constitutes the characteristic mark of modern science, but if there is such an outstanding mark, I think it must be the abolition of infinity.

It is only fair to state that this writer is not yet prepared to apply his remark to the psychic or moral world. He is like a great many physicists in drawing this line. In the spiritual world he is unable to find that the infinites, or the impossible objects of knowledge, have been abolished.

But for that matter, it is difficult to see how they have been abolished anywhere. Certainly they still reign in the world of mathematics, which is logically prior to the world of physics and chemistry. It is the infinites in mathematics which must still cause us to have our qualms. We shall be obliged to abolish them there before we look for their abolition anywhere else, and before we set about preparing our minds to abandon humility forever.

The modern mathematical theorists have offered a definition of infinite which is technical and, at first sight, rather difficult.

An infinite may be defined according to this school perhaps about as follows: A quantity is infinite if, when it has been divided into any number of unit parts whatever, any one of those parts may in turn be divided similarly into the same number of parts of itself, so that the original parts and the parts of the parts have a one-to-one correspondence.

This is at first sight obscure. I should think that this is essentially a natural history of the infinite, or a psychology of the notion of infinite as it arises in our minds. It seems to refer especially to the infinite divisibility of a quantity, or to the infinitesimal which is a sort of inverted infinite. For it says that we may keep on dividing the parts, or the parts of the parts, without ever stopping; so that any whole is evidently capable of having parts below and beyond any that we can possibly arrive at. But on the other hand it implies also the notion of infinite componability and of the infinitely large. For it suggests that we may start with the parts and compose them into a whole; then substitute the whole for the part and compose a whole of wholes; and so on going upward, till we see that there are wholes componable out of wholes above and beyond any that we can possibly arrive at.

When we have worked out the meaning of this definition, therefore, we come to the conclusion that it is the definition of a serial effort which can never be completed. It carries the whole theory of the locus, or of the draught, such as the applied sciences are incessantly preparing. The material which constitutes the locus or draught must be perfectly or infinitely plastic; that is, it must be capable of representing, in the ascending scale, any aggregate of quantity however large; and in the descending scale, any particle of quantity however small. For any given unit quantity, there must be a corresponding unit quantity on any scale of magnitude, whether above it or below it. But the definition carries an alarming confession. For it assumes that there are magnitudes beyond any to which we have risen, and parvitudes below any to which we have descended: a universe whose exterior limits are not assignable, and whose interior is not exhaustible. Such is the universe as mathematical theory construes it.

This definition is an extreme generalization or abstract of the mathematical infinites. But we will return to a lower plane of mathematical theory, and examine some types of the infinite series as they appear to the layman. And we must insist that, whether we are in mathematics or in some science far less abstract, infinite is a term with a very plain psychological meaning. A magnitude is declared to be infinite only when we see that our organs of knowledge are not capable of grasping it. Or more practical still, a project of knowledge is infinite only when we see that it is destined, for reasons that are constitutionally insurmountable, never to be completed. We do not employ this term except as a final confession of defeat. And doubtless we cannot employ it without deep emotional consequences, for it is a pronouncement upon the ultimate relations which we as would-be knowers bear to a world which is here ostensibly for us to know.

There seem to be essentially two types of the infinite mathematical series; probably both are expressed at once in the one-to-one formula above.

Let us consider first the fundamental numerical series, 1, 2, 3, 4, 5. . . . This is called an infinite series, and it is infinite in a rather terrifying sense—if an old-fashioned one—that still has, for the lay mathematician, its logic. Infinite means here: exceeding or containing every finite. If we did not have this infinite series, there might be quantities with which we could certainly make acquaintance, yet to which we could not give a numerical value. The great value of the numerical series therefore lies in the fact that there is no possible quantity which is not contained in the series, and which may thus become finite and comprehensible and measurable. *The infinite series is the instrument by which finitude is conferred upon every given object.*

And precisely the same considerations apply, *mutatis mutandis*, to the inverse numerical series which derives from it: 1/1, 1/2, 1/3, 1/4, 1/5. . . . Here infinite means less than any assignable quantity, and the value of the series lies in its power to assign finite distinctitude to any quantity however small; or *in its power to make an object out of any part of an object.*

But the unfavorable aspect of the numerical series, or of its inverse, is quite apparent. It is finite at the point where it contains the given object and looks backward: but then as an infinite series it reaches on and points to further objects. No object is locable or numerable except on the assumption that the locus or the numerical system reaches on beyond it. The bounded or concave implies the unbounded or convex. Each historical event is finite in time, and each historical object is finite in space, but time and space are infinite, being the loci, and quite prepared to take account of yet more history and yet further materiality. In other words, it is the assumption of these two infinite series, if we take them together, that the universe can be neither bounded nor exhausted.

The numerical series therefore may represent one kind of infinite with which we become acquainted in mathematics. There is another kind.

The other kind of infinite series is found in such serial efforts as try to express a surd, like the square root of 2; or such as try to express with a decimal denominator a rational number whose denominator is not commensurable with decimal denominators. I shall take for example the series 0.3333 . . . . , and try to show how painful are its implications for us; painful regardless of the fact that it arises out of a very usual and homely sort of project.

Perhaps we were not dismayed by the suggestion of the numerical series as to those aspects of the universe which are still beyond our experience and not accessible to our knowledge; like territories which are only provisional and schematic, or blank spaces on the draught, waiting in the dark till they may receive our visitations. We may comfort ourselves with the thought that as fast as we invade these regions they become finite for us!

But the series 0.3333 . . . . is of much more practical importance, and therefore more disturbing. It represents simply our attempt to express by a decimal notation the perfectly finite quantity 1/3. The attempt has not succeeded. *The quantity 1/3 is not measurable by any system of notation whose ratios are in denominations of 10 and the powers of 10.* And this is a startling predicament. For we have committed ourselves, on the promise of wonderful economies in our thinking, to a decimal notation; and it serves us as well as some other notation would do; but here it fails us.

The number 1/3 could have been expressed successfully by a duodecimal notation, or system of notation whose denominations would be 12 and the powers of 12; but then the number 1/5 would have been impossible of expression; and the number 1/7 could not be expressed by either decimal or duodecimal system.

The distressing frequency with which we encounter surds or incommensurables under our decimal system may be quickly indicated by some statistics. Of the first 10 numbers, only 6 may serve as denominators which can be expressed by the decimal system; of the first 100 numbers, 15; of the first 1,000 numbers, 29; and of the first 10,000 numbers, only 45. Beyond that point, of course, a still more overwhelming majority of numbers, if they become denominators, produce under the decimal system the infinite series.

What does this unexpected flaw in our basic mathematical technique indicate with respect to the possibility of a body of precisely articulated or finite knowledge? We may be sure it is not a favorable sign.

The failure of the decimal system to express the quantity 1/3 stands for all the notorious failures of our sciences to embody the concrete objects of our sensible experience. For example, it stands for the failure of geometry to define the configuration of a lake, or a mountain, or even the merest pebble. *The pebble is too stubborn for the geometer: it is an infinite.* However minutely or microscopically he may study the parts of its surface, he will find no law, no type, no denominator by which their values are all commensurable. His determinate or ideal reductions are much too simple. His geometry is impotent.

Likewise the impossible effort 0.3333 . . . . stands for the failure of the manufacturer, who is allied with the physical scientists, to realize his dream of the perfect homogeneous material. His simple instruments are attempting to reduce a complex material to their own terms; but it continues to defy them and to display its novelties; and after all his care his final products are not uniform. In this case the quantity 1/3 is the natural material, while the quantity 0.3333 . . . . is the artificial product as the manufacturer has made it over according to prescription. But the natural property persists in it; and the artificial object as defined in his advertisements is not quite the object that exists actually, until we have restored to it its original property; that is, until we have confessed that 1/3 is not the same as 0.3333, but is precisely 0.3333 1/3, and nothing short of it; or 0.3333 plus 1/3 of 0.0001.

But the infinite decimal series stands all the better for the grosser failures of the less precise sciences, the biological and social ones. Here the scientists are of course more humble, and make somewhat less sweeping claims to power. These sciences theorize about their objects, and sometimes attempt to manipulate them. But the objects resist their treatment, and involve the formulas constantly in hazard and error. *The quantity 1/3 is the biological variation,* or the individual who inevitably exceeds the definition of his biological species in his quality: the Socrates who cannot be comprised within the universal man. Or here—whether we deal in matters biological, psychic, economic, political, military—the quantity 1/3 is the variety which composes any individual living object anywhere, and makes it exceptional and intractable.

More summarily still: The mathematical enterprise intends to construe the world as a completely determinate system of objects. But the energy of a surd, such as the infinite decimal fraction 0.3333 . . . . , asserts the freedom of the object to escape determination. *So a surd symbolizes the stubborn concreteness of objects.*

What becomes then of our thesis, that every object may be obliged to present itself as a finite quantity in a scheme that has a single qualitative ground? Again we must note the reservation with which this thesis must be taken. *Any object placed within a scheme is likely to exhibit additional qualities foreign to the scheme.*

We may now contrast more precisely the decimal series 0.3333 . . . . with the numerical series 1, 2, 3, 4, 5. . . . The numerical series is a cardinal series which means to furnish numerators for all magnitudes of the same denomination; but the decimal series is an ordinal series which means to furnish a common denomination for all denominations. The numerical series compares the quantities of the same quality; the decimal series compares the different qualities. The numerical series represents the draught which locates the objects upon a common ground; the decimal series is the formula which effects the passage of an object from one draught into another. But the numerical series is infinite, and so is the decimal series. The infinitude of the numerical series terrifies us because it suggests that no final knowledge is possible of the sheer aggregates or particles of an extended homogeneous material. The infinitude of the decimal series terrifies us because it shows us that the variety of quality within any local object is not capable of being reduced to a homogeneous material.

The Pythagoreans invaded even numbers, to show, in the most unlikely place in the world, the demonic energy of the concrete objects. They were wonderfully sensitive to the qualitative distinctitudes of the numbers. We are evidently more obtuse. We are inclined to forget that our mathematics, the archetype of all our systematic knowledge, is infected with the presence of surds, against which the mathematical enterprise cannot prevail.

And what is mathematics prepared to do toward enabling Dr. Radin to abolish the decimal infinites? Mathematics may of course reject the decimal scheme and try another. But then we must remember what the intention of any scheme is, and see whether other schemes will escape censure. A scheme is a simplification, and it means to permt an economy of observation. The decimal scheme is extremely economical, since it requires us to give attention only to ten different digits, and represents all the higher numbers by compounding these digits over and over. And so why not a scheme, let us say, which would provide a common denomination for the numbers 2, 3, 5, 7, and therefore for all numbers through 10? *The scheme which would provide this service would be a scheme with* 210 *digits instead of*

10. Evidently it would not be a scheme at all in the common sense: it would be far more impracticable than a Chinese alphabet. And besides, for many of the digits above 10 this scheme would not provide a common denomination.

And what sort of scheme would be that *which undertook to measure all quantities,* and obviate all such infinite series as 0.3333 . . . . ? Clearly we would have to employ a denomination to which all denominations would reduce. Our digits would then extend not from 1 to 10, nor from 1 to 210, but from 1 to that number which is the Lowest Common Multiple of all the prime numbers that we have ever known. We would have to record all the numbers that have been historically encountered, and take the L.C.M. of the prime numbers among them: and so our digits would greatly exceed in number the largest numerical aggregate ever encountered. These digits would constitute our base, and the successive powers of the top digit would constitute the orders of our new notation. Such a scheme would indeed be adequate to represent all known quantities within a single notation. But we might be exhausted in making a single application of it. The known world would require for its representation a draught many times larger than the world; a body would have to be drawn on a scale greatly exceeding its sensible minuteness; and the numerical notation of even a trifling quantity might require more time and room than has yet been allotted to any mortal mathematician. Furthermore, this all-inclusive denomination, though very vast, would be still finite and rigid; and therefore it would be shattered in that moment when we encountered a fresh body that increased the number of bodies in the world by one. We would have to have immediately a new system of notation, and we would have to revise all existing draughts and numerical valuations.

But as a matter of fact, we have seen that we require for our use a numerical series that is infinite, or capable of

enumerating any possible finite object that we may encounter. Therefore it may as well be confessed at once that
we must surrender our hope of a system of notation that
will provide a universal denominator which is finite. The
L.C.M. of any series is at least as large as, if not larger
than, the last number of the series, and the L.C.M. of the
infinite series is *a fortiori* infinite, or incapable of attainment.

This conclusion bears heavily upon the prospect of breaking down the absoluteness by virtue of which the different
systems of knowledge decline to enter into relations with
each other. It is contrary to our sense of economy to expect
it. It is also theoretically impossible.

There is an absoluteness somewhere, then, that resists the
ordinary mediation of number.

It is quite true that absoluteness does not inhere in the
objects regarded under the same kind, or by the same
science: they become simply the quantities of a quality. But
among the kinds, the qualities, the separate sciences, there
is a variety which will not disappear. This variety focuses
specifically in the concrete object, and inevitably causes it
to exceed the simplicity with which the object is invested
under any single system. It confers upon the object the only
absoluteness with which we are acquainted. The only absolute is the concrete object.

The scientists may not do much theorizing about the
matter, but they evidently realize very deeply that the
effectiveness of their labors depends on their separateness
from the labors that go on in the other sciences. *It is clear
enough that they intend to have their sciences remain separate sciences.* There is no master-science which will embrace
them all.

In mathematics, then, we have two kind of infinites. They
have their characteristic forms, in each case a serial form

which stands for the vanity of an effort. One series—the one we treated last—attempts to reach the unattainable denominator which will define the variety of the concrete object. The other series attempts to reach the unattainable numerator which will define the range or extent of the objects in which a quality may embody itself. To exhaust the quality of the object which we are examining is one thing; and to set the bounds, upward and downward, to the range of its connections with other objects of its kind is another thing. These seem to be the two projects which our knowledge assigns to itself in its ambitious moments. The one is a project in quality, the other is a project in quantity; but both are infinite projects.

We resent these infinites. They thrust us into an endless process as soon as we take them seriously. How far are we going to continue in an infinite series? If we go far, we harness ourselves to a treadmill and carry on an operation without any attention to the economic law of diminishing returns—we doom ourselves to exhaustion. But on the other hand we are led into error if we stop with some early member of the series as a sufficient representation of the whole. It is as if we had wearied, in our mathematics, of the term $0.3333 . . . . ,$ which we could never employ without distraction and embarrassment, and decided to call it simply 0.3333; but in the practical assumption that it was as well to drop that part of the infinite decimal process fraction which lay beyond the fourth place there was a pure self-abandonment to certain error.

From this dilemma, the ordinary method by which we escape practically is through the improvisation of a ghost. A ghost, from our present point of view, is our embodiment of the infinite series. We have already seen how we embody in ghostly form that which is supersensible yet finite. All the more must we embody that which is infinite. We decline to pursue the infinite series to the point of futility;

we will not be so dishonest as to construe some finite part of it for the whole; so we think of it under a finite form. And this would not be distinguishable from the procedure just named, except that this finite form is fabulous, or admittedly make-believe. Being a sensible form it is finite; but being fabulous it frankly testifies to infinity.

For one kind of infinity, namely, the infinite intensive series which tries to exhaust the variety of concreteness, the ghost which we employ is a kind of demon.

Demon is the Greek *daimon*. A demon to the Greeks was miraculous and patently unhistorical, but he was not very much like the great Gods, Zeus and Apollo, who were also unhistorical but ghosts of rather another order. There was a multiplicity of demons, and no demon had remarkably large dimensions; but each demon stood for the secret, or ineffable, or transcendental individuality of some individual and private person. Socrates had his demon, which presided over his mind and told him the strange things he must say. Possibly Socrates felt obliged to claim a demon in order to defend himself against the devouring Sophists and scientists who thought, each in his own way, that his definitions had extracted the essence that was Socrates and left nothing behind. As the official residence of a demon, Socrates could answer that his variety was something supernatural, which they were not going to exhaust.

Ordinarily we take a person entirely for granted, as conforming to some convenient definition which we have given him, or as fitting precisely into some place that we have assigned him. But when we are moved to picture his inexhaustible variety, and his unpredictable contingency, it is as a demon that we represent him. We think then of his genius, which is the Roman variety of the demon; or of his soul; or of his magical nature; or of his gifts; or of his afflatus or inspiration; or of his fairy-like or ogre-like

being; or of his charm; or, if he is a lady, of his enchant-
ing or bewitching qualities; or of his spirit; or of his
divinity. These objects, and all their like, are ghosts, and
they are devised for the purpose of respecting and defending the infinite personality of the person.

Proper names, on the whole, intend to do the same service
to their bearers. They are just a little sub-demonic. But if
a proper name is going to do this, it ought in logic either
to carry a magical connotation, like the name Theodora, or
else it ought to be strictly private and have no connotation
at all. It ought then to be like the names Gibraltar and
Aldebaran: proper in the strict sense, as the *proprium* or
exclusive property of the bearer, and quite removed from
the half-definitive or half-common names like Smith and
White. But then any proper name is likely to succeed much
better than a common name in recalling to us *the sense of
its concrete owner*. So that a proper name, if it is not too
obviously definitive, is a weak, and not very assertive, form
of the demonic term; and denotes to us an object that is
at least a mystery, if not outrageously and monstrously a
ghost.

As being clearly outside the historical order of beings
with which we are familiar, the demon is of course a sort
of monster when we conceive him, though not necessarily
an odious one. He is the sacred person picturized, but the
picturization must not be too fixed, and must not be taken
for fact. It is the business of a historical object to be articulate and precise, not the business of a super-historical object
or ghost. We need not try to define for all the course of
our thinking the sprightly divinity who presides over the
infinite variety of an individual, for he is frankly beyond
definition. He is the quasi-knowable form under which we
spontaneously elect to take cognizance of the unknowable.

A demon is especially our recourse when we think of an individual person, like ourselves. But what of the individual thing? The tree as an infinite variety had for the Greeks its dryad, the mountain its oread, the fountain its nymph. But in all these cases the divinity was extremely like a human being in form: monstrous enough from the point of view of the tree, mountain, or fountain that was being likened to it, but an easy form that the ghost might assume for the benefit of human beings themselves. This was an advantage in respect to representation that the lower natural orders possessed over the human order. Their presiding principle might well be a person, but that which presided over a person had to be a sort of super-person, hard to define: a divinity or a demon.

Of course we are a little more loath to testify to the infinite variety of the concrete thing, than to that of the concrete person. The dignity of personality is bound to be superior to the dignity of thinghood, if a person and not a thing is attempting to express them both. Socrates is concerned primarily to maintain his own freedom from determination. And being, in his usual possessive rôle, himself the would-be determiner of things, he may even be disinclined to admit the ultimate freedom of the thing. But eventually he will be compelled in honesty to do so. And then the form under which he can most easily make this admission is to attribute to the thing a quasi-personality.

The impersonal objects which we regard have a usual and, from one point of view, an unfortunate history. When the object is new, we do not readily reduce it or quantify it. Nevertheless, we give it a term, which prescribes for us the form under which we shall regard it. But it is for a little while, all the same, a new object, and we linger over it when we refer to it. However precise and quantitative the term means to be, we feel that it stands for a novelty, and we do not hurry over it, but stop and reconstitute the object for a moment in our memory as a substantial and sensible object; so that it means to us not only the quantity of a quality, but to some extent also the sensible if vanishing object. But the novelty wears off. The terms are routine terms, and provoke in us less and less the sense of their objects. They become more and more the symbols, tags, identification-marks, and definitions, the substitutes for the sensible experience; and they bear less and less of meaning, or of the diffuse qualitative connotation. The common fate of a term is to lapse into a routine symbol. Or perhaps we should say, the common fate of an impersonal object, when thrown upon our tender mercies, is to receive a term, to enter through the term into our routine experience, and to be disqualified. But we may recover the sense of the object ordinarily, if we will boldly personify it, or attribute to it the dignity of a person. For persons have fared a little better than things against the severe indignities inflicted upon them by the sciences. In the modern style, dryads, oreads, and nymphs have gone nearly out of use. In our period things have suffered the extreme of humiliation, and come to be generally disesteemed as simply *the objects for our sciences to possess and for ourselves to use.* The demonic terms have largely disappeared. Personal or sub-demonic terms have had to replace them, and these are mostly found in poetry and the literature of children, where they exist on the sufferance of a scientific public. These personal terms nevertheless persist unquestionably in our thinking. They are those personifications of things that have been condemned under what has been called the "pathetic fallacy": for example, a breath of wind; the laughing waters; the brooding forest; the vengeful lightning; the devouring sea; the stubborn stone. Objects thus evoked are perfect ghosts, with a fabulous investment of substantial quality. In these forms, the objects which were their originals are effectively removed from the categories under which they were being determined.

There is one other important aspect of demons. The demons have generally, at least in our Occidental background, been reckoned as evil. At any rate they have been reckoned as irresponsible, and unethical. This is very easy to understand. A demon is the embodiment of variety and freedom who resists determination. He is therefore very uneasy company for the determiner who would like to put him into his determinate system. Goodness and evil, after all, mean only the tractability or intractability of objects to our desires. God himself is reckoned as good, only as his will is favorable to our instinctive human enterprises. To be good is to be good for, or to be good to. So a demon is necessarily to be deplored from the practical, social, or scientific point of view: *a demon is a devil.* In a docile society, before demons went out of fashion, a person who was unsocial and eccentric seemed very naturally to be possessed by a demon; or else he was mad, which was often only a little less vivid way of saying the same thing; he was anarchical, dangerous, and evil. Summing up these adjectives, I should think his supreme and inclusive quality was: he was irrational. A person always seems irrational when his behavior is free or contingent or unaccountable. But if his individuality is very marked, his irrationality is socially odious, and he is a public evil.

And as for the things, if the dignity of spirit is attributed to them at all, it is nothing better than evil spirit. Materiality has been very generally conceived as the irrational, and therefore demonic, opposer of good scientific enterprises: that is, of course, when its opposition is threatening, and the enterprises are about to fail. Then we are capable of feeling an intense animus against the devils that inhabit our material, and make it so various and insubordinate.

The only ghosts to which modern scientists are very much addicted, perhaps, and certainly the only ghosts which science has ever loved, are ghosts of quite another kind. There are no demons openly testified to in science now, though there used to be. But frequently there are ghosts in science, who differ from the demons precisely as the infinite numerical series differs from the infinite decimal series which attempts to represent a surd.

Let us start again with a sensible object, as it actually occurs to us in our daily experience. The object probably occurs to us primarily as one of a class of objects; that is, as a defined object, or a given quantity of a certain quality. As such an object, we may employ it in the usual routine with a minimum of attention. But if we are more reflective, we ponder the situation for a moment, and we are quickly caught up into one of two kinds of the infinite series. One of these two infinite series we have just considered. The object appears to us to be constituted of more qualities than the one carried in its definition, and in fact to be a concrete object or infinite variety of qualities. And this produces for us the infinite series. We look inward on the object, undertake the impossible task of finding all its qualities, and presently bring the effort to a conclusion by the bold hypothesis: *This infinite variety is a demon.*

But there was more matter for reflection here than that. The defined object is a member of a class of objects. We find ourselves going outward from the object to its connections, and attempting to define its quantitative range. But this again produces the infinite series, at which we labor until we bring the task to a close by an equally bold hypothesis: *The infinite quantity of this system is a Logos.*

In naming this type of ghost Logos, I revert evidently

to the usage of the Platonists of the early Christian era; but I also employ a term which has the closest affiliations with the grandiloquent language actually affected by scientists of our day.

The Logos presents no difficulties to the mind if we proceed by distinguishing it from the logos. The logos itself is nothing but the definition of the object, from which we said a moment ago we had started. The logos is the common word as it is found in the dictionary, which represents the object as a precise quantity of a certain quality. The logos of water is H_2O; the logos of middle C in our music is the vibration-frequency 256; the logos of falling bodies on the earth's surface is some other formula; and the logos of a certain fish is thymallus signifer.

It is but too easy to repeat unthinkingly such logoi as these, taken out of books or out of the mouths of technicians. When we repeat one of them we are not necessarily aware of the vast and laborious system of precise comparisons which lies behind it, and which is the condition that permits us to have it at all. It is certain that many of us, those with a tinge of the anarchist and the freeman, or of the esthete enamored of the particularity of his objects, who sniff at the routine of the practical and professional mind, are capable of employing the logoi for all they are worth when the occasion of profit arises, without any compunctions of gratitude towards the collective scientific labors that have made them the standard conveniences they are. For example, our esthetic man falls sick, hires the doctor, follows tediously his commonplace prescriptions, and gets well again feeling as contemptuous as ever towards the medical profession. This is not a kind of conduct to admire particularly.

But what is much more important, these disaffected spirits, so militant in their freedom, are capable of using the logoi without being sensible of *the quantitative magnificence with which, as universal terms, they apply to their innumerable objects without exception.* This is to exhibit serious philosophical obtuseness.

The scientists are temperamentally more sensitive to quantitative implications. They see in the object not merely a logos, or object with an immediate practical aspect, but an object existing within an infinite but ordered world of its own kind. Thus the object as chemical logos is not really detachable from the whole world of chemistry; nor middle C from the whole world of sound-physics; nor the particular motion of a body from the world of all objects that have mass; nor the fish from the world of ichthyology. Only as members of these worlds do the objects, encountered as logoi, have their existence.

So the scientists pause in their routine, suspend the practical attitude, and indulge in a reflection. It is quite analogous to the reflection of the esthetic man recovering his concrete object, but it takes a different direction, and in fact seeks to recover not the concrete but the universal.

Upon such reflection, the object is but an instance of the universal, or an indifferent item of a whole. Let us not forget, says the scientist, to think the whole. The Logos is precisely the ghost under which he thinks the whole: it is the way he conceives the whole as a power which dominates its parts. What a Whole it must be to dominate its innumerable parts! We must not only be conscious of this falling body, but remember the whole quantitative aggregate of falling bodies, which energizes every one of its members; we must think now of Gravitation. We were interested most immediately in an evolving biological organism; but the organism was a case of evolution; and now we must think of the infinity of the cases and attribute to this infinity the name and potency of Evolution itself. Any object is an instance of a rule, but wonderful must be the authority of the Rule. Now a rule, said Aristotle, simply has a distributive validity, or is nothing except what is common within the instances;

but then a Rule is also the existence of a King; and if his act is nothing but distribution, think what an infinite act, and what a Distributor he must be!

Those vast aggregates, when thought as manifesting themselves actively within their parts, are genuine ghosts. They are not historical and actual entities, but fabulous and hypothetical ones. They are fictions which are meant to represent as powerfully as possible a truth. The truth is that the range of the quality observed in the logos is not limited to the object but has an infinite number of applications, like the fundamental numerical series. The fiction is the representation of this infinite system by a fabulous being: a Logos, a Word, a Principle, a Law, a Cause, a Whole, a Universal, a Platonic Idea—or God himself, construed as the aggregate and energizing unity of all the masses, or the forms, or the wills, or the objects within some other classification.

The best outward sign that permits us to detect the fact that such a ghost is in the thinking of the scientist is his capitalization of the word. The scientist does not appear to need a new term, such as those that would represent a demon. He can manage with his regular scientific term, if he may fill out its meaning to his taste,—especially if he may convert the common term into a proper term, and turn the logos into a Logos. *He does not require the word God in order to be religious, but his infinite and active quantities are his Gods.* With his flair for great magnitudes, the scientist is apt indeed to be religious. However, there is a disadvantage in his equivocal terminology, for he is likely not to know that he is dealing with ghosts at all, since he has no specifically ghostly or fabulous terms. He is likely to imagine, for example, that there is no God, but that there is indubitably Evolution, or Progress: when God, Evolution, and Progress may well be names of the very same sort, and represent the same kind of object.

The Logos as a practicable ghost, I should think, is quite personalistic or animistic, though with a different connotation than the demon. A Logos is a Great Man; a Great Scientist; a Great Ruler; what he has that makes him a ghost is a kind of personality. The Logos by which scientists most persistently represent their ghost, perhaps, is Law: but Law is all but as personalistic as Law-giver. It is only arbitrarily that we elect to discover the former without going back a little further to the latter. Law is authority, and we cannot think the authority of the law without thinking the Author of Law—unless we stop thinking before we conclude the thought. In philology, *logos* means in Greek the universal word, or class word, but word itself is personalistic: when word becomes Word, it is the Fiat of the Creator. *Nomos* is the ordinary Greek for the word law. But *lego* and *nemo*, the root terms of *logos* and *nomos*, are closely related, meaning to collect and to distribute, and indicating indifferently the mathematical act of a personal mind. And *logos* is of course closely connected with *legis*, the Latin for law.

But if both are personalistic, in what way does Logos the universal ghost differ from demon the concrete ghost? Both import into the object an unhistorical property, in so far as both represent the object as a form of the person. The demon represents the object as a qualitative variety, and is able to represent it as person because a person notoriously offers such a variety. The Logos represents the universal as a single quality presiding over an infinite realm of quantity, but this also is one of the aspects of a person; for a person may have such a fixed and compelling purpose as to convert every one of his innumerable experiences into a purposeful experience; such a person will objectify Determination, Consistency, Will, and Unity. *A person is not only the best example in our acquaintance of the various, irrational, and free, but also the best example of the sys-*

tematic, constant, rational, and determinate. It is in the latter sense that the scientist endows his universal with a quasi-personality. The Logos is after all a very appropriate name to ascribe to a logical ghost.

The Law is the word of the Law-giver, who is a person. And sometimes this person may even be regarded as a Father, or Paternal Principle. But not on the assumption that this Father possesses the human frailties which are embodied in the vacillating demon of personality. As Father he lays down the law and requires obedience. His infinity has reference to the prodigious extent and consistency of his authority, for his children however innumerable do not modify its rigor; and he imposes his paternity completely upon them, as if these were children with no mother; for they exhibit only the paternal favor, and are quite exceptional children as a Mendelian might view them.

The Platonic Idea was a grand specimen of the ghost Logos. Of course the ghosts of Plato's thinking are confusing to us. Ghosts are generally apt to be that; for it is difficult to perform that psychological analysis which determines exactly what the terms really mean to us, and enables us to see what part is actual and what part is factitious. But it seems clear that Plato's Ideas were forms of the Logos as here represented. The Platonists by the time of Christ had certainly replaced the Platonic Ideas by the Logoi of the Stoics, and regarded them as entirely equivalent.

Plato's Ideas were animated universals. The Idea of a table, said Plato, displaying the courage of his convictions by electing a most unfavorable example, was the real table. It inhabited somewhere in the heavens; and it was only copied—badly copied at that—in the tables that the draughtsman drew or the tables that the artisan made out of the wood.

Aristotle properly criticized this view on historical and

scientific principles. Such an Idea cannot be actual; what is actual in experience is only a table, with the implication of others of its kind that always attends our sense of a universal. But what Plato did when he saw the table was to stop and think the other tables, the infinity of all possible tables; speculate on the productive power that produced so many tables; and hypothesize a Platonic Idea, Ghost, or Logos, to serve as the legislative or paternal Cause.

CHAPTER FOURTEEN

THE HOLY GHOST

No one was ever more enraptured with universals than was Plato. He elevated them from ideas to Ideas, and formed them into a sort of celestial Hierarchy expressing progressively the being of God. The Ideas took their rank in this Hierarchy according as they suited Plato's humane set of values, with Goodness at the top. But then a great difficulty rose, and infected the happiness of this charming theogony. Plato might worship what God he pleased, and it was readily understandable if he worshiped the God who was Logos. But as a realist, Plato was obliged to admit that the Divine Ideas were greatly contaminated when they had to descend into the mundane particulars, and express their precious essence in sensible objects. God as a Hierarchy of Ideas had to incarnate himself in a material, and the material was too intractable. *God as Goodness was not omnipotent.*

Plato fell inevitably into a dualism, by which God, who as Goodness was qualitatively very simple though quantitatively infinite, was forced to contend ineffectually against an evil or enemy principle inherent deeply in the constitution of materiality. It is not everywhere, nor always, of course, that Plato bears such witness to the power of evil. It is occasionally, and sometimes. It is particularly in the Timaeus. Here Plato has recourse to a mythical representation which grievously qualifies his simple faith, but at the same time preserves the integrity of his critical mind.

God is the Father, the masculine, cosmic, and rational Creator. But the material is the Mother, who is feminine, anarchical, and irrational. (We would add, with Plato's permission: The Father is the personification of Quantity, and the Mother is the personification of Quality.) It is upon such a Mother that God must beget his children, the objective creatures which we know on earth as nature. They partake of the being of both the parents; and so far as biology can generalize them, in equal degrees.

The Occidental mind, one is prompted to remark at this stage, in sharp distinction to the Oriental, has evidently accepted the Platonic Ideas without the Platonic reservations. *The Occidental God is a Logos:* infinite in his dimensions but pure in his quality, and entering ineffectually into the life of the world. That is to say, the Occident grows more and more scientific in temper, and is devoted to grandeur and simplicity as its ideal. The Occident has Platonized itself, and yet has not adopted the whole witness of Plato. For Plato went far enough in this direction, but then he came back to earth. Virtually, he confessed that his God was a Demigod.

It must be remembered on behalf of our Occidental scientists, however, that in exhibiting such varieties of the Logos as we have seen they are essentially religious. It is probable that nearly any given scientist of today will pause in his scientific routine to animate and contemplate his Logoi or Universals, and this is by an impulse that is common or human, and is generally called religious. Religion is a kind of contemplation, and has of course both intellectual and emotional elements. But the objects of its contemplation seem peculiarly obliged to be great magnitudes. Religion evidently is concerned with objects of very great dimensions: supersensible, planetary, solar, cosmic, and quantitatively infinite. So science leads to God, and the God that science worships has at least the prime dignity of a God, that he is sufficiently imposing in his stature.

But the Gods of science are not so great in another sense. As the specific Movers, Authors, and Legislators, they are Simple Persons. They have a "single-track" mind, and know but one thing at a time. They are far too rational and predictable: so much more so than is, for instance, any single sensible object in the world. It is very comfortable to believe that they rule the world, since we understand so well their technique; for it would follow that we can do some ruling of our own. But the skeptical mind does not take hold of such a belief with much conviction.

Opposed to the ghosts of quantity and purity are the concrete ghosts. They are very local ghosts, but they have variety. They are not so much for contemplation as religious objects, as they are for contemplation as esthetic objects. They gratify that impulse of the mind, perhaps not so common an impulse with us as the religious impulse, to contemplate for its own sake the object as a concrete object, or as an inexhaustible complex of attributes. Hence the demon or concrete ghost. The demon is inscrutable. various, baffling, and evil as well as good

The demon will hardly do for a religious object, being not nearly big enough. He has no majesty, which is an effect of grandeur. He has only mystery, which is an effect of variety. His greatness is intensive, not extensive. Artists with their many-mindedness, such as landscape painters and lyric poets, are devoted to him, but to Puritanical religionists he inclines to be odious, and to all religionists he is unworthy.

But a great stroke is possible here. If the Universal Ghost has the theological dimensions but not the esthetic variety, and if the Concrete Ghost has the variety but not the dimensions, and if the mind has sufficient hypothesizing power, as unquestionably it has a great deal of this power: Why not invest the Logos with a hypothetical demonism, or, if you will, invest the Demon with a hypothetical universality, and create the Hypothesis of all Hypotheses, or the Ghost of Ghosts? *This great Ghost will be the Logos of all the Demons, or the Demon of all the Logoi.* He will be a Person in both the senses of a person: in his freedom and in his magnitude. He will be, I am convinced, that formidable being to which the ladder of Hegel led: *the Concrete Universal.*

This is evidently a stroke of genius. It obviates at once that weakness which has so often proved fatal to religions: the unearthly and impracticable purity of their God. It also removes the limitation which has so often crippled art: the localism or point-like isolation of the esthetic object. It enables our act of worship to partake of the substantiality of esthetic experience. And it enables our arts to rise to the dignity of worship.

But it must be borne severely in mind that this Ghost of Ghosts, as an object for our contemplation, is still tolerably synthetic. The component ghosts, the persons of two such widely different orders, have to be firmly held together, for either one is likely to slip out of the union and leave the other there alone for our regard. Possibly our psychic history, if we should be attempting to contemplate this compound ghost, would be that we alternated between regarding him in his aspect of Logos and regarding him in his aspect of Demon. The Hegelians, who have possessed him beyond a doubt, have always seemed to represent him too glibly, to win him too easily, and their facility has generally exposed him to suspicion. Hegel himself grievously offended Schopenhauer by the rhetorical ease of his dialectic, though Schopenhauer himself, in his esthetic doctrine, seems to have erected Hegel's own Concrete Universal for his devout contemplation.

Especially is the true Ghost apt to degenerate speedily into his mere Logos, if the religionist is not very patient and very humble. And the religionist must beware, for this is the Holy Ghost, and one must not commit the sin against him. The sin against the Holy Ghost, I should judge, consists peculiarly in withdrawing the demonism from his nature: in reducing him back to pure Logos.

We may approach this Holy Ghost from either side, it might seem. We may reach him from the side of theology, if we start with some Logos, some one rational Ghost, and compound him with other Logoi, laboriously adding attributes to his barren purity. Or we may reach him from the side of art and demonology, which does not look like so propitious a side for that purpose. For we may start with the local demons in their intense brightness of personality, increase their dimensions by a process of grouping, till they become Little Gods, and then put this polytheistic group into one Whole.

But at all events we must insist on the term Holy for this greatest Ghost. For Holy evidently means partaking of the whole or embodying the whole. And so the Holy Ghost has all the powers of all the Logoi, and all the properties of all the Demons.

The Jews possesesd their sense of the Holy Ghost firmly. To the authors of the Old Testament God was ineffable for the most part, but his active manifestation was through his Holy Ghost, which was represented preferably as *ruah*, meaning wind. It is the critical property of wind that it bloweth where it listeth. The energy of God in creating the world out of the void was like that of a mighty wind beating upon the face of the waters. The New Testament authors faithfully kept to the same representation, which became the *pneuma* of the Greek. Wind, like spirit or personality, seemed to them to serve well as the representation of majesty combined with contingency. It is a significant fact, and it has proved rather detestable to Occidental theologians with their special interest in the Logos aspect, that the Holy Ghost for the Old Testament authors, and for Christ himself speaking his native Aramaic, was of the feminine gender. But this was the right gender for defending the demonic and irrational aspect of his being.

But the New Testament authors very nearly lost the Pneuma, or the Holy Ghost, out of their excessive devotion to the Logos as personified in Christ. God as Pneuma exceeded God as Logos, but they would have preferred him in the simple capacity of the Logos for the very reason that in this guise they found him rational and humane. This was a natural favoritism of theirs. It was like the desire of the early Christians that Christ should become the military Savior of Israel; or the desire that, failing that, or having died without accomplishing that, he should soon make his second coming; or the desire that, if he did not intend to rule over this world at all, he should destroy it, and rule eternally over one that answered to his purpose. These desires stand in a series according to the order of choice, and the Christians who under compulsion have had to abandon one of them have generally elected the next.

And that was the very beginning of Occidentalism: the substitution of Logos the Demigod for the Pneuma, the Holy Ghost, the Tetragram, the God of Israel.

The Fathers carried this tendency further, and the Christian bodies have more or less generally sanctioned the usurpation. And so Christ now rules over the Occident instead of God. But if this is according to some expressions of the New Testament authors, it is not according to some others. For there is certainly a sufficient justification in the New

Testament for the view that Christ's noble rôle in the story, a rôle almost unique in religious literature, was this: *to be the Demigod who knew he was a Demigod and refused to set up as a God.*

At any rate, the Orthodox or Eastern Church, nearest to the source of our religion, which was an Oriental source, has consistently declined to represent Christ the Logos as coördinate with the Holy Ghost. In rejecting the famous Filioque clause of the Western canon, this Church has maintained that the Holy Ghost proceeds from God the Father (that is, the God of Israel) but not from God the Son: an admirable doctrine rightly entitled to the name of orthodoxy.

Perhaps the most critical moment in our history—if we had to fix precisely upon one—was just such a moment as that: *the moment when the Roman Church sanctioned the doctrine of Filioque.* In that moment Occidentalism emerged as a definitive historical polity which was to glorify the rational principle and deny the irrational principle. Since then the world has been for the Occident a rational and possessable world, while the irrational and evil world which the Orient contemplates has vanished from our horizon. Western empire has developed out of that choice, and Western science, and Western business. But empire, science, and business have been sponsored all along, with a tolerably consistent loyalty, by a Western Church. This institution has trimmed the doctrine to suit the deed

The Holy Ghost has an ancient and continuing office to perform: he is a Comforter, a Helper, or a Paraclete. So this office is defined historically in our own religious tradition. The Holy Ghost is offered to us in the New Testament as part of the religious equipment of our Christianity, and there he is promised as a Paraclete.

But it is interesting to observe that this is the very office which we would assign to him as following from our own independent study. For it is a matter of course that any ghost is for comfort, or has his existence in order to be enjoyed by the mind. That is what ghosts are for. A Paraclete in the sense of the Greek word is one who is called in or invoked to keep us company. So it is in order to see whether, and how, the Holy Ghost—whom some might prefer to know as the Concrete Universal or the Absolute—is among all the ghosts the specially comforting one for us.

The teachings of Jesus and of those followers who wrote the New Testament abound in brilliant ghosts of many sorts. Hardly of sorts unfamiliar to the orthodox rabbinical speculations of Judaism; nor of sorts unfamiliar to other contemporary Oriental theologies; but strange and bewildering to the modern Western mind. Thus we read in the New Testament of, among many others, the Father and the Son; the Father, the Word, and the Holy Ghost; the spirit, the water, and the blood; the Son of Man; the Kingdom of God; the true vine, with its husbandman and its branches; the cursed fig tree; the judgment of the world; the Paraclete who is the Spirit of Truth. These ghosts illustrate the power and fascination which the ghostly has for the mind: for men pore over them fearfully and lovingly and for long periods at a time. Among the historic idealisms which have moved the thought of the world these are of the first order of importance. But they also illustrate a certain weakness that may attach to ghostly exercises. The hard Occidental mind has often gloated over this weakness, and by reason of it tried to discredit entirely this particular set of ghosts.

What weakness? These New Testament ghosts are shifting, confused in outline, overlapping in their identities; when taken one at a time, colorful and appealing; when taken all together, disorderly, and impossible to entertain systematically.

I do not know whether it is more right to say that the

exuberance of the New Testament in the matter of ghosts is at fault, or the dryness of the Occidental mind that contemplates it. It is clear that the Oriental mind immediately knows a ghost when it sees one, and rejoices in that ghost frankly, and scarcely thinks of making systematic knowledge out of him. An effort, such as this is, to work out a natural history and a logic of ghosts is doubtless a pure Occidental performance that would seem to Orientals a strange and tedious labor of love. But while this performance was appearing superfluous to the eyes of quick Orientals, their energetic play with figures would be at the same time appearing very fantastic to me. They are as incapable of my Puritanical rigor as I am incapable of their freedom of imagination.

At any rate, there is hardly any such thing as a *theology,* in the Western sense of a system of religious concepts, which has ever successfully defined, ordered, and assimilated all the great ghosts which throng that brief document, the New Testament. Its wealth exceeds our grasp, and it is because the theologians have failed so badly—though sometimes honestly and charmingly—in this task, that there is always fresh work for private initiative.

Christ, as the Son and the Word, is the subject of the New Testament, both in its narrative and in its exegetical parts. (This is a platitude.)

The most thrilling passages which concern that central figure, whether for the interested secular reader or for the theologian, are those portions of the four Gospels which record the words of Christ between the triumphal entry into Jerusalem and the arrest and crucifixion. To these passages we have to go to find the heart of any Christology. For here we find those intimate counsels to the chosen disciples *which were deliberately uttered as last counsels.* We have Christ reviewing his own mission, and consenting not without reluctance to his own destiny, now nearly accomplished. (He is about to be "lifted up" in a manner which they have not yet conceived.) He knows the misconceptions which they in their simplicity cherish of his mission, and he would like to enlighten them, but is afraid of revealing "more than they can bear." So he chooses carefully the commandments which he is to lay upon them against the day of his departure, and the images under which they are to keep him in their minds afterwards. It is quite according to our sense of the dramatic that in each of the Gospels these last confidences receive such a full and lingering treatment.

The Gospels have many differences, and much the most profound one is the fourth one. In this one alone we have the promise that after the departure of Christ there will come to the faithful the Holy Ghost, who will be their Comforter or Paraclete. The doctrine of the Paraclete is John's contribution to Christianity.

But just here we are astonished at what we read. For we learn that *this Paraclete who will come is the Spirit of Truth.* This is a remarkable thing either for Christ to have said or for John to have written. To talk about the Spirit of Truth is quite Greek; it is quite philosophical; it is more Western than it is Eastern; *it is Hegelian.* This ghost is not nearly so colorful and Oriental a piece of imagery as most of the New Testament ghosts. Christ and John are talking to us here in our own language. When we encounter a ghost defined as a Spirit of Truth, we feel as if we were meeting with such unexpected words as these: "The Holy Ghost, the God whom the Jews revere, is the same ghost that Hegel shall acknowledge in his dry tongue as the Concrete Universal or Absolute."

But of course Christ's apprehensions were realized: he had indeed revealed more than the disciples could bear. It turned out speedily that the Holy Ghost had been deeply misunderstood. We see this upon reading the Acts of the Apostles, which is the account of the missionary origins of the Church immediately after Christ's death. The Holy Ghost who was promised them had fired the imaginations of the disciples— but not in his character of the Spirit of Truth. In the first parts of the Acts the Ghost doubtless receives a fonder doctrinal emphasis than at any subsequent period in the history of the church, and a more mistaken one.

To be filled with the Holy Ghost, as all the preachers in the early chapters of the Acts were supposed to be, was to possess magic and to be able to work wonders. The Paraclete who could bestow this power must have seemed a very useful Helper indeed. But that was because they had missed the point of Christ's promise. To the extent that they had wished to be filled in order to enjoy the magic power, they were believers of the most gullible sort in a most meretricious doctrine: believers who had persuaded themselves *that their Ghost enjoyed an objective status and was a Ghost who could and would be good to them.* The early Christians, like a good many later ones, expected that nothing would be beyond the power and inclination of the Holy Ghost to accomplish for them. They were doomed to disappointment, and cult of the Holy Ghost was to lose much of the favor with which it was regarded by its first fanatical adherents.

So goes the account of the Holy Ghost in the earlier Acts. Then Saul of Tarsus enters the story, and the book becomes mainly a chronicle of his doings. At this point a great refinement is to be observed in the way of regarding the Holy Ghost, for Saint Paul was not the man to be under illusions as to the ghostliness of his Ghost. The notion that the Christians had to put out of their minds was the notion that the Paraclete was going to help them in some material way. It was not for this that Christ had promised him; and Paul knows it very well.

The Holy Ghost is but a ghost. But on the other hand, let us remember that *he is a ghost in a world that we have peopled thickly with ghosts;* and that he is quite the supreme ghost if we will compare him with the others. We may as well dismiss the question of his ghostliness, and concern ourselves with seeing how he is a better Comforter than other ghosts.

One might naturally think there were many ghosts who were pleasanter company to keep, who offered to furnish us with sweeter illusions and better comfort, than this Holy Ghost who is the Spirit of Truth. For truth is one of the most uncomfortable things to live with. It reminds us continually of our impotence. It never flatters us in the least.

Of all the ghosts given to Christians, it is evident that the most successful competitor against the Holy Ghost for their favor was the Father Ghost. With the Father Ghost, of course, goes inseparably the Son Ghost. The Father is our Father, and the Son is ourselves. It is a paternal relation in which we are hopefully involved. For God's act of paternity had no human importance and was not even hypothesized until religionists were prepared to identify the only-begotten Son with humanity. The Son was incarnated in the form of man, and dwelt among men, in order to teach them to know God as their Father.

And such has been the delightfulness of this way of thinking, that we may perhaps say that Christians generally have found they had rather dwell on the Father and Son than to dwell on the Spirit of Truth; and that the third member of the Trinity has about become obsolete for the modern Westerners. Of course it is possible for Christians to think of themselves as very weak and infantile sons, and God as an awful and unapproachable Father. But if he is too awful, he is not a Father after all, and this is a ghost that might as well be abandoned. However austerely this term can be taken, the temptation to take it in its homely sense has been more than we could resist. Historically, we have become more and more *familiar* with this Father, and our theology has become tame and ingenuous, lacking the stern doctrine of the Spirit of Truth.

Evidently John, who made so much of the Father and the Son, was like Plato. He at length, and perhaps with some reluctance, made the wholesome addition of a Spirit of Truth, just as Plato had at length added an irrational Mother Ghost. But John's whole teaching has not been always adopted—again the very thing that has happened to Plato, if we may judge by most of the varieties of Platonism.

Father and Son are the same kind of ghost: for both are forms of the Logos. The essence which is common to them is the human order of will and intelligence, transmitted by the Father and received by the Son. Our bias on behalf of these ghosts is perfectly transparent. They suggest to the meanest and meekest of Christians that God's will is the good will of a Father towards their little projects. But to more ambitious Christians, including the belligerent scientists, the suggestion is that God's intelligence is the intelligence which they have inherited, and that the universe is rational for them since its Author is their Father. They are his inheritors: and to think the least of their regal perquisites, they can well afford to imagine themselves in a privileged position towards the universe. This is the kind of image we have in our minds when we put forwards the great Occidental boast. It is behind our militant progressivism, our ceaseless drive for material power, and our occupation with mechanical toys that testify to our cunning.

Father and Son compose a Godhead that is patriarchical in its constitution. The absence of the feminine element is remarkable, and makes it one of the purest patriarchies ever imagined. The ruling concept in a patriarchal society is that the son inherits the powers and properties of the father. In fact, it assumes that the son *repeats* the father and that paternity is the perfect transmission of the stable essence from one generation to the next. This is very pretty, but we scarcely pretend that in our actual human societies it ever quite obtains. For the deposit of the father's seed in an alien being is precarious for the seed, and a grievous necessity for the father from the dynastic point of view. We are not good Mendelians at heart, since we honor the male above the female in our lineage, and will not regard them in their mathematical equivalence. Probably we would be glad if there were no mothers meddling with the creation of the offspring, and if only virgin fathers were concerned in it. Then heredity would be rational, and the inheritance would be determinate. Under the honors we pay to paternity in our patriarchal society, it seems likely that we are really indulging a deep metaphysical partiality for rationality, simplicity, and science.

For the mother-concept means for us traditionally the source of variation and error. Fatherhood is a good symbol for rational sequence, for cause and effect, but motherhood is a symbol for irrational sequence and contingency. And if we were plunged suddenly into a matriarchal system, with its preference for the mother over the father, our habits of mind would be thrown into confusion. There would be many metaphysical implications bound up in this preference which would be entirely novel to us, and repulsive and uncomfortable. They would be very stern implications.

The Holy Ghost, however, is not a feminine image. He is Wind—the spirit of contingency. It is in this shape, and not that of woman, that he complements the Father-and-Son relation in the Godhead.

But if we had a feminine image, or a Mother Ghost, to embody this spirit for us in Christianity, it seems in order to remark that the image would not be the tender one which the Roman Catholics cherish. The feminism of Rome is not the assertive cult of the femina which the term means generically. It is not characteristic feminism such as is denoted in Goethe's *das Ewig-Weibliche*. The Holy Mother of the Italian sacred paintings is not the inscrutable woman who is represented in Leonardo's desperate picture of the Mona Lisa. The Holy Mother is the perfect or model mother as defined for a patriarchal system. She is obsequious and subordinate to the Father, like a loyal nurse, or foster-mother. She is determined not to imprint her image on the Child. She will weep over his misdemeanors and intercede a little with the Father, but does not really intend to interfere with heroic designs. Completely self-effacing, she is ambitious only for the Child, and anxious that he should enter fully into his inheritance. Nothing could be quite so fantastic as to try to make Mary the theological equivalent of the Holy Ghost, or to see in the Holy Family of the paintings the equivalent of the New Testament Trinity.

Representing as he does the demonic qualifications, the Holy Ghost was an appropriate addition to the Godhead at a critical time. The inscrutable and awful God of the Jews, whose name was the ineffable Tetragram, was being reduced to a Father, who had acknowledged man as his son and heir, and upon whose goodness man was quite ready to presume. But the rational and humane essence which he had imparted through the act of paternity, and which he and man therefore shared in common, had not exhausted his nature, nor defined the entire process by which he governed his universe. There was also an essence, an exceedingly energetic one, which was irrational and contingent, for all that human reason could do to compass it, and either indifferent or cruel, for all that it seemed to sympathize with human desires. So the Holy Ghost was the ghost who came to bear witness of God in his fullness.

And it was in that sense that he was a Comforter. The comfort that he brought was the comfort of being possessed with the Spirit of Truth: the comfort that comes when the mind has had the courage to look realistically upon the world. Perhaps this is the peace that passeth understanding.

The comfort that the Father Ghost brings, or any other Logos, is a specious and dangerous comfort. The Father Ghost is not the whole of God, but only a part or a Demigod. He may be our partisan and our parent, but we must not expect too much from him, for he will not be very effectual against the powers opposed. Comfortably depending upon his amiable intentions, we lay up for ourselves a very uncomfortable disillusionment. If we miss this disillusionment it will be by incurring a fate unhappier still: by persisting in an illusion to the point where we deny the evidence of our senses and the validity of fact itself. Not very far on that road lies Christian Science; a little farther lies insanity.

Nothing is really gained by flattering ourselves. We are going to have ghosts in our employment who are to embody for us the aggregate force and tendency of the world as it bears upon our destiny. But that ghost is the truest who is the fullest and most comprehensive, and that ghost is the best who is the truest. If we are content with a lesser though a handsomer ghost, we shall sooner or later have to remark that events occur which are foreign to his fine intentions, and for which we are quite unprepared. The shock is too dangerous.

To support this position, I could go back to Job, or the Greek drama, or Shakespeare; but actually I find myself generally going to a modern poem which seems to discuss the problem of comfort with a good deal of practical wisdom. I will quote a pointed passage from an admirable context that deserves to be quoted in full. It is from a poem of A. E. Housman's:

Therefore, since the world has still
Much good, but much less good than ill,
And while the sun and moon endure,
Luck's a chance, but trouble's sure,
I'd face it as a wise man should,
And train for ill, and not for good.

But this is not the whole comfort furnished by the Spirit of Truth. The saints and the mystics have experienced him much more profoundly even than that. Along with a proper humility goes love; and love is not the negative response that consists in enforced renunciation, but the positive and energetic sentiment that delights in contemplating that which it cannot fully understand nor hope to master.

I would hesitate to introduce this romantic term if it were not so thoroughly a religious term—and if its propriety had not been so clearly established by Plotinus in theory, and by Dante and many mystics in fact. Romantic love is among the most delightful of our experiences; most of us would probably name it as the most massive and satisfying of all— provided at least that we do not confine the term to the love between the sexes, but extend it to the love of nature, of works of art, and of God. But this romantic love is not what it might first seem to be, and it may be quickly per- verted. At the base of romantic love there is probably an impulse fundamental in our biological constitution, *to be in rapport with our environment.* In the psychological terms of Schopenhauer, this is the impulse *to have knowledge with- out desire.* Love is conditioned on respect for the object, and what it loves is to contemplate the infinite variety of the object: its demonic and invincible individuality.

So God in his fullness, whether Holy Ghost, Concrete Universal, or Spirit of Truth, is the God whom we can never familiarly nor intelligibly possess. And this is doubt- less the only real God there is. Certainly this is the only God we can ever really love.

Epilogue

CHAPTER FIFTEEN

BY WAY OF A PROGRAM

IT is painful to bring my book to its logical conclusion. For this conclusion will seem at least a little bit ignominious as a climax to the study. I have no heroic proposals to bring forward, no splendid crusade to agitate.

But it is necessary to be as honest as possible. There can be no advantage in making false representations, or indulging excessive hopes.

All around us in the Western world we may observe the local varieties of one consistent movement: the disintegration of the Kingdom of Heaven. Everywhere the Gods that have come to us by inheritance are being uncrowned, and retired to a sort of private life where they are only plain Principles. The philosophers do not like the Gods, and have had much to do with this movement. But the scientists like them still less, and so little that they do not even permit them to withdraw gracefully from their high position and become Principles: the scientists would simply cut their heads off and be done with them. The philosophers find themselves in an embarrassing and untenable position therefore. They are in the middle. On one side are the ardent religionists who want their Gods to rule them. But on the other side are the naturalistic rabble, who are so jealous of the rule of the Gods that they propose to wipe

out even the Principles, seeing in these a sort of blood royal
who might at any time set up as Gods again. So there are
fierce hatreds and conflicts over the matter in our Western
society,—which issue steadily to the disadvantage of the
Gods, the discomfiture of the religionists, and the increasing
authority of naturalism.

That is one picture of our contemporary social history.
But it is probably a little bit over-dramatized, it looks
rather more colorful and warlike than the actual course
of events. So I will put the matter in another way.

Sometimes we hear only a few very bitter words being actually said. But there is something which ought to appall us
more than any bitter words and fratricidal deeds of arms that
might be taking place between the two camps. And that
is the way in which they fraternize with each other, so
contrary to the ethics of good soldiers: the way in which
their hostilities are becoming a mere formality, while the
religionists are coming gradually to a perfect understanding with the anti-religionists in which they are the losers and
the anti-religionists are the winners. The priests themselves
have lost heart and are not handing on the priestly tradition. They have in effect come to this arrangement with
the naturalists: "If you will leave us the name and honor
of our Gods, we will surrender to you their powers and
see that you are not interfered with in your naturalism
and your secularism."

That is the intent of the new theology, which makes
Christ supreme over all other Gods. For Christ is the spirit
of the scientific and ethical secularism of the West.

To give tangible evidence that this is the way matters
are going, I will cite a little pamphlet that is in circulation:
"A Service of Communion—suggested for use in liberal
churches." The author is Mr. Leroy E. Snyder, of the

Rochester Unitarian Church of Rochester, New York. The service proposed is so completely in harmony with the watered theology of the advanced moderns that it is easy to fit it into the picture of almost any big city church in Protestantism as it worships on this Sabbath morning.

There are ten pages of an elaborate ritual, with choir, processional, litany, and sacrament.

But it is after this manner that the minister pronounces the Call to Worship:

We are met together that we may worship God.

The name of God is the name of the most high God who has been worshiped, throughout the ages, under many names and forms. He is the false gods and the true God; the many, and the one and only God. He has spoken through the wise and good of all ages, through holy men, through saints and prophets and martyrs of a thousand holy causes. He has died a thousand deaths, to be born anew of a thousand dreams of man. He is the sunset and the dawn. He is the voice that speaks within us when honor and love and beauty urge us to the highest endeavor. He is that within us which is nearest and closest, which we cannot weigh or measure, or name by any name unless it be his. He is that which speaks even in the hearts of those who deny him, which is at the seat of their doubt, the very question with which they front the Universe. For he is the spirit of life and growth, of power and progress, which touches us at every point, to which we are mysteriously joined in our unconscious selves, which is wonderful beyond words and beautiful beyond dreaming, in our highest aspirations, our deepest emotions, our noblest and most compassionate impulses.

We are met that together we may worship God.

God is not worshiped only in temples made with

hands. He is not worshiped only when the prayer and praise of many ascend together. He may be worshiped by one alone, and in many ways. He may be worshiped in voiceless meditation in the inner sanctuary of the soul, curtained by quiet and repose. He may be worshiped under the golden sun or the gray clouds of day, or in the dark silences of the night. He may be worshiped in the majesty of mountains, or in the rhythmic beat of the surf upon an ocean shore. He may be worshiped in the depths of the woods, or in the ordered beauty of a garden. He may be worshiped in the slow moving tide of a great river, or in the clamorous music of a mountain stream. He may be worshiped in the green and flower-studded freshness of spring meadows, or in a fair land white-mantled with snow. He may be worshiped in the creative genius of man and his ceaseless search for light and truth; in great art and in true craftsmanship; in the memorials of all who have made new paths for mind or spirit.

It is evident that there is no courage, and no commitment, behind such an eclectic rigmarole as this. The God is compounded of any and all Gods that ever were thought of, and no offense is done to any. I have never before seen in print such an inclusive religious ceremony.

When we come to the Litany, we find the minister continuing in the same strain—still synthetic and innocuous —while the choir renders for its responses some Old Testament passages taken literally or, if it suits better, paraphrased.

And presently:

Minister:

We celebrate thee in man, in whom thy life hath grown through impotence and strife to power and dignity. We celebrate thee in heroism and sacrifice, in love and human fellowship. We celebrate thee in all high strivings of the soul of man, in all his aspirations toward that divinity which is his destiny and end.

Choir:
What is man that thou art mindful of him?
And the son of man, that thou visitest him?
For thou hast made him but little lower than God,
And crownest him with glory and honor.

Here we have the subtle destructive touch of Protestantism as it Occidentalizes its ancient theology. The minister celebrates God in man, as man aspires "toward that divinity which is his destiny and end." And the choir replies that God has made man "but little lower than God." This is according to neither the Septuagint nor St. Paul, who represented man as "a little lower than the *angels.*"

Nothing could be better evidence of the general drift of the Protestant bodies. The faith is disintegrating from within: it is not only the victim of enemies without.

When our churches worship as they do in this manner, they lead me to the reflection that perhaps in respect to religion we are today in much the same position as was the Greece of Plato's time.

For Plato was ashamed of the old Greek Gods. The myths were a little too ridiculous, or too stale, for his taste. The Gods seemed to him to be about played out. They had had a great many hard knocks. Yet he saw that religion was essential to a unified and happy State, and to his own happiness. His mind was constantly upon it. He continued to compose myths, he played with many myths, and in general he loved myths. But he never committed himself to a single set of myths, and so he went without a religion.

Or would it be more accurate to say that we are in the same position as the Greece of the age of Aristotle? For the ritual from which I have been quoting is vaguely aware of a great many and very various myths that the world has enjoyed, but scarcely abandons itself for a single moment to any one of them. It has not the mythical competence even of poetry, which does form powerful images, and surrender to them, although it does not stand by them but runs too freely from one to another. This is a pale ritual —its allusions to myth are as faint and dry as can be—its esthetic quality is at the minimum of vividness. And this suggests Aristotle rather than a poet like Plato.

For Aristotle had no myth at all in his system. His God was nothing but a Principle: without properties and circumstances. The breakdown of religion which we find in Plato consists in the effort to replace it with a sort of comparative religion, with a colorful and various poetry, or with a Gnosticism. But the breakdown which we find in Aristotle is one step further on: a severe Western rationalism has been at work and reduced the myths to metaphysics.

We have moved far from the habits of those days and those climates to which the Scriptures were congenial. Culturally their language and their images seem strange to us now. And we have heard so much fun made of them! There is a real effort required now to enter into them sympathetically even when we consider that metaphysically they are sound. Perhaps we would greatly relish, and indeed it is probable that we are continually on the lookout to see if we will not discover somewhere, a brand-new myth, not shopworn, not yet ridiculed, and not unrepresentative of what little taste we may have yet for the enjoyment of myths. But that is an event upon which it is impossible to make any calculations.

A new religion being totally impracticable as a thing to propose, the only recommendation that it is in my power to make is this one: We had better work within the religious institutions that we have, and do what we can to recover the excellences of the ancient faith. The churches must be turned from their false Gods towards their old true Gods —whenever, and however, and so far as this proves to be practicable.

Is it possible then for all the religious institutions yet to be saved? There is undoubtedly a good deal of difference in their respective chances of obtaining this happiness. The further they have come from orthodoxy, the smaller their chances.

But why should one not dispose of this vexing problem by saying, ever so simply: Let the West go into the Greek communion, where orthodoxy still largely prevails.

Like other dispositions that are excessively simple, that solution is not in the least practicable. The West will scarcely do what I might ask in this matter. At best only a few Westerners might do it. Where is this Greek communion? It is too far away from my part of the world, and I would have to expatriate myself to join it, or lead an emigration of a few like-minded fellow-citizens to go and become Greeks. The only local example of a church of this faith with which I have any actual acquaintance is situated in a Wyoming mining town: I cannot pronounce the names of its members, I can scarcely exchange with some of them any conversation in the same tongue, and I find very little in common with them except that, so far as I understand, I admire their Gods. The thought of joining them is, in brief, abhorrent.

Or why not advise the Western world to enter the Syna-gogue, if the Synagogue might be so kind as to receive it, and find the God of Israel in his greatest purity? Once more, and with all respect, the word suggests itself: ab-horrent. For better for worse, a man is a member of his own race, or his own tribe. He will have to prosper or suffer as it prospers or suffers. The religion that he requires must have the character of being his own social institution. If there is not a religious institution that suits him quite near at home, he will have to go without one.

Besides, there might be some disagreeable questions to raise and answer. Would Judaism admit Christ the Logos into its Godhead, even in his subordinate capacity? And does Judaism still cherish the ancient God of Israel in his stern and inscrutable majesty? Or has Judaism softened him down, and degraded him, and identified him with its rather secular and commercialized existence?

I will mention another possibility. Why should not the Western world go Roman? But again that is too simple. My Western world does not want to do anything of the kind. The history of the Western world is a history of political separation from the Roman church, which is now definitely a rejected polity (as well as a faith), and against which we have for a good many generations cultivated a powerful antagonism. We have prejudices; and if I for my part might overcome these prejudices, would my community as a whole do this also? I have friends, and I hear of men whose sound judgment I esteem highly, who are going back to Rome. Sometimes I may feel envious of their spiritual advantages. But the most of my friends and kind are not doing this and will not. Therefore I am not willing to do it, and neither will I advocate it.

And next: Why not bid the West go Anglican, or Episcopal? I am now getting much nearer home—much nearer to the actual milieu in which I live. I am an Anglophile, and I wish my country might be more so. But I am not so Anglophile as I am American. And I find myself sometimes, as I find my neighbor more frequently, abhorring Anglicanism and Episcopacy. For reasons perhaps that are social and political, and inarticulate but deep—for inherited reasons. Therefore I propose no such thing. I still seek the religion that will be the expression of the social solidarity of my own community.

There is Presbyterianism; and Methodism; and Baptistry; there are plenty of other sectarian possibilities. These bodies are evidently close to the genius of my kind of community. But they have declined rather far from orthodoxy, as I see it—and as what Western religious body has not? They secularize themselves more and more every day. It is hard to give them an endorsement.

There are two objectives at which the religious purpose of an intelligent private citizen has to drive. One is scarcely more important and indispensable than the other. But while it might well be possible to realize one of them, it is, according to our present prospects, almost impossible to realize both of them at once. One is a religion to which the private citizen might by personal conviction be intensely loyal, with Gods whom he may fear and love, and whose commandments represent for him the deepest wisdom. The other is simply a religion with the sanction of his own natural society behind it.

Under these circumstances it will be a bolder man than I who has an extremely specific or concrete proposal to offer to the Western cis-Atlantic world seeking its religious expression.

I have already made the best suggestion I can; it is a comparatively tame one, it does not look in the least heroic, and it does not promise any quick and spectacular consequences. But I will repeat it, a little more fully, and it will have to be the only contribution that I know how to offer.

With whatever religious institution a modern man may be connected, let him try to turn it back towards orthodoxy.

Let him insist on a virile and concrete God, and accept no Principle as a substitute.

Let him restore to God the thunder.

Let him resist the usurpation of the Godhead by the soft modern version of the Christ, and try to keep the Christ for what he professed to be: the Demigod who came to do honor to the God.

INDEX